An Introduction to Real-Time Systems: From Design to Multitasking with C/C++

An Introduction to Real-Time Systems: From Design to Multitasking with C/C++

R. J. A. Buhr
Department of Systems and Computer Engineering
Carleton University
Ottawa, Ontario, Canada

D. L. Bailey
Department of Systems and Computer Engineering
Carleton University
Ottawa, Ontario, Canada

Prentice Hall, Upper Saddle River, New Jersey 07458

Library of Congress Cataloging-in-Publication Data

Buhr, R. J. A.
   An introduction to real-time systems / R.J.A. Buhr, D.L. Bailey.
      p. cm.
   Includes index.
   ISBN: 0-13-606070-6
   1. Real-time data processing. 2. C (Computer program language)
3.C++ (Computer program language) 4. Bailey, D. L. (Donald L.)
II. Title.
   QA76.54.B85   1998
   004' .33--dc21   98-25878
                                                        CIP

Acquisitions editor: **Laura Steele**
Production editor: **Rhodora Penaranda**
Managing editor: **Eileen Clark**
Editor-in-chief: **Marcia Horton**
Director of production and manufacturing: **David W. Riccardi**
Copy editor: **Patricia Daly**
Cover director: **Jayne Conte**
Cover designer: **Bruce Kenselaar**
Manufacturing buyer: **Donna Sullivan**
Editorial assistant: **Kate Kaibni**

©1999 by Prentice-Hall, Inc.
Simon & Schuster / A Viacom Company
Upper Saddle River, New Jersey 07458

The author and publisher of this book have used their best efforts in preparing this book. These efforts include the
development, research, and testing of the theories and programs to determine their effectiveness. The author and
publisher make no warranty of any kind, expressed or implied, with regard to these programs or the documentation
contained in this book. The author and publisher shall not be liable in any event for incidental or consequential damages
in connection with, or arising out of, the furnishing, performance, or use of these programs.

Printed in the United States of America

10 9 8 7 6 5 4 3 2 1

ISBN   0-13-606070-6

Prentice-Hall International (UK) Limited, *London*
Prentice-Hall of Australia Pty. Limited, *Sydney*
Prentice-Hall Canada Inc., *Toronto*
Prentice-Hall Hispanoamericana, S.A., *Mexico*
Prentice-Hall of India Private Limited, *New Delhi*
Prentice-Hall of Japan, Inc., *Tokyo*
Simon & Schuster Asia Pte. Ltd., *Singapore*
Editora Prentice-Hall do Brasil, Ltda., *Rio de Janeiro*

To Heron Cay, where many pages of this book were written.
Ray Buhr

To Lori, who never complained when I said,
"I think I'll spend a few hours working on the book."
1 Cor. 13
Don Bailey

Contents

Preface

This book was written to fill a need for a textbook capable of introducing, to third-year students in a Computer Systems Engineering (CSE) bachelor degree program, a systems engineering approach to the development of software for real-time systems. The term *real-time system* has, to us, a very broad interpretation that includes examples as wide-ranging as board-level communication products, consumer appliances controlled by embedded computers, telephone switches, air traffic control systems, on-line banking systems, and enterprise-support systems for intranets. This book aims to help our CSE students (and other types of students) to learn common system problems and solutions that underlie a bewildering diversity of applications and software technologies.

The book should also be of interest to industrial professionals because of the unique slant it provides on designing real-time systems.

The course for which this book was developed centers around a programming project, but systems thinking, not programming, is the main point of the course. The course presents a set of concepts, issues, and techniques that will prepare students for dealing with the variety and complexity of actual real-time systems. The principles are intended to be portable to programming technologies other than the one used for this course, and to more than just programming. Programming is just the means of making the principles concrete.

Because programming is not the main point of the course, the criteria for choosing a programming technology to support the course are simplicity and familiarity, not expressive power. All we require is a minimal language, backed up by a minimal real-time kernel to support multitasking. This means that a competent student with minimal sequential programming background can successfully deal with the programming side of the course (and this book). More important than advanced sequential programming experience is experience programming interrupt handlers for input/output (I/O) devices of the kind found in ordinary personal computers, some knowledge (not necessarily deep) of concurrent processes and semaphores, and an ability to form mental models of the relationship between a program on a page and its execution (we have found that students who only scrape through early programming courses often lack this ability and have difficulty with the material as a result).

The case study that serves as a running example in much of this book is based on a project students have done in this course, in groups, for a number of years. It is a small computer-communication system that is rich enough in real-time system issues to be interesting. Such a project can appear overwhelming to students who view it as a conventional C-style programming assignment, to be coded as a whole. To survive they must undergo a paradigm shift in the way they think about software. They must come to understand that they cannot code the desired overall behavior directly, as they could with programming assignments in previous courses; that the desired behavior *emerges* at run time through the collective efforts of a set of relatively simple, cooperating components, without central control; and that the difficult problem is not coding the components, but understanding how to make them work together in the face of unpredictable events, failures, and concurrency. The whole approach of the course, the project, and this book is designed to help students make this paradigm shift.

To assist this paradigm shift, we use a set of expressive, easy-to-learn, home-grown design notations that build explicit bridges from real-time system requirements, to cooperating components, to interrupt-driven, multitasking programs, and also provide traceability in the other direction. The nature of these notations is outlined in Chapter 1, along with the reasons for choosing this particular set from among many possibilities. We have chosen *not* to use the emerging standard notation known as UML (Unified Modeling Language) in this book for two reasons: UML is still a moving target in the real-time area; and UML provides both more and less notation than we need. Some UML-based books have already appeared, including one on "Real-Time UML" (Douglass, Addison Wesley, 1998). However, our objective is not to "cover" UML as the Douglass book does, but to introduce real-time system problems and solutions using only enough notation to do the job, which, we think, requires both more and less than UML currently offers. We plan to document the relationship between this book's notations and UML—a cross reference will eventually appear on the book's Web site. (See www.omg.com for documentation of UML—v 1.1 is the latest version as this book goes to press—and see the end of this preface for our Internet addresses). Chapter 11 has more to say on the subject of notations.

PROGRAMMING

The book uses, for its programming examples, a C-like subset of C++ that we call *skinny C++*, so the material is as accessible to C programmers as it is to C++ programmers. Skinny C++ is basically C with a few other "better C" features of C++ (for example, C++ I/O streams), but without any of the advanced features of C++, such as classes or templates. We have chosen to use the "better C" features of C++ for pedagogical reasons. However, the differences are not great enough to get in the way of using the book with plain ordinary C, if desired.

Support for concurrent processes is provided by a simple, home-grown, real-time kernel called Tempo written in full C++. For the purposes of this book and the course for which it has been designed as a text, full C++ is deliberately hidden behind a skinny C++ interface. Tempo is publicly available over the World Wide Web (see the end of this preface for Internet addresses).

Tempo programs may be developed and run under the MS DOS or Windows operating systems (this has been tested for Windows 95 but not yet for either Windows 98 or Windows NT—any new information on these versions of Windows will be posted on our Tempo Web page).

The availability in this book of code for a version of the computer-communication system that we said earlier had been used as a course project for many years does not invalidate the continuing use of this system for the same purpose. Details of the requirements are easily changed to make the code—and the emergent system behavior—sufficiently different that straight copying of old code is easily spotted. Students may still try to edit old code (including the code of this book), but an instructor can easily make this difficult enough that only students with deep insight will find it worthwhile. Such students will gain valuable experience with an important subject—code reuse—so this is not necessarily something to be discouraged.

SCOPE OF THE MATERIAL

This book focuses on *learning for the first time* how to think about, design, implement and test real-time systems, using "soft real-time" systems as the example. Soft real-time systems do high priority things first when bursts of events occur but, in contrast to "hard real-time" systems, do not attempt to guarantee response times. In soft real-time systems, overall behavior emerges from the collective actions and interactions of a set of event-driven, semi-autonomous, cooperating, prioritized, concurrent processes. The design notations enable the book to introduce advanced issues associated with such systems in an understandable way, issues such as interference, critical races, resource contention, fault tolerance and priority inversion, so that readers will get an appreciation of how to deal with these issues during design, implementation, and testing. The design notations also enable the book to demonstrate in an understandable way, through examples, important aspects of the flow from real-time requirements to solutions.

Outside the scope of the book are advanced technical topics in the real-time area, such as scheduling strategies for soft real-time or hard real-time systems, and object-oriented design patterns for real-time software. Although this book touches on many advanced issues by means of examples, systematic treatment of these issues as subjects in their own right is outside its scope. Also outside its scope is the *prescription* of step-by-step methods for going from requirements to solutions (the focus is on systems thinking, not the development process). An example of a well-known book that treats the development process is Jacobson's "Object-Oriented Software Engineering" (Addison-Wesley, 1992).

CHAPTER-BY-CHAPTER OUTLINE

As appropriate for an introductory book with this slant, the chapters flow through the material in a spiral fashion, introducing system issues and notations gradually in the first loop of the spiral in Chapters 1 through 4 and then revisiting them in subsequent loops of the spiral in later chapters. To provide a solid jumping-off point for novices in this area, Chapters 2 through 4 present the material in a bottom up fashion, beginning with small code examples and gradually introducing design notations and system issues in passing. Chapters 5 through 8 then present examples in a top down fashion, showing the flow from requirements to solutions. However, the book may also be read out of order: *Advanced readers* may bypass the spiral organization by reading Chapter 1 and Chapter 5 first, and then reading the rest of the chapters in any convenient order, using Chapters 2 through 4 primarily as references for concrete examples. *Novices* may impose there own spiral approach on the order of reading the material in Chapters 5 through 8 by skipping all the material on use case maps (UCMs) on first reading. This approach focuses on solutions first, leaving for a second reading the process of arriving at solutions through the use of UCMs; it may be followed without loss of continuity with respect to understanding solution details.

> **Chapter 1. A System View of Real-time Software.** This chapter explains the diversity of real-time systems and then outlines the book's approach to stepping back from this diversity to expose complex issues in a way that is general and scales up. In this approach, real-time systems are represented in three views: source code, wiring diagrams (called collaboration graphs), and path diagrams (called use case maps). The chapter explains the general nature of the relationship between the views and why these views are particularly important for real-time systems.
>
> **Chapter 2. Programming with the Tempo Kernel: Concurrent Processes.** This chapter introduces programming with the Tempo kernel. It shows how to use Tempo to create processes and how to write concurrent programs in which Tempo processes use only the most basic form of interprocess communication (IPC), namely semaphores. The objective is to introduce Tempo, not to go deeply into concurrent programming or IPC. The collaboration graph notation is gradually introduced to show how to characterize programs as systems after they have been explained as programs.
>
> **Chapter 3. Programming with the Tempo Kernel: Processing Real-time Events.** This chapter explains how to add interrupt service routines to Tempo programs to handle real-time events. It continues to introduce elements of the collaboration graph notation to explain programs as systems.
>
> **Chapter 4. Programming with the Tempo Kernel: Advanced IPC.** This chapter explains how to use the full range of Tempo IPC facilities. It continues to introduce

elements of the collaboration graph notation to explain programs as systems.

Chapter 5. Basic Design Notations. This chapter provides self-contained explanations of the basics of all the design notations used in the book (components, collaboration graphs, and use case maps) and relates the notations explicitly to the programming techniques introduced in previous chapters. The notations abstract away from dynamic situations in code involving pointers, creation and destruction of processes, and so forth, to give a system view that is structurally static. We do not represent systems as structurally dynamic just because the programming technology does things dynamically, but only if they are structurally dynamic in some more fundamental way (such systems are deferred to Chapter 9).

Chapter 6. Design Case Study: Message Transfer Utility (MTU). This chapter explores the design of a computer-communication system example, beginning with use case maps and ending with collaboration graphs. To focus on how to use the notations to deal with the big picture, it ignores many details.

Chapter 7. Design Case Study: Refining the MTU. This chapter refines the case study by adding details that were ignored in the previous chapter. For example, it treats failure and recovery in some detail. Again, the development is from use case maps to collaboration graphs.

Chapter 8. Implementation Case Study: Programming the MTU. This chapter gives highlights of how to implement the MTU from collaboration graphs developed earlier using the programming techniques that were introduced in the early chapters.

Chapter 9. Structurally Dynamic Systems. This chapter shows how to use the same design notations as in Chapter 5, with some extensions, for systems that are structurally dynamic in a large-scale, coarse-grained fashion. The extensions are not major, but the issues are sufficiently deep that introducing the extensions earlier would likely confuse rather than enlighten, by giving the misleading impression that the extensions are needed in all situations where the programming technology does things dynamically.

Chapter 10. A Look Inside the Tempo Kernel. This chapter opens up the Tempo kernel to show how it accomplishes its purpose. This is the only chapter that requires significant knowledge of C++. Knowledge of this chapter is not required to understand the rest of the book, but the material is interesting enough in this context that it merits inclusion here for the benefit of those who know C++ (although even those who don't can get a sense of how Tempo works from this chapter).

Chapter 11. Perspectives on Issues. This chapter wraps up the book by discussing the relevance of the material that has been presented to development practices in the "real world."

Appendix A. Tempo Reference Manual. This appendix summarizes the kernel functions and their use. The second part of this appendix gives helpful tips for avoiding the most common programming problems that novice real-time programmers often encounter.

Appendix B. Collaboration Graph Reference Manual. This appendix summarizes the collaboration graph notation, relates it to Tempo, and gives helpful hints for using the notation.

Appendix C. Programming Interrupt Controllers and UARTs. This appendix summarizes details of device programming that are needed for the MTU case study.

INTERNET ADDRESSES

Send email corrections and comments about this book to the following Internet address:

bailey@sce.carleton.ca

Find downloadable Tempo code, new information about Tempo, and corrections to this book (if any are needed) at the following Web site:

http://www.sce.carleton.ca/ftp/pub/RealTimeBook

Find information about related subjects, including related publications, at the following Web sites:

http://www.sce.carleton.ca/faculty/buhr.html
http://www.sce.carleton.ca/faculty/bailey.html

ACKNOWLEDGMENTS

Research supported by the National Research Council of Canada, Bell Northern Research, and the Telecommunications Research Institute of Ontario contributed to the development of the material in this book. We also acknowledge helpful technical discussions, comments, support, and encouragement during the development of some of this material from (alphabetically): Daniel Amyot, Francis Bordeleau, John Bryant, Don Cameron, Ron Casselman, Gary Driver, Bill Foster, Ric Holt, Curtis Hrishchuk, Ivar Jacobson, Gerald Karam, David Kennedy, Doug Lea, Michel Locas, Luigi Logrippo, Andrew Miga, Trevor Pearce, Mike Petras, Francois Pomerleau, Russ Pretty, Bob Probert, Bran Selic, Fahim Sheikh, Terry Shepard, Mark Vigder, D'Arcy Walsh, Steve Watson, David Wilson, and Murray Woodside. We thank students in Carleton undergraduate course 94.333 and graduate course 94.586 who served as test subjects for some of this material over several years. Thanks also to students from industry who tried the techniques at work, championed them among colleagues, and provided us with feedback. We thank Carleton's Department of Systems and Computer Engineering for providing a stimulating environment in which to develop ideas.

Thanks are due to the following reviewers, who read parts of early drafts of the manuscript and offered many suggestions for improvements: Colin Atkinson, University of Houston (Clear Lake); Greg Bond, University of British Columbia; Don Cameron, Bell Northern Research; Ric Holt, University of Toronto; Spiros Mancoridis, Drexel University.

Finally, we thank the following members of the editorial team at Prentice-Hall for their advice and their patience: Laura Steele, Rhodora Penaranda, Bayani DeLeon, Patricia Daly, and Kate Kaibni.

R. J. A. Buhr
D. L. Bailey

A System View of Real-Time Software

*I*n general, a *system* is a set of components that collaborates to achieve some common purpose. A *real-time system* is a computer-based system that must resolve a number of difficult issues simultaneously: rapid response; continuous operation; bursty stimuli; failure of its own components and connections; uncertainty about communication and processing delays; uncertainty about the state of the environment; possible geographical distribution; and the possible need to adapt over time (while continuously operating) to changing requirements and circumstances. A real-time system typically resolves these issues by means of collaborations among components that are not individually aware of the big picture.

Examples of real-time systems are as wide ranging as board-level communication products, consumer appliances controlled by embedded computers, telephone switches, air traffic control systems, on-line banking systems, and enterprise-support systems for intranets. Components include physical components, such as sensors, actuators, keypads, display screens, and communication chips, and software components, such as objects, concurrent processes, and agents. Programming languages include assembly language, C, C++, Smalltalk, Pascal, Fortran, Ada, Java, and many more. Runtime environments range from language-specific runtime systems to general-purpose operating systems. How are we to make sense of such diversity to get at common issues?

We do so in this book by stepping back from the diversity to expose complex issues in a way that is general and scales up. The purpose of this chapter is to explain the approach in a general way, to provide context for the remaining chapters. While doing so, concepts and terms will be introduced that you may only fully understand when you have finished the book and implemented some software, so don't expect this chapter to *explain* everything.

1.1 OUTLINE OF THE APPROACH

For an introductory book, our approach is unique. Real-time systems have three representations in this book: source code, wiring diagrams (called collaboration graphs), and path diagrams (called use case maps).

   The following figure gives a sense of the nature of these descriptions and provides a starting point for understanding how they may be used together. The stylized pictures are used in this and other diagrams of this chapter to *symbolize* the things named underneath them. A diskette is not source code, but a picture of a diskette provides a convenient symbol for source code, because source code exists as files on storage media. Similarly, although requirements may be expressed by more than prose documents, a picture of a prose document symbolizes the nature of requirements definitions as somewhat informal descriptions, an important element of which is prose.

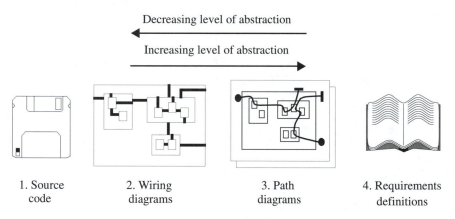

Decreasing level of abstraction

Increasing level of abstraction

| 1. Source code | 2. Wiring diagrams | 3. Path diagrams | 4. Requirements definitions |

   In the preceding figure, moving from right to left lowers the level of abstraction; this is the direction of designing from a blank sheet, with the source code as the end product. Moving from left to right raises the level of abstraction; this is the direction of understanding existing code in system and requirements terms.

1.1.1 The First Level of Description: Source Code

Source code is the means of implementation but not the main point of the book, so we keep it as simple as possible. We use a C-like subset of C++ with a small C++ kernel to support concurrent processes. There is nothing fundamental about this choice, except to keep the programming side simple. Almost any other programming language familiar to the reader would do as well, including full C++, Java, or Ada. Languages such as these are the Ferraris of the programming world. They are useful and worth learning in their own right, but they would absorb our attention to the point of distracting us from the system issues that are our central concern. For our purposes, the mundane C Volkswagon suffices.

We say *the code is not the system*, meaning that source code kept on storage media is not the same thing as the system that comes into existence when the source code is compiled, linked with a kernel, and loaded into some target environment. *Systems* exhibit emergent properties that are often difficult to see in source code. The components that drive system behavior are often somewhat implicit in source code (for example, processes—see Section 1.2.1).

This book begins with code in Chapters 2 through 4, but only because experience has shown that the best way of getting the intended message across to our intended audience is by proceeding from the concrete to the abstract. Gradually, as the book proceeds, the emphasis shifts away from code as the starting point, but code is always used to make system abstractions concrete.

1.1.2 The Second Level of Description: Wiring Diagrams

Wiring diagrams of software are used for viewing the system as a set of collaborating components. Section 1.2 provides more details, but the general idea is as follows. Boxes represent software components and connectors represent the means of intercomponent collaboration. In the stylized diagram in Section 1.1, only one connecting line is shown between each pair of connected components, to symbolize the *concept* of a connector, but in general there may be many connectors and they may have different shapes to indicate different types of interaction. Similarly, only rectangular boxes are shown for components, to symbolize the concept of a component, but, in general, the shapes used to represent different types of system components vary (for brevity, we shall often use the term *box* as a synonym for *a shape representing a system component*, without implying that the shape is rectangular).

1.1.3 The Third Level of Description: Path Diagrams

Path diagrams are used for viewing the system as a whole. Section 1.3 provides more details, but the general idea is as follows: Path diagrams show stimulus-response paths threading through the components. They leave out connectors and all the implications that go with them, thus treating them as deferred detail and replacing the detail with a more abstract view.

1.1.4 The Fourth Level of Description: Requirements

A fourth level of description, requirements, requires no new notation. Path diagrams bridge the gap between requirements and solutions. They also bridge the gap between so-called functional and nonfunctional requirements. The latter term refers to whole-system properties, such as performance and fault-tolerance. Because path diagrams are used for viewing the system as a whole, they are capable of including so-called nonfunctional requirements in their scope. For example, performance is related to traversal times along end-to-end paths through the system, and fault tolerance is related to the ability to survive failures that may occur along the paths. Path diagrams also provide a starting point for devising test strategies and test cases.

1.2 WIRING DIAGRAMS

The wiring diagrams we use are of a relatively common type in the software industry, although with some special nuances; they provide a way of understanding the running code as a *system* of interacting components (the boxes).

Implicit in the definition of a system as a set of collaborating components is the idea that some components must be *active*—meaning they must have autonomy and be able to operate concurrently.

1.2.1 Processes as Representative Active System Components

Active system components are typified by concurrent processes. We assume that readers of this book have encountered concurrent processes before, but will be unfamiliar with our way of representing them as system components by means of a diagramming notation.

The systems of this book are, in essence, systems of processes. There may be other types of components in a system to provide support to processes (particularly important ones are interrupt service routines, or ISRs), but processes provide the conceptual core.

Processes provide an illustration of our observation that "the system is hard to see in the software." Processes are runtime units that are often not directly visible at the source-code-packaging level because they are often created at runtime by mechanisms outside the programming language (as is the case with the processes of this book). Even if they are visible in the programming language as types or classes, the system is hard to see because it does not come into existence until instances are created at runtime, there may be many instances of each type or class, and the collaboration is hidden in code bodies. In general, the concept of a *system* component does not necessarily align with the concept of a piece of source code that is packaged as a unit for separate compilation, development, or reuse (for example, modules, source files, and classes).

The term *process* is used in this book with several shades of meaning, ranging from concrete to abstract. At the concrete end of the range, a process is a specific type of software component supported by the particular programming technology of this book. In the middle of the range, a process is a generic name for a concept that goes by other names in other programming technologies (for example, *thread* in Java, *task* in Ada, *actor* in a CASE tool for real-time system design called ObjecTime, and *concurrent object* in some object-oriented programming technologies). At the abstract end of the range, the term is used for a general concept of an active system component, expressed by a design notation. The design notation enables us to conceptualize any system as a set of collaborating processes (and other supporting components).

The use of processes as a central concept in this book does not mean that programs without processes cannot be real-time programs. A real-time program may be no more than a sequential main program and a set of interrupt service routines. However, using processes as an organizing concept is useful for many reasons that will be outlined later. Furthermore, the *concept* of a system being composed of processes is not violated by processless programs. A main program is, conceptually, a lone process. A set of collaborating computers, each with a lone process of this type, is, in effect, a set of collaborating processes.

Thus this book aims to provide a very general view of real-time systems as systems of collaborating processes. The term *collaborating* is important, because it rules out systems that use processes only to time-share independent, sequential application programs on a single processor.

A lot of baggage accompanies processes, such as interprocess communication (IPC) techniques that enable processes to interact, real-time clocks that enable processes to deal with failures by timing out when expected events fail to arrive (from the environment or other processes), interfaces to physical input/output (I/O) devices that enable processes to control I/O, and interrupt service routines (ISRs) that pass physical events to processes.

Although the process concept is widely understood by experienced practitioners, processes can seem mysterious to novices, who may have trouble seeing where processes are required, and who may become confused by the confusing variety of process terminology and IPC techniques that exist in practice. Therefore, a major concern of this book is demystifying processes.

Having established processes as our main type of system component, we can now go back to calling system components just *components*, using the term to include any operational unit in a running implementation (for example, processes, objects, ISRs, and groups of any or all of these, called *teams* in this book).

1.2.2 Collaborating Components

We use wiring diagrams to show the *collaborating-component* aspect of real-time systems. The essence of a wiring notation is illustrated in the next diagram using rectangular boxes to stand for any type of component (we sometimes call the boxes in diagrams like this *neutral shapes* to signify an intended lack of commitment to component type). Chapter 5 describes a wiring notation with a number of different possible shapes for boxes and connectors. Other wiring notations exist that may differ in detail (although not in general intent).

The neutral shapes in the next diagram suffice to indicate the general nature of any wiring notation used for system design. Boxes represent system components (for example, processes) and connectors ("wires") represent paths for interactions between components (for example, for sending and receiving messages). Offsets between internal and external wires in glass-box views (views in which internal components are shown) symbolize the interposition of a component's intrinsic behavior between external and internal wires. The intrinsic behavior of a component (for example, the mainline of a process) is not shown as an internal component but is imagined as residing in the box edges.

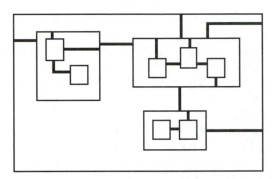

Think of the boxes as *code boxes*, meaning that code associated with the boxes must be executed to cause work to be done inside them and interactions to take place between them. The key phrase here is *code associated with the boxes*—keep in mind that the boxes may not literally represent code. For example, different processes may have the same code mainline, so thinking of process boxes as literally representing the code would be incorrect; we must perform some mental tricks to think about software in system terms.

Because we think of the boxes as code boxes, data are pushed down as detail in these diagrams. Data are viewed as being stored in code boxes or flowing over connections, but the code boxes *themselves* do not represent data.

The wiring model requires commitment to the interface operators of components (for example, operators to send or receive particular types of messages), the quantities transferred (for example, messages), and the internal logic of components that implements collaborations (for example, receives a message over one connection and consequentially sends one over another).

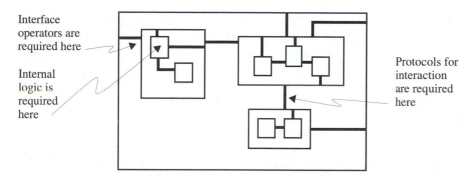

The definition of these elements provides a starting point for the creation of source code.

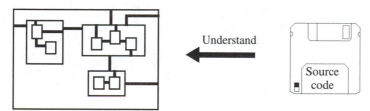

Completed source code can be understood in system terms by means of wiring diagrams.

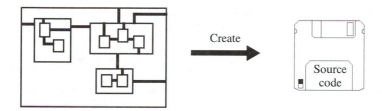

With practice, a person starts to think of wiring diagrams as systems and the source code as just the means of implementing them. The diagrams are abstractions that may be quite hard to see in the code but accurately represent the systems that exist while the code is running.

1.2.3 Relationship to Real-Time Systems

How do wiring diagrams help us to deal with the issues of real-time systems? A real-time system must respond to unpredictable stimuli from its environment in a timely fashion while operating reliably and continuously in the presence of failures in its own (perhaps distributed) components and connections, and uncertainty about the state of its environment.

Wiring diagrams help us stand back from code details to see the system in terms of stimuli that trigger actions inside components, actions that in turn have effects on other components. The diagrams are sufficiently abstract to be equally useful for representing a software system running on a uniprocessor or a geographically distributed system. The boxes and connectors are identifiable as potential failure points in the system and thus provide a framework for understanding where mechanisms to recover from failures should be placed.

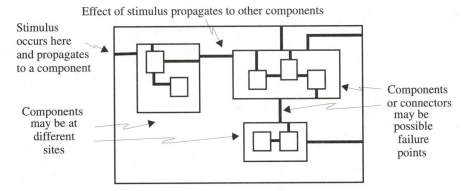

Wiring diagrams are very useful for detailed design of systems, because they provide a framework for defining and understanding details of components and interactions. However, wiring diagrams are not particularly useful for understanding whole-system properties such as performance and the effects of failures on whole-system operation. Such properties are often thought of as nonfunctional because they arise from the collective behavior of many components and cannot be pinned down to any particular component. Wiring diagrams are not particularly helpful because they provide a component-centric view (next diagram). Many details have to be put together from many component-centric views to understand whole-system properties.

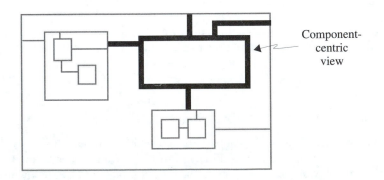

Novices may have trouble realizing the significance of this point, because the examples they see (including the ones in this book) are likely to be too small in scale. The issue becomes very important when systems are large enough that many tens or even hundreds of diagrams are required to describe them (including not only wiring diagrams, but also other types of diagrams, including ones not used in this book). For such systems, getting lost in component-centric details is very easy.

1.3 PATH DIAGRAMS

The path diagrams we use are a novelty in an introductory book. They provide insight into real-time system issues at the whole-system level, issues that are associated with stimulus-response sequences. Examples of such issues are achieving fast stimulus-response times, recovering from failures in the middle of such sequences, and dealing with bursts of stimuli that may require many sequences to be processed at once, and that may produce emergent behavior that is difficult to understand at a detailed level, such as races among activities triggered by different stimuli of a burst.

Path diagrams are used to remove some of the magic that seems to be required to deal with such issues at the level of wiring diagrams and source code. They are also helpful for thinking of so-called nonfunctional requirements in functional terms.

Path diagrams are two levels of abstraction removed from code and probably also new in concept to most readers, so keep in mind that they are not being *explained* here, only motivated. Chapter 4 and the subsequent case-study chapters explain and apply them. Path diagrams represent stimulus-response paths directly. They show cause-effect sequences as paths, without regard to how the paths are realized by connectors, interfaces, and component logic (next diagram). The original cause is a stimulus at the start point of a path (a filled circle). The final effect is felt at the end point of a path (a bar). In between, a path traces cause-effect sequences from component to component (symbolized by the pointing finger in the diagram, which is not part of the notation).

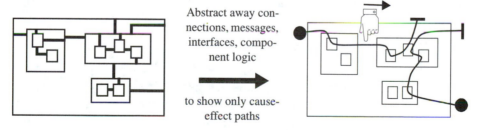

Abstract away connections, messages, interfaces, component logic

to show only cause-effect paths

Here is an example of how such diagrams help us to see the big picture for an implemented real-time system (this is an example, not fully explained, of the kind of issue treated in Chapters 4 through 7). Imagine the boxes are processes. Imagine that a burst of stimuli occurs while a particular process among many is running (the stimuli would be seen by the software as interrupts). The first stimulus of the burst could cause the currently running process to be preempted to enable a higher-priority process to deal with stimulus. Imagine that the preempted process is one stage in a pipeline of processes along a path from an earlier stimulus (a pipeline is one among many possible process architectures). Imagine the preempting process as belonging to a different pipeline along a different path. In effect, the paths are concurrent and preemptable, not just the processes. Thus a burst of stimuli can cause many paths to be in progress concurrently. When the burst passes, the paths will be completed, one after the other, as dictated by the process scheduling rules. A set of processes tries to keep progress going along such a set of paths, in a decentralized, collaborative fashion, without any process seeing the big picture. This seems and is potentially complex in wiring-diagram terms, but is much simpler in path terms.

A designer must stand back from wiring-diagram-level details to understand how to realize paths correctly. Path diagrams help, by enabling the designer to think in a high-level way about issues such as end-to-end response time along paths, interference along paths, race conditions between paths, and failures causing paths to be unable to complete.

• Paths determine response times
• Paths help identify interference issues

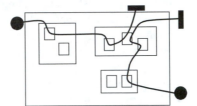

• Paths help identify implications of failures
• Paths help identify race conditions

As described in Chapters 6 and 7, we may use paths for discovering processes and process architectures from application requirements (a pipeline of processes is one kind of architecture, but there are many others, for example, master-slave, and collaborating peer); for building failure detection/recovery into the process architectures; for making tradeoffs between different architectures (for example, based on judgments about performance); for deciding on required IPC mechanisms; and for integrating components other than processes into the architectures.

Alternative solutions   Make tradeoffs between alterna-tives

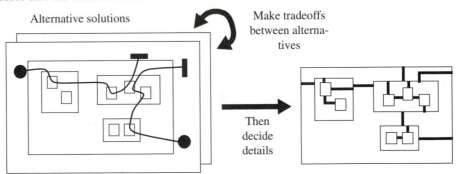

Then decide details

Path diagrams provides a starting point for removing the mystery from designing and implementing real-time software with processes. Stimulus-response paths are given independent, concrete representation to serve as a basis for discovering processes to real-ize them. Once processes are discovered, they become the centers around which other types of components coalesce during the design process. In this way, the special issues of real-time systems are kept to the forefront.

1.4 STRUCTURALLY DYNAMIC SYSTEMS

Wiring diagrams are nothing if not fixed, so using them as design models seems to imply that systems must have fixed structure. Actually, what it means is that *conceptualizing* them this way is often useful. In many software technologies (including the one of this book), software "wires itself" after it starts to run. For example, processes are dynamically created by other processes and their identifiers passed to still other processes for IPC pur-poses. You will look in vain in the code for anything that is literally like a wire, but a wir-ing diagram is a useful fiction if the effect is to establish IPC relationships that endure for a time (perhaps for the lifetime of the system).

However, writing a program that continually "rewires itself" as it runs is often as easy as writing one that does not. The programming techniques are no different; the differ-ence is in the details. Furthermore, there may be good reasons for writing such programs (e.g., error recovery, device installation, downloading software from elsewhere). The effect may be viewed in terms of wiring diagrams that continually change form while the system is running (analogous to morphing in computer animation). Components and wires may both change over time (as shown in the next diagram), or only wires may change (the same components may be continually forming themselves into different collaborating groups for different purposes, each group with a different wiring diagram).

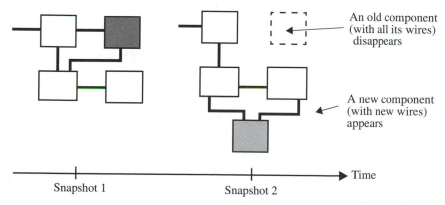

An old component (with all its wires) disappears

A new component (with new wires) appears

Time

Snapshot 1   Snapshot 2

Although structural dynamics may sound like an exotic property not normally encountered in run-of-the-mill systems, software often routinely does things so dynami-cally—through the use of pointers to provide access to components like processes and objects that may be dynamically created at any time and accessed from different places in the code at different times—that continual "rewiring" may seem to be the rule rather than the exception.

One reason for saying something about structural dynamics so early in the book, even though notations for it are not presented until Chapter 9, is that the subject is unavoidable. Even the simplest programs of this book "wire" and "rewire" themselves in some sense. However, many programs may have system-level wiring diagrams that are effectively fixed on a large scale, even when small-scale, fine-grained details are continually changing. For example, a program that may be viewed as having a fixed wiring diagram at the level of processes and IPC may be structurally dynamic at the level of message objects passed between processes. *The trick is to know what to include and what not to include in the system picture.* Structural dynamics should be included in this picture when it is relatively large scale and coarse grained (for example, reinstalling large units of software for error recovery purposes, installing drivers for new devices, downloading software applications from elsewhere), but not when it is as small scale and fine grained as creating and destroying message objects.

Another reason for mentioning this topic early is to warn readers that the obvious way of looking at structurally dynamic systems—morphing wiring diagrams—is not the best way. Too many diagrams are required and the approach does not scale up. Better approaches are described in Chapter 9, including an approach with path diagrams.

A final reason for mentioning this topic here is to say that another reason for choosing path diagrams as one of only two main visual notations for this book is their expressiveness about structurally dynamic systems. Such systems are becoming too important in modern software, including in the real-time system domain, for structural dynamics to be left to details. Learning how think about structural dynamics in a high-level way from the start seems like a good idea.

1.5 "REAL-TIME" VERSUS "FAST"

It has taken us a while to get to the point where we can confront this issue directly, but we needed to establish some background first. Clearly, from all we have said, the term *real-time* means more than just "fast." All programs must be fast enough to meet the requirements of their users, but simply saying a program must be fast does not make it a real-time one. For example, a program to invert matrices must be fast, but we would not normally characterize it as a real-time program (unless, perhaps, the program was organized as a set of processes running on multiple computers and multiple inversions were going on at the same time in response to different stimuli of different degrees of urgency and importance).

Real-time means dealing directly with system issues such as physical distribution, unpredictable stimuli, failures in components and connections, and uncertainty about the state of the environment, and with the effects of these issues on the system's performance and robustness. *Fast* is part of real time, but not the only part, and must be traded off against other issues.

The use of processes does not guarantee a program will be *fast.* However, it provides a way of dealing with the issue by enabling performance to be tuned by adjusting process

priorities, the number of physical processors, and relationships between ISRs and processes, without having to change tested code.

Processes have always been important for soft real-time systems and, with the emergence of better scheduling techniques, are becoming increasingly important for hard real-
time systems. The difference lies in the scheduling techniques—which are outside the
scope of this book—not in the concept of processes.

1.6 OTHER NOTATIONS

This section is included here mainly for general interest. With the exception of *timing diagrams*, nothing in the rest of the book depends on it. The two main types of diagrams used
in this book have been deliberately selected from among many possibilities. Other possibilities are suggested in stylized form in the following figure and explained after the figure.

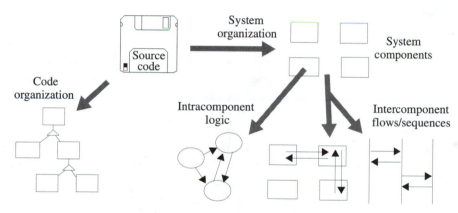

One type of diagram shows the organization of source code. For example, the organization of object-oriented programs written in languages such as C++ centers around
classes and class hierarchies, and *class relationship diagrams* (represented here by a stylized tree structure of the kind used to show inheritance relationships among classes) may
be used to show this organization. However, the unique issues of real-time systems center
around behavior and such diagrams do not give much insight into behaviour, so we do not
use them.

Other types of diagrams that focus more on *system* organization/behavior are more
useful for exposing the unique issues of real-time systems. State-transition diagrams or
Harel statecharts may be used to describe intracomponent logic. Flow/sequence diagrams
of various types may be used to show intercomponent flows and sequences (of quantities
such as messages or data), either as arrows between component boxes or as sequences of
arrows between component timelines (the latter type of diagram is often called an *interaction diagram* or *message sequence chart*).

However useful such notations may be, they are not used in this book (except for a
very brief use of state transition diagrams) because we think that, for the purposes of this
book, the notational issues they raise would be out of proportion to the insights they would
give to novice readers.

The two main notations we have chosen to use in this book are particularly powerful for giving insight into the special issues of real-time systems, and are mostly sufficient for this purpose. The logic of our components is usually simple enough that code (or pseudocode) suffices to describe it, making the use of diagrams for intracomponent logic mostly unnecessary. The wiring notation is easily augmented by notations and sequence numbers to indicate intercomponent flows and sequences. Occasionally we show inter-component temporal sequences using a particularly simple form of diagram called a *timing diagram*, in which temporal sequences are indicated by square-wave shapes. Timing diagrams are sufficiently simple and obvious that they raise few notational issues.

Other notations than the ones of this book may be easily learned and used by the reader in a supplementary fashion once the notations of this book have been internalized.

1.7 SUMMARY

In this chapter we have

- Defined a system as a set of components that collaborate to achieve an overall purpose, and a real-time system as a particular kind of system in which many issues must be resolved simultaneously, such as performance, failure detection and recovery, geographical distribution, and self-modification.
- Explained that concurrent processes are the cornerstone components of real-time systems in this book, for many practical and conceptual reasons.
- Motivated and explained the nature of the three levels of description of real-time systems used in this book: source code, wiring diagrams (for viewing the system as a set of interacting components), and path diagrams (for viewing the system as a whole in terms of stimulus-response paths threading through the components).
- Explained that diagrams are needed because "the system" is an abstraction that is hard to see in the code and that wiring diagrams are a convenient fiction, because there is no concept of "wires" in code.
- Explained that wiring diagrams and path diagrams have been selected, from among many possible diagram types, because, in our opinion, they give the most insight with the least number of diagrams into the special issues of real-time systems.
- Explained that path diagrams provide a bridge between requirements and solutions.
- Identified *structural dynamics* as an important issue that emerges even from very simple programs.
- Explained the difference between *real-time* and *fast*.
- Explained that this book does not aim to *cover* the field of real-time systems, in the sense of explaining all techniques in use in the field, but only to introduce novices to the core issues of the field through a set of techniques that will scale up and can be used in conjunction with other techniques.

CHAPTER 2

Programming with the Tempo
Kernel: Concurrent Processes

*T*his chapter introduces programming with the Tempo multitasking kernel that underlies all the programming examples of this book. To demonstrate the fundamental concepts, we present the source code for several complete programs. Along the way, we introduce visual notations as a means of stepping back from the code, to help us explain program organization and behavior.

All the programs in this book are written in what we call *skinny C++* (the subset of C++ that corresponds roughly to C), so you don't need to know anything about C++ classes or objects to understand our examples. Our skinny C++ code is essentially standard C, except that we use C++ stream input and output instead of C's standard I/O library. Although we use a familiar programming language, our multitasking programs are organized and designed very differently from conventional (sequential) programs. Neither C++ nor C provide support for concurrent programming, so we use Tempo to provide the abstractions needed for multitasking programs. Tempo supports the creation and management of concurrent processes. It also provides mechanisms for those processes to synchronize and communicate with each other.

2.1 TEMPO PROCESSES—A FIRST EXAMPLE

Figure 2.1 is a Tempo program consisting of a single process that simply displays the string, "Hello, world!", on the system console. At start-up, Tempo creates a single process from `Main()` and then transfers control to the process. The process starts execution at the first statement in `Main()`. After printing its message, `Main()` exits and returns control to Tempo. Tempo then destroys the process and terminates.

```
// ch2ex1.cpp - a process that prints "Hello, world!"

#include <iostream.h>
#include "tempo.h"

// The root function for the Main process
void Main()
{
    CS(cout << "Hello, world!" << endl);
}
```

Figure 2.1 The "Hello, world!" program as a Tempo process.

The `#include` statements refer to two *header files*, `tempo.h` and `iostream.h`. The statement

```
#include <iostream.h>
```

causes the compiler to read the contents of file `iostream.h`, which contains the declarations for the standard stream input and output facilities supplied with C++. The interface to Tempo is defined by `tempo.h`; the compiler reads this file when it encounters

```
#include "tempo.h"
```

Because `tempo.h` is enclosed by quotation marks, the compiler starts searching for the file in the subdirectory where the `.cpp` (source code) file is located.

The next section of code is a function called `Main()` that defines the Main process. Every Tempo program begins execution in a Main process. Each Tempo program must have a `Main()` function (with an uppercase "M"), in the same way that every sequential C++ program has a function called `main()` (with a lowercase "m"). We refer to `Main()` as the *root function* for the Main process. This particular `Main()` contains a single statement:

```
CS(cout << "Hello, world!" << endl);
```

The statement inside the parentheses is a C++ stream output statement. It will be familiar to C++ programmers and is easy to understand for C programmers (it simply replaces a call to the standard I/O library's `printf` function). The output operator "`<<`" writes the string "Hello, world!", followed by an end-of-line character, to the standard output stream `cout`.

CS, on the other hand, is not part of normal sequential C or C++ programming. CS is unique to Tempo: It is a macro that is defined in `tempo.h`. Any program statement enclosed by this macro's parentheses (in this case, the stream output statement) is executed in a *critical section*. The need for critical sections will be explained in Section 2.3, but for now it is enough to know that each program statement that performs input or output or calls one of the standard C++ library functions must be in a critical section. The Tempo programs in the sections that follow provide additional examples of using the CS macro.

A conventional C or C++ program begins execution in a function called `main()`, so why is there no `main()` function in Figure 2.1? The answer is, `main()` is part of the kernel because it is the same for all Tempo programs. Tempo's `main()`, shown in Figure 2.2, initializes the kernel, creates the first process from `Main()`, and arranges for this process to start executing. You do not need to understand `main()` to write Tempo code, but knowing it aids understanding of the relationship between Tempo programs and C++.

```
void main()
{
    // initialize kernel data structures
    initialize_Tempo();
    // create the first process from user's Main()
    Main_process = create_process(Main, 0);
    // start Main process executing
    become_idle();              // this call never returns
}
```

Figure 2.2 main() for all Tempo programs (part of the Tempo kernel).

The `initialize_Tempo()` function in Figure 2.2 is called once, from `main()`, to initialize the data structures inside the kernel. Function `create_process()` in Figure 2.2 is one of several Tempo functions for managing and coordinating processes. Function `main()` calls `create_process()` to create a single process that starts execution at the first statement in the root function `Main()`. The value returned by `create_process()` is a *process id* that identifies the newly instantiated process. Function `main()` then calls `become_idle()` to turn itself into Tempo's idle process (the idle process is explained in Section 2.2.1).

2.1.1 Creating Additional Processes

Every Tempo program has a single process that is created by the kernel at start-up from the `Main()` function, but any Tempo process can create additional independent processes.

```
// ch2ex2.cpp - creating a process that prints
//               "Hello, world"

#include <iostream.h>
#include "tempo.h"

void hello();

void Main()
{
    Process process1;

    process1 = create_process(hello);
}

// The root function for process1
void hello()
{
    CS(cout << "Hello, world, from process1" << endl);
}
```

Figure 2.3 Creating a Tempo process.

The program presented in Figure 2.3 reworks the previous example to show how this is done. `Main()` calls Tempo's `create_process()` function, supplying it with the address of `hello()`:

```
process1 = create_process(hello);
```

Tempo creates a single process that starts execution at the first statement in the root function `hello()`.

2.1.2 Process Termination

`Main()` does not call `hello()` or wait for it to finish. When `create_process()` returns, we have two independent processes: one executing `Main()`, the other, `hello()`. After creating the new process, `Main()` simply exits to Tempo and is destroyed; meanwhile, the process executing `hello()` prints its message.

What happens when `hello()` finishes? In a conventional program, `hello()` would simply return to the function that called it, but `hello()` is not explicitly called. The explanation is simple: When the root function of a process returns, it passes control back to Tempo, which destroys the process. A Tempo program terminates when all processes have been destroyed. There are two processes in this example, so the program doesn't terminate until both `Main()` and `hello()` have returned.

Not all processes have to return. Often, a process is cyclic, meaning that its root function has an infinite loop and implying ongoing execution until something outside the process terminates the execution of the Tempo program. That something is the kernel function `terminate_multitasking()`, which can be called by any process to halt the currently executing Tempo program and exit to the operating system. This way of shutting down a Tempo program containing cyclic processes is much simpler than the alternative of asking each process (using the techniques presented in Section 2.3) to terminate, until all processes are destroyed and the program terminates. (The program in Section 4.2 illustrates how this function is used.)

2.1.3 Program Preparation and Execution

Program development uses common programming tools (we use Borland's C++ development environments) running under a common operating system (we use MS-DOS, but programs can also be developed in the Windows 95 or Windows NT environments). Object code for the application program is linked to the Tempo kernel; then the entire application is loaded into memory as an ordinary, sequential program running under the operating system. After initialization, the Tempo program effectively takes over the machine; that is, all of the software and hardware resources are devoted to executing a single, multitasking application. Figure 2.4 is a *uses diagram* showing the software and hardware layers in a computer executing a multitasking Tempo program. It shows that the developer's skinny C++ code uses the Tempo kernel to manage processes.

Tempo is not a complete operating system when compared to, say, MS-DOS or Unix. Specifically, Tempo does not provide functions to manage the system memory pool or to perform console and file input/output; that is why we refer to Tempo as a kernel. Tempo could be used as the kernel of a full-fledged operating system, but for the real-time programs we describe in this book, this is unnecessary.

In practice, the absence of memory management and I/O support in Tempo is not a problem. The C++ run-time library contains routines for managing dynamically allocated memory and performing stream I/O to files and the system console. The functions in this library are built on top of the operating system, which remains resident and usable while a Tempo application executes. Figure 2.4 shows that the application's processes and the kernel both use the services provided by the underlying layers, by calling C++ library functions.

I/O device drivers may be added outside the kernel to handle hardware that is not supported by the operating system. Figure 2.4 implies that Tempo processes can perform low-level I/O operations by reading and writing these devices, and as we shall see in the next chapter, interrupt service routines associated with these devices can use Tempo services to synchronize and share data with processes.

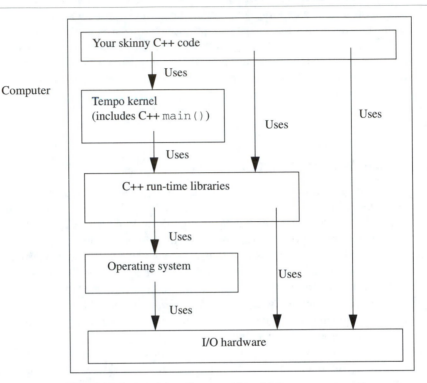

Figure 2.4 Layers in a Tempo multitasking program at run time.

Figure 2.5 compares the source code of a sequential C or C++ program and a concurrent Tempo program:

A sequential C or C++program	A concurrent Tempo program
• must have a `main()` function	• must have a `Main()` function (the root function for the Main process)
	• may have other functions that serve as root functions for other processes
• may have other functions	• may have other functions

Figure 2.5 Source code components of sequential C/C++ and concurrent Tempo programs.

2.1.4 Tempo Kernel Functions

The interface between processes and Tempo is a set of 23 skinny C++ *kernel functions* (see Figure 2.6).[*] We list these functions here, without detailed explanation, to give a quick overview of the nature of Tempo. Detailed descriptions of what each of these functions do are presented in Chapters 2, 3, and 4 and Appendix A.

Kernel startup & shutdown
initialize_Tempo();
become_idle();
terminate_multitasking();
	Initialize kernel and create Main process
	Create the idle process
	Halt the Tempo program and exit to O/S

Process management
pid = create_process(root_function);
pid = create_process(root-function, priority);
process_sleep(num_ticks);
	Create a new process with priority 0
	Create a new process
	Put calling process to sleep

Semaphore management
sem_id = create_semaphore();
sem_id = create_semaphore(initial_count);
wait_semaphore(sem_id);
signal_semaphore(sem_id);
	Create a new semaphore with initial count 0
	Create a new semaphore
	Wait on a semaphore
	Signal a semaphore

Event queue management
signal(pid, queue);
queue = wait();
send(pid, queue, msg, ack_queue);
queue = receive(msg, pid, ack_queue);
reply(pid, queue, reply);
mask_queue(queue);
unmask_queue(queue);
	Signal a process queue
	Wait for a signal from any process
	Send a message to a process queue
	Wait for a signal or a message from any process
	Reply a message to a process queue
	Mask an event queue
	Unmask an event queue

Timeout management
status = wait_semaphore(sem_id, timeout);
queue = wait(timeout);
queue = receive(&msg, &pid, &ack_queue, timeout);
	Wait on a semaphore, with timeout
	Wait for a signal, with timeout
	Wait for a signal or a message, with timeout

Interrupt management
saved_flags = disable_ints();
enable_ints();
restore_flags(saved_flags);
	Disable interrupts at the processor
	Enable interrupts at the processor
	Update processor flags register

Figure 2.6 Tempo kernel functions. *pid* is a process identifier and *sem_id* is a semaphore identifier.

---

[*] The interface functions of a full-fledged operating system are more commonly known as system calls or system primitives, but we use the term kernel functions exclusively when referring to the interface to Tempo, to distinguish them from the services (system calls) provided by the operating system layer beneath Tempo (see Figure 2.4).

2.2 PROGRAMS WITH MULTIPLE PROCESSES

In the Tempo program shown in Figure 2.7, the Main process creates two other processes, process1 and process2. Each process prints a message 10 times and then terminates.

```
// ch2ex3.cpp - two processes that write to the console

#include "tempo.h"
#include <iostream.h>

void process1root(), process2root();

void Main()
{

    Process process1, process2;

    // create two concurrent processes.
    // process1 has higher priority than process2
    process1 = create_process(process1root, 1);
    process2 = create_process(process2root, 0);
}

// root function for the first process
void process1root()
{
    for (int i = 0; i < 10; i++) {
        CS(cout << "Process 1 here, i = " << i << endl);
    }
}

// root function for the second process
void process2root()
{
    for (int j = 0; j < 10; j++) {
        CS(cout << "Process 2 here, j = " << j << endl);
    }
}
```

Figure 2.7 A Tempo program with three processes.

In this example, we pass two arguments to create_process(). The second argument specifies an integer *scheduling priority* for the newly created process:

```
process1 = create_process(process1root, 1);
process2 = create_process(process2root, 0);
```

The lowest scheduling priority is 0; higher integer values correspond to higher priorities. Priorities affect the order in which processes are scheduled for execution by Tempo.

In this example, `process1` is assigned a higher priority than `process2`, so Tempo arranges for `process1` to run before `process2`. In this example, `process1`, once started, executes to completion before `process2` is scheduled for execution, as shown in Figure 2.8.

```
Process 1 here, i = 0
Process 1 here, i = 1
Process 1 here, i = 2
Process 1 here, i = 3
Process 1 here, i = 4
Process 1 here, i = 5
Process 1 here, i = 6
Process 1 here, i = 7
Process 1 here, i = 8
Process 1 here, i = 9
Process 2 here, j = 0
Process 2 here, j = 1
Process 2 here, j = 2
Process 2 here, j = 3
Process 2 here, j = 4
Process 2 here, j = 5
Process 2 here, j = 6
Process 2 here, j = 7
Process 2 here, j = 8
Process 2 here, j = 9
```

Figure 2.8 Output from the two processes in Figure 2.7.

2.2.1 Sharing the Processor between Processes

Processes that run on a single processor are not physically concurrent. At any time, the computer is executing instructions from a single process. The role of a multitasking kernel is to provide the illusion of concurrency by causing the processes to execute in an interleaved manner. How this is accomplished will be examined several times in the remainder of this chapter. Here is a first look.

Look again at the output shown in Figure 2.8. From the preceding description, you might expect to see output from one process interleaved with the lines printed by the other process, but as the figure shows, `process2` doesn't start until `process1` has finished printing its message ten times. When `process1root()` returns, Tempo destroys `process1` and then schedules `process2` for execution. So if this is a multitasking program, why does Tempo let `process1` to run to completion before allowing `process2` to execute?

When Tempo schedules a process for execution, the process executes until it voluntarily relinquishes the processor (by calling a kernel function), terminates, or is preempted by a higher-priority process. (In Chapter 3, we will see how process preemption can be triggered by real-time events delivered by hardware interrupts.) In Figure 2.7, `process1` executes first because it has a higher priority than `process2`. None of the statements in `process1root()` call Tempo kernel functions, and the program handles no real-time events, so there is no opportunity for Tempo to give the processor to `process2` before `process1` finishes. When `process1` terminates, Tempo regains control and starts `process2` executing.

```cpp
// ch2ex4.cpp - two processes that write to the console

#include "tempo.h"
#include <iostream.h>

void process1root(), process2root();

void Main()
{
    Process process1, process2;

    // create two concurrent processes
    // process1 has higher priority than process2
    process1 = create_process(process1root, 1);
    process2 = create_process(process2root, 0);
}

// root function for the first process
void process1root()
{
    // amount of time for process to sleep
    const unsigned int NUM_TICKS = 5;

    for (int i = 0; i < 10; i++) {
        CS(cout << "Process 1 here, i = " << i << endl);
        process_sleep(NUM_TICKS);
    }
}

// root function for the second process
void process2root()
{
    for (int j = 0; j < 10; j++) {
        CS(cout << "Process 2 here, j = " << j << endl);
    }
}
```

Figure 2.9 Using `process_sleep()` to relinquish the processor.

Observe that there is no *timeslicing*. Timeslicing means the kernel schedules processes in a round-robin fashion, allowing each process to run for a fixed amount of time.

Timeslicing is one way to share a processor between multiple processes, but many multi-tasking kernels designed for real-time applications, including Tempo, do not use timeslicing. Instead, they rely on real-time events to make processes ready to run and preemption of lower-priority processes to ensure that processes that need processor time urgently get it. The assumption is that high-priority processes will be written to execute only for a short time.

Real-time events will enter the picture in Chapter 3, but for now we can show the nature of their effects by using Tempo's `process_sleep()` kernel function. Most Intel-standard computers have a timer device that is programmed to "tick" at 18.2 times per second. Tempo uses this timer to provide various timing services to processes. One of these, `process_sleep()`, allows processes to give up the processor for a specified number of ticks. The program in Figure 2.9 is identical to the previous example (Figure 2.7), except that the kernel function call `process_sleep(NUM_TICKS)` has been added to `process1root()`.

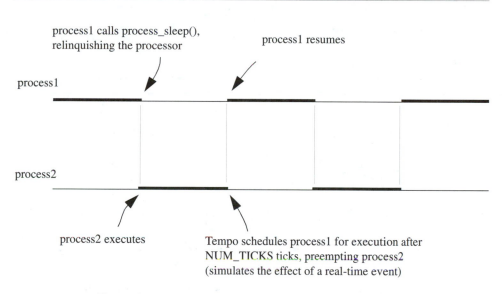

Figure 2.10 Context switching between process1 and process2.

The timing diagram in Figure 2.10 illustrates how control is interleaved between higher-priority `process1` (executing `process1root`) and lower-priority `process2` (executing `process2root`). After printing a line of output, `process1` calls `process_sleep()`, informing Tempo that it wishes to relinquish the processor for NUM_TICKS ticks of the timer. Because `process2` is eligible to run, Tempo suspends execution of `process1` and causes `process2` to execute. We refer to this transfer of control as a *context switch* between the two processes. `Process2` executes until `process1` has slept for the requested amount of time. Tempo wakes the sleeping process by making it eligible to run; then, because `process1` has higher priority than the currently executing process, `process2` is preempted and `process1` resumes execution.

As a model of the effect of real-time events this example is limited, because the preemption of `process2` is the direct result of an earlier action by `process1` (putting itself to sleep for a fixed length of time); however, it gives the general idea, because the precise point in `process2`'s execution where the timer will wake `process1` is unpredictable.

Figure 2.11 shows the situation in which the sleep period is so long that `process2` terminates before `process1` wakes up. The diagram shows that the program contains an *idle process* in addition to `process1` and `process2`. This idle process is created when the `main()` function, hidden inside Tempo, calls `become_idle()` (Figure 2.2). The idle process has a lower priority than any user-defined process, so the processor executes the idle process when no other process is eligible to run.

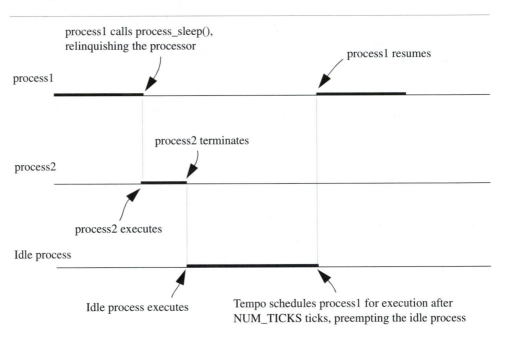

Figure 2.11 The idle process runs while there are no other processes to run.

In Figure 2.11, when `process2` terminates, Tempo schedules the idle process for execution while `process1` sleeps.

The point of this example is to demonstrate context switching, not to suggest using calls to `process_sleep()` to achieve the effect of timeslicing. In Tempo programs, we rely on real-time events to preempt processes. This will be presented in Chapter 3.

2.2.2 Processes with the Same Root Function

The same root function can be used to define more than one process. The effect is to create multiple process instances that execute the same code. The program in Figure 2.12 is similar to Figure 2.7, except that it specifies processroot() as the root function for both process1 and process2. As in Figure 2.7, process1 has a higher priority than process2, so it will run to completion before process2 is scheduled for execution. (We can't determine from the program's output which process executes first, because both processes execute the same code and therefore output the same message. As an exercise, think about how the processes could use local variables to establish their identity dynamically.)

```
// ch2ex5.cpp - create two processes from one
// root function

#include "tempo.h"
#include <iostream.h>

void processroot();

void Main()
{

    Process process1, process2;

    process1 = create_process(processroot, 1);
    process2 = create_process(processroot, 0);
}

void processroot()
{
    for (int i = 0; i < 10; i++) {
        CS(cout << "Process here, i = " << i << endl);
    }
}
```

Figure 2.12 Creating two processes from the same root function.

The following points should be noted about processes with the same root function:

- Different instances can have identical or different priorities.
- Different instances have their own copies of the root function's local variables. The variables that are local to this function are not shared between processes. Instead, private copies of these variables are created for each process.

2.2.3 What Is a Tempo Process?

A summary of the properties of Tempo processes will now be helpful.

Processes Viewed from Outside the Kernel

As code, a Tempo process consists of a function, known as the *root function*, and a variable of type `Process` (essentially a pointer to a data structure maintained by Tempo that contains information about the process). A root function has no parameters and does not return a value (we enforce this in our examples by declaring the return type as `void`.)

A process is explicitly created by calling Tempo's `create_process()` kernel function. We have seen two ways to do this:

```
process_name = create_process(root_function);
process_name = create_process(root_function, priority);
```

Each call to `create_process()` returns a *process id* that identifies the newly created process. This value may be ignored or saved in a variable of type `Process`. As we shall see, several of Tempo's kernel functions require us to specify a particular instance of a process by passing the process id as an argument.

When an instance of a process is created, it executes independently of and concurrently with the other processes in the program. Concurrently means that we think of all the ready-to-run processes as running at the same time; only one at a time actually runs.

Each process has its own stack that stores the root function's local variables, the return addresses of the function calls made by the process, and local variables that are declared in these functions. A process' stack, together with current contents of the processor's registers, is referred to as the *context* of the process.

When a root function returns, either by running "off the end" of the function or by executing a `return` statement, the process is destroyed. Unlike a normal function call, there is no calling function that resumes execution; instead, there is simply one less process in the system.

Tempo provides preemptive, priority-based process scheduling. Each process has a fixed priority that is assigned when the process is created. Process priorities range from 0 (the lowest priority) to n (the highest priority); currently, n is 4. If no priority is specified when `create_process()` is called, the process is assigned a default priority of 0. Any number of processes may have the same priority. For each priority level, Tempo maintains a queue of processes that are eligible to run. During scheduling, the process at the head of the highest-priority, nonempty queue is selected for execution. While this process executes, it is referred to as the *current process* or *active process*. The active process continues to run until it relinquishes the processor by calling a kernel function that *blocks* the process (in other words, the process gives up the processor until Tempo is informed that a a particular event has occurred and makes the process eligible to resume execution). Another way for an active process to relinquish the processor is for it to call kernel function that makes a higher-priority process eligible to run. When this happens, the active process remains eligible to run. Finally, an active process will be preempted when a real-time event causes a higher-priority process to become eligible to run. Note that preempting a process does not block it.

```cpp
// ch2ex6.cpp - processes and function calls

#include <iostream.h>
#include "tempo.h"

void f1()
{
    CS(cout << "Process " << my_id() << " executing f1()"
            << endl);
}

void p1root(), p2root();

void Main()
{
    Process proc1, proc2;

    proc1 = create_process(p1root, 1);
    proc2 = create_process(p2root, 0);
}

void p1root()
{
    CS(cout << "Process " << my_id()
            << " executing p1root()" << endl);
    f1();
}

void p2root()
{
    CS(cout << "Process " << my_id()
            << " executing p2root()" << endl);
    f1();
}
```

Figure 2.13 Functions are executed in the context of the calling process.

Although Tempo processes are created from functions, a process and a function are not the same thing. Processes can call ordinary functions (that is, functions that are not root functions), but the called functions do not become processes. The program in Figure 2.13 demonstrates this. Main() creates two processes, called proc1 and proc2. The root function for proc1 displays its process identifier (the value returned by my_id()) and then calls f1(), which also prints the identifier of the currently executing process.

As shown in Figure 2.14, the same process id is printed by `p1root()` and `f1()`, confirming that both functions are executed by the same process. Next, the root function for process `proc2` executes, prints its identifier, and calls `f1()`. This time, the function prints `proc2`'s process identifier, because `proc2` is the active process. We can summarize these results this way: *When the active process calls a function, the function is always executed in the context of that process.*

```
Process 12348 executing p1root()
Process 12348 executing function f1()
Process 27192 executing p2root()
Process 27192 executing function f1()
```

Figure 2.14 Output from the processes in Figure 2.13.

This also applies to calls to Tempo kernel functions. Tempo is not itself a process. When an active process calls a Tempo kernel function, the functions inside the kernel are executed in the context of that process. In other words, calls to Tempo kernel functions use the calling process's stack; Tempo does not have its own stack that it uses when its functions are called. A Tempo kernel function will not always return immediately—the active process may relinquish the processor while inside the kernel, causing a context switch. If this happens, the call does not return until the process is scheduled for execution and resumes executing the kernel function. In any case, the important thing to remember is that kernel code is always executed in the context of the currently executing process. This holds true even when functions that handle interrupts, known as interrupt service routines, make kernel calls, as we shall see in Chapter 3.

The Kernel's View of Processes

Here is a high-level look at what happens inside Tempo (see Chapter 10 for more).

When `create_process()` is called to form a new process, Tempo creates a process descriptor (PD) to store information about the process. Tempo maintains a separate PD for each process. Exactly one process is active at any time; consequently, one PD corresponds to the currently executing process, while all other PDs contain information about the processes that are either ready to run or blocked. Inside the kernel, process management is largely a matter of updating these process descriptors and moving them into and out of queues.

When Tempo performs a context switch between two processes, it must first save enough information about the active process so that its execution can eventually resume exactly where it left off, suspend the active process, and transfer control to the other process. To do this, Tempo first stores copies of the processor registers in the active process's PD. The register contents will change when the next process executes, so Tempo must save their current values while the active process is still executing. Next, Tempo loads the registers from the second process's PD, which causes control to transfer to that process.

Context switching includes changing process stacks (remember, Tempo allocates a separate stack for each newly created process). This is accomplished when Tempo saves the processor's stack pointer in the active process's PD and reloads it from the second process's PD.

Tempo also uses a process's PD to store the internal state of the process. Process states are only changed by the execution of Tempo kernel function calls; these functions may change the state of the calling process, the state of another process, the state of both processes, or may not make any state changes at all. Process state transitions are closely related to context switching, as shown in Figure 2.15, which summarizes the state transitions corresponding to the Tempo kernel functions introduced so far.

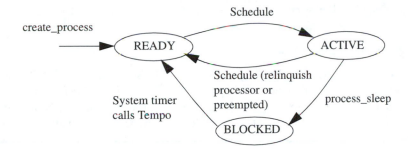

Schedule: a call to a Tempo kernel function that causes the kernel to schedule the processor among ready-to-run processes.

Figure 2.15 Process state transitions.

- Each new process is created READY (eligible to run).
- A READY process becomes ACTIVE when it is scheduled for execution; for example, when all other processes with equal or higher priority call Tempo and relinquish the processor. This transition also happens when a process preempts a lower-priority ACTIVE process (as described later).
- A transition from the ACTIVE state to the READY state occurs when the active process relinquishes the processor (by calling a Tempo kernel function that causes a higher-priority process to become ready) or when the ACTIVE process is preempted (a higher-priority sleeping process becomes READY and is scheduled for execution).
- By calling `process_sleep()`, the ACTIVE process puts itself into the BLOCKED state.
- After the system timer counts the requested number of ticks, it calls Tempo to move

the BLOCKED process to the READY state. If this process has the highest priority of all READY processes, it is given control of the processor (becomes the ACTIVE process), preempting the lower-priority ACTIVE process.

- Transitions labeled "schedule" correspond to the process scheduling operation described earlier and are always the result of calls to Tempo kernel functions.

2.3 INTERPROCESS COMMUNICATION USING SEMAPHORES

For practical purposes, processes that execute completely independently of one another are of little use. From time to time, processes must communicate with one another. Tempo provides *semaphores* and *event queues* to accomplish interprocess communication (IPC). Semaphores are described in this chapter and event queues are presented in Chapter 4.

2.3.1 The Nature of Semaphores

The *semaphore* is a mechanism for the simplest form of IPC, synchronization. A Tempo semaphore consists of an integer counter, two operations called *wait* and *signal*, and a list of processes, organized as a first-in, first-out queue. When a process requests a wait operation and the semaphore count is 0, the process is blocked (by being placed at the tail of the semaphore's queue). If the semaphore counter is positive, wait simply decrements the counter and the process continues executing. The signal operation complements wait. Signaling a semaphore causes the blocked process at the head of the semaphore queue to be removed from the list; that process is now eligible to run. The semaphore counter keeps track of the number of signal operations that occur when no process is blocked on the semaphore. If a semaphore's queue is empty when it is signaled, the semaphore counter is incremented by one.

Processes create semaphores by calling the `create_semaphore()` kernel function. The following statements create a semaphore with an initial count of 0 and save the semaphore id in variable `sem`:

```
Semaphore sem;
sem = create_semaphore(0);
```

To wait on this semaphore, processes call Tempo's `wait_semaphore()` function:

```
wait_semaphore(sem);
```

The semaphore is signaled by calling Tempo's `signal_semaphore()` function:

```
signal_semaphore(sem);
```

Think of processes as being analogous to people and a semaphore as being analogous to a place to which a person (process) travels to synchronize with another person (process). Imagine that the place contains a jar (the semaphore counter) and traveling processes carry tokens. By "traveling" to a semaphore, the process indicates that it is willing to wait there until it receives a signal from another process. If the jar is empty when the process arrives, it must wait until another process deposits a token in the jar. Signaling a semaphore corresponds to placing a token in the jar. The waiting process can then remove the token and continue.

The signaling process may arrive at the semaphore first, before the arrival of the process that is willing to wait—remember, in the real world, people don't necessarily arrive at places in the expected order—in which case the semaphore counter is incremented (a token is left in the jar) and the signaler continues on its independent way. When the process that is willing to wait arrives at the semaphore, it sees that the semaphore has already been signaled, so it decrements the semaphore counter (removes a token from the jar) and resumes its travels, without waiting.

What happens if a semaphore is signaled several times before a process arrives to wait there? Each signal is counted (several tokens accumulate in the jar), and each process that is willing to wait removes one signal.

Figure 2.16 extends Figure 2.15 to include the process state transitions corresponding to the signal and wait operations.

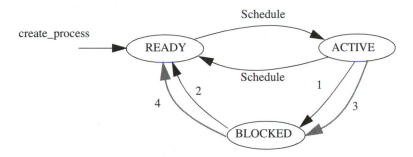

1. The active process calls process_sleep()
2. System timer calls Tempo
3. The active process calls wait_semaphore()
4. An active process calls signal_semaphore()

Schedule: a call to a Tempo kernel function causes the kernel to schedule the processor among ready-to-run processes.

Figure 2.16 Process state transitions.

Semaphores may be used to provide three different kinds of synchronization, as explained in Section 2.3.2, 2.3.3, and 2.3.4:

- event signaling (Section 2.3.2).
- synchronizing interprocess data transfer (Section 2.3.3).
- mutual exclusion (Section 2.3.4).

2.3.2 Semaphores for Event Signaling

Figure 2.17 shows how a process uses a semaphore to inform another process that an event has occurred.

```cpp
// ch2ex7.cpp - event signaling

#include "tempo.h"
#include <iostream.h>

void p1root(), p2root();

Semaphore sem1;

void Main()
{
    Process p1, p2;

    sem1 = create_semaphore(0);
    p1 = create_process(p1root, 1);
    p2 = create_process(p2root, 0);
}
// p1root - waits for an event from a lower priority
//          process
void p1root()
{
    CS(cout << "Process p1: waiting for an event" << endl);
    wait_semaphore(sem1);
    CS(cout << "Process p1: received event" << endl);
}

// p2root - signals an event to a higher priority process
void p2root()
{
    CS(cout << "Process p2: signaling an event" << endl);
    signal_semaphore(sem1);
    CS(cout << "Process p2: terminating" << endl);
}
```

Figure 2.17 Event signaling between processes.

Main creates a semaphore, sem1, and two processes, p1 and p2. The higher-priority process, p1, executes first and blocks when it waits on sem1, because the semaphore count is 0. The lower-priority process, p2, now executes and signals the semaphore, causing p1 to continue.

Diagrams can help us understand concurrent programs as systems better than code spread across several pages can. Figure 2.18 shows the system organization of the program in Figure 2.17 using a notation called *collaboration graphs*, which is treated in depth starting in Chapter 5. The processes and semaphore are labeled with the identifiers used in the program. Doing this helps us relate the design to the program.

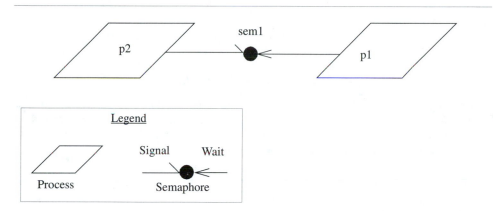

Figure 2.18 Collaboration graph for the program of Figure 2.17.

Note that this is not a literal picture of a program for the following reasons. A process symbol represents the *concept* of a process, not the literal way the process appears in code (a root function, a Process variable, and the associated code inside Tempo). Similarly, a semaphore symbol represents the *concept* of an interprocess connection over which signals flow, not the literal way the semaphore appears in code (a Semaphore variable and the associated kernel code).

To avoid clutter, Figure 2.18 does not show initialization. Figure 2.19 introduces some initialization notation. It shows that Main creates the two processes and one semaphore. Each thick, dashed arrow labeled with a "+" is an *assertion* that the component at the head of the arrow is created by the component at the tail. The bracketed names indicate the kernel function to be called to implement the assertion (normally these are not shown, because they are implied by the diagram). Observe that the assertion arrow does *not* represent an interaction with the component to which it points (interaction is not possible with a component that does not yet exist).

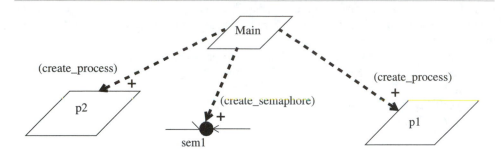

Figure 2.19 Collaboration graph for program initialization.

2.3.3 Semaphores for Interprocess Data Transfer

Suppose a producer process produces items of data and a consumer process consumes them. Data can be transferred between the two processes through a shared buffer object that stores one item of data. The producer repeatedly produces new data and stores them in the buffer, while the consumer gets each new value from the buffer and prints it. To synchronize their use of the shared buffer, the processes must ensure that two conditions are met. One is that the consumer must wait for the producer to update the buffer before it prints the new value. The other is that the producer must wait until the consumer gets the value before it stores a new value in the buffer. Thus, a producer and a consumer interacting through a single-item buffer proceed in a lockstep fashion.

A Tempo program for the lockstep producer/consumer is shown in Figures 2.20 and 2.21. The program begins with the declaration of a buffer object that is shared by the processes. (The term *object* is defined in Chapter 4, but in this chapter, it's sufficient to think of an object as software component that provides a data abstraction.) In C or skinny C++, the buffer object consists of a single integer variable, `buf`, and interface functions `store_item()` and `retrieve_item()` to access that variable (in full C++, it would be an instance of a C++ class).

Figure 2.20 also contains `Main()`, which creates the producer and consumer processes. The producer and consumer synchronize their accesses to the shared buffer using two counting semaphores, `produced` and `consumed`, which are also created by `Main()`. Semaphore `produced` has a count of 1 when the buffer contains a new value that has not yet been printed. The value of `consumed` is 1 after the value retrieved from the buffer has been printed.

```cpp
// ch2ex8.cpp - synchronized producer/consumer processes

#include <iostream.h>
#include "tempo.h"

// begin single-item buffer object
//    The object shared by the producer and consumer
//    processes consists of an integer variable
//    and two functions that operate on it.
static int buf;

// store_item - store item in buffer object
void store_item(int item)
{
    buf = item;
}

// retrieve_item - return the value stored in
//                 buffer object
int retrieve_item()
{
    return buf;
}
// end single-item buffer object

void produce(), consume();

Semaphore produced, consumed;

void Main()
{
    Process producer, consumer;

    produced = create_semaphore(0);
    consumed = create_semaphore(1);
    producer = create_process(produce);
    consumer = create_process(consume);
}
```

Figure 2.20 Lockstep producer/ consumer example (part 1 of 2).

The consumer process executes the code in consume() (see Figure 2.21). By calling wait_semaphore(produced), it waits until the buffer has been updated. After displaying the new value, the consumer calls signal_semaphore(consumed), indicating to the producer that it is finished with the buffer.

```
void produce()
{
    for (int i = 0; i < 10; i++) {
        wait_semaphore(consumed);
        CS(cout << "producer: produced "
                << i << endl);
        store_item(i);
        signal_semaphore(produced);
    }
}

void consume()
{
    for (int i = 0; i < 10; i++) {
        wait_semaphore(produced);
        CS(cout << "consumer: consumed "
                << retrieve_item() << endl);
        signal_semaphore(consumed);
    }
}
```

Figure 2.21 Lockstep producer/consumer example (part 2 of 2).

Function produce(), the root function for the producer process, complements the code executed by the consumer. This process first waits until the buffer has been printed by the consumer process (wait_semaphore(consumed)). It then stores a new value in the buffer and calls signal_semaphore(produced) to inform the consumer that a new value is available.

Thus, the producer and consumer processes proceed in lockstep fashion, synchronizing in two places. The producer signals the consumer each time it updates the buffer object, and the producer is signaled by the consumer every time the buffer object is printed. In this example, consumed's initial count is 1 and produced's initial value is 0, so the producer process will be the first process to access the buffer object.

Figure 2.22 shows the system organization of the producer/consumer example and introduces additional elements of the collaboration graph notation. The buffer object is represented by a box with rounded corners. The arrows pointing at the buffer object represent the concept of a function call-return connection and imply the existence of functions to call. The arrows show that the object's functions are called by both the producer and consumer processes. The parameter arrows show that store_item() is passed an integer value and retrieve_item() returns an integer value.

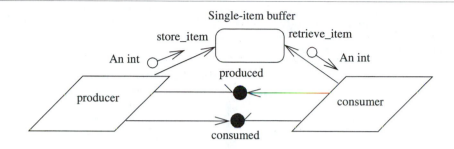

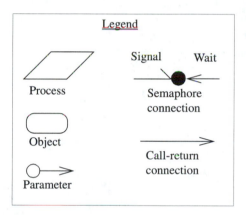

Figure 2.22 Collaboration graph for the lockstep producer/consumer program.

The diagram allows us to step back from the lines of source code to focus on the interactions between the processes. It clearly shows how the consumer and producer synchronize buffer operations using the two semaphores. As before, this is not a literal picture of a program.

Figure 2.23 shows explicitly the relationship between the code and the collaboration graph. Collaboration graphs support system design by allowing us to visualize how multi-tasking software is organized as a system. It might seem that a visual notation that is more closely tied to the programming language—one that provided shapes that directly represent functions, function calls, variables, pointers, and so on—would be preferable for capturing program designs. In practice, a notation like this would not be sufficiently far removed from the programming language for system design.

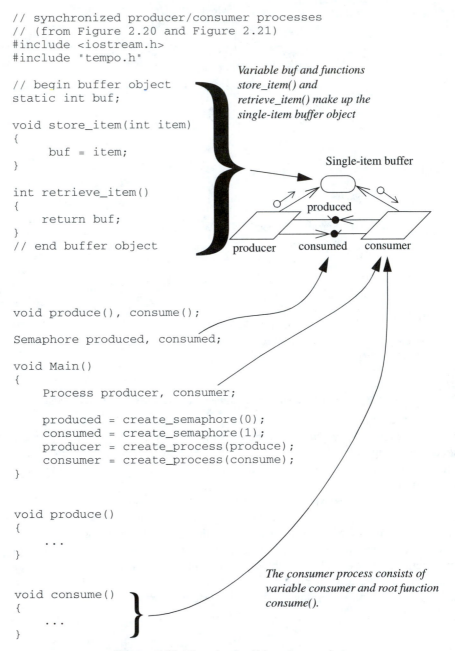

```
// synchronized producer/consumer processes
// (from Figure 2.20 and Figure 2.21)
#include <iostream.h>
#include "tempo.h"

// begin buffer object
static int buf;

void store_item(int item)
{
     buf = item;
}

int retrieve_item()
{
    return buf;
}
// end buffer object
```

*Variable buf and functions
store_item() and
retrieve_item() make up the
single-item buffer object*

Single-item buffer

produced

producer   consumed   consumer

```
void produce(), consume();

Semaphore produced, consumed;

void Main()
{
    Process producer, consumer;

    produced = create_semaphore(0);
    consumed = create_semaphore(1);
    producer = create_process(produce);
    consumer = create_process(consume);
}


void produce()
{
    ...
}

void consume()
{
    ...
}
```

*The consumer process consists of
variable consumer and root function
consume().*

Figure 2.23 The role of collaboration graphs.

Figure 2.24 shows how the lockstep producer/consumer program is initialized. `Main` creates the consumer and producer processes and the two semaphores. Don't confuse the thick, dashed arrows with connections. As noted earlier, these arrows assert that one component creates another and do not imply component interactions over the paths indicated by the arrows.

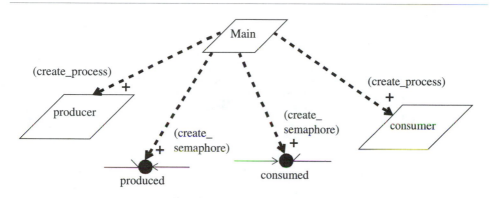

Figure 2.24 Initializing the lockstep producer/consumer example.

2.3.4 Semaphores for Mutual Exclusion

Replacing the single-item buffer object in Figure 2.20 with a shared buffer object that holds multiple items permits the producer and consumer to produce and consume data at different rates. The producer and consumer processes no longer execute in a lockstep manner. The multi-item buffer acts as a first-in, first-out queue, so the consumer removes items from the buffer in the same order in which they were produced.

If both processes attempt to use the buffer simultaneously, the buffer data structure may be damaged. To ensure that the processes do not interfere with one another, the operations on the buffer must be *mutually exclusive*; that is, the lines of code for each operation must be executed so that only one process at a time operates on the buffer. The term *critical section* is used to describe a sequence of program statements that must be executed this way. Concurrent processes must cooperate to ensure that only one process at a time executes the code in a critical section. Synchronization to protect a critical section is called *mutual exclusion*.

```cpp
// mbuf.cpp - multi-item buffer object

#include "tempo.h"
#include "mbuf.h"

// begin multi-item buffer object
// A semaphore ensures mutual exclusion on the buffer.
Semaphore buffer_mutex;

// a simple ring buffer is used to hold the data
const int SIZE = 5;     // # elements in buffer
static int buffer[SIZE];
static int in_index, out_index, count;

void store_item_(int item)
// store item in buffer object
{
    wait_semaphore(buffer_mutex);
    buffer[in_index] = item;
    in_index = (in_index + 1) % SIZE;
    count++;
    signal_semaphore(buffer_mutex);
}
int retrieve_item_()
// remove item from buffer object
{
    int item;

    wait_semaphore(buffer_mutex);
    item = buffer[out_index];
    out_index = (out_index + 1) % SIZE;
    count--;
    signal_semaphore(buffer_mutex);
    return item;
}

void init_buffer_() // initialize buffer object
{
    // set up the indices into the buffer
    in_index = 0;
    out_index = 0;
    count = 0;          // initially, the buffer is empty
    buffer_mutex = create_semaphore(1);
}
// end multi-item buffer object
```

Figure 2.25 A multi-item buffer object.

Figure 2.25 presents the code for a multi-item buffer object and shows how a semaphore can be used to enforce mutual exclusion on a shared object. Within the object, data are stored in a ring buffer, and the code that accesses this buffer must be executed in a critical section. A single semaphore, `buffer_mutex`, is created when `init_buffer_()` is called to initialize the ring buffer. The buffer object's interface functions, `store_item_()` and `retrieve_item_()`, are responsible for enforcing mutual exclusion. The calls to `wait_semaphore(buffer_mutex)` and `signal_semaphore(buffer_mutex)` inside these functions bracket the critical sections. Because `buffer_mutex` is initialized with the value 1, the first process that calls `wait_semaphore()` will proceed directly into the critical section without blocking. Other processes that attempt to enter the critical section will wait on the semaphore— the semaphore count remains 0 until the semaphore is signaled. As it leaves the critical section the process calls `signal_semaphore()`; this will unblock a waiting process and allow it to enter the critical section.

Until now, the code for each of our Tempo programs has been stored in a single `.cpp` file, but the skinny C++ file in Figure 2.25 is not a complete Tempo program. It contains the code for the multi-item buffer object but does not have a Main process. When converting collaboration graphs to code, a common programming convention is to put the code for an object in its own compilation unit—that is, a source (`.cpp`) file and its associated header (`.h`) file.

Figure 2.26 shows the header file for the multi-item buffer object. It contains the external declarations for the three interface functions provided by the object.

```
// mbuf.h - declarations for the multi-item buffer object

void store_item_(int item);
int retrieve_item_();
void init_buffer_();
```

Figure 2.26 Header file for the multi-item buffer object.

Figure 2.27 introduces the notation for an object whose interface functions enforce mutual exclusion on the object. By drawing the multi-item buffer with a double outline we imply that it is "protected" (that is, mutual exclusion is enforced by a semaphore). The mutual exclusion semaphore is not shown. Protected objects like this are called *monitors* and are described further in Chapter 4.

store_item_   retrieve_item_

Multi-item buffer

Figure 2.27 Collaboration graph notation for a monitor.

Figure 2.28 is a collaboration graph for a producer/consumer program that uses the multi-item buffer. Because the buffer has a fixed capacity, there are synchronization requirements in addition to mutual exclusion: The producer must not deposit data into a full buffer and the consumer must not attempt to remove data from an empty buffer. When the buffer is full, the producer must wait until the consumer removes data from the buffer before it stores a new value. If the buffer is empty when the consumer attempts to retrieve an item, it must wait until the producer adds data to the buffer.

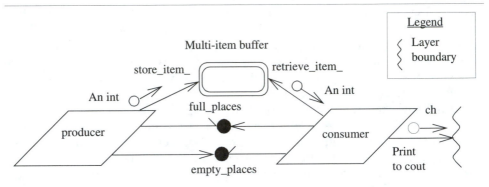

Figure 2.28 Producer/consumer with a multi-item buffer.

The synchronization is provided by the semaphores `full_places` and `empty_places`. Semaphore `full_places` counts of the number of items that are in the buffer. When the buffer is empty, a waiting on `full_places` causes the consumer to block. Semaphore `empty_places` counts the number of unused places in the buffer. When the buffer is full, waiting on `empty_places` causes the producer to block.

The system in Figure 2.28 is a generalization of the one in Figure 2.22, as follows: The buffer now holds multiple items, and mutual exclusion has been added to it. Lockstep execution of the processes has been removed by using counting semaphores. Semaphore `full_places` is a generalization of semaphore `produced`, and semaphore `empty_places` is a generalization of semaphore `consumed`.

Figure 2.28 shows a new graphical symbol, a wavy line. The wavy line is the destination of print calls. A stream output statement in the program causes a call to the C++ run-time system. Because we regard the run-time system as a layer underneath our program, we do not show it as a box in the figure. However, any arrow representing a function call path, such as the print arrow in this figure, needs a destination for the call. The wavy line symbolizes the existence of such a destination without explicitly showing the actual destination. The wavy line is called a layer boundary. The concept is that the call crosses the layer boundary and disappears into the layer. Layer boundaries were not explicitly shown in earlier collaboration graphs, to reduce clutter, but one is used here to highlight that data items produced by the producer are ultimately sent by the consumer to the external environment (the computer's console).

```
// ch2ex9.cpp - synchronized producer/consumer processes

#include "iostream.h"
#include "tempo.h"
#include "mbuf.h" // import multi-item buffer object

void produce(), consume();

Semaphore full_places, empty_places;

void Main()
{
    Process producer, consumer;

    full_places = create_semaphore(0);
    empty_places = create_semaphore(SIZE);
    init_buffer_();  // initialize the buffer object
    producer = create_process(produce);
    consumer = create_process(consume);
}

// producer
void produce()
{
    for (int i = 0; i < 10; i++) {
        wait_semaphore(empty_places);
        CS(cout << "producer: produced "
                << i << endl);
        store_item_(i);
        signal_semaphore(full_places);
    }
}

// consumer
void consume()
{
    for (int i = 0; i < 10; i++) {
        wait_semaphore(full_places);
        CS(cout << "consumer: consumed "
                << retrieve_item_() << endl);
        signal_semaphore(empty_places);
    }
}
```

Figure 2.29 Producer/consumer with multi-item buffer.

The code for this version of the producer/consumer program is provided in Figure 2.29. Because the buffer object is initially empty, semaphore full_places is initialized to 0 and semaphore empty_places is initialized to SIZE.

2.3.5 Mutual Exclusion and the CS Macro

We now turn our attention to the CS macro that we introduced in Section 2.1. Recall that we stated that input and output statements and statements containing calls to functions provided in the C++ compiler's library must be enclosed in this macro to ensure that they are executed in critical sections. Why is this necessary?

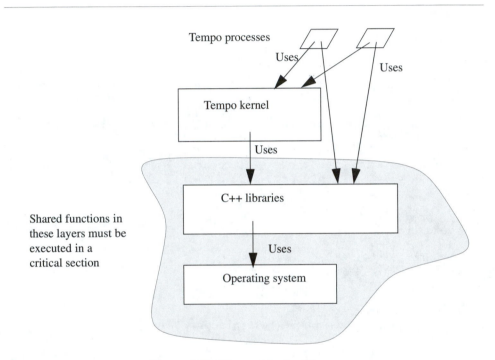

Figure 2.30 The need for the CS macro.

Figure 2.30 shows the relationship of the processes in a Tempo program to the real-time kernel, the standard C++ function library, and the computer's operating system. Suppose that the active Tempo process is preempted by a higher-priority process while it is executing a library or operating system function. If the higher-priority process calls a function in the library or operating system layers, problems may result unless the code in the layer is *reentrant*. This isn't guaranteed in our program development environment (Borland C++ and MS-DOS), so Tempo processes must treat the library and operating system layers as serially reusable. They must synchronize to ensure that no more than one process is executing code from these layers at any time; in other words, all calls by processes to the underlying software layers must be placed in critical sections. The CS macro provides the required mutual exclusion.

For example, a process that contains this statement

```
CS(cout << "i = " << i << endl);
```

executes the following code:

```
wait_semaphore(Tempo_mutex);
cout << "i = " << i << endl;
signal_semaphore(Tempo_mutex);
```

The calls to the library functions corresponding to the "<<" operator are bracketed by wait and signal operations on the `Tempo_mutex` semaphore, which is created by Tempo when it starts. If the process is preempted while executing in the critical section, any other process that executes the CS macro will block on `Tempo_mutex` until the first process resumes, finishes writing its output, and signals the semaphore.

2.3.6 The Priority Inversion Problem

The system in Figure 2.31 has a high priority process, P_h, a medium-priority process, P_m, and a low-priority process, P_l. Each process is eligible to run, and because P_h has the highest priority, it is scheduled for execution. Eventually, P_h blocks on semaphore S to wait for a signal from P_l. When P_h blocks, P_m is scheduled for execution. P_l cannot signal S until P_m relinquishes the processor, allowing P_l to be scheduled.

This situation, in which a lower-priority process prevents a higher-priority process from running, is known as *priority inversion*. In this example, P_m prevents P_l from running and, as a consequence, P_l cannot unblock P_h by signaling S.

Priority inversion and solutions to this problem are advanced topics in the area of real-time schedulability theory, so a complete treatment is beyond the scope of this book. Interested readers are referred to the books by Gomaa and Levi, which are listed in Appendix D.

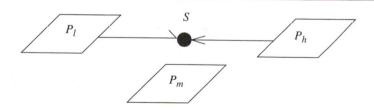

Figure 2.31 The priority inversion problem.

2.4 PACKAGING COMPONENTS

The program in Figure 2.29 is representative of a wide range of real-time systems containing one or more producer and consumer processes that transfer data through multi-item buffers. The code for the producer and consumer processes is often specific to a particular application, but a multi-item buffer for transferring data between processes is sufficiently general purpose that its design can be reused. A fixed-size buffer that enforces mutual exclusion and synchronizes data transfer between processes is such a fundamental concept in concurrent programming that it is known simply as a *bounded buffer*. In this section, we show how to package components into higher-level design abstractions, using the bounded buffer as our example.

Figure 2.32 shows the collaboration graph for a producer/consumer program with three components: a producer process, a consumer process, and a bounded buffer *team*. A team is a grouping of related processes and objects into an operational unit. We say that Figure 2.32 presents a "black box" view of the bounded buffer team's organization because its internal details are hidden from the producer and consumer processes. Labels *store_item* and *retrieve_item* refer to interface functions provided by the team that are called by the processes. The parameters beside the call paths indicate the data that are passed from the producer to the buffer team and from the buffer team to the consumer.

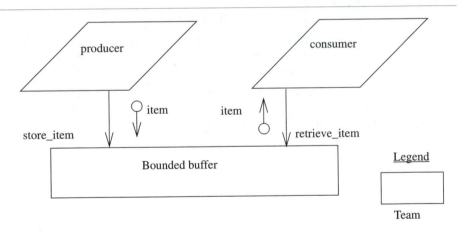

Figure 2.32 Bounded buffer team: black box view (operational organization).

Figure 2.33 refines the previous figure to provide a glass box view of the internal organization of the buffer team after initialization is finished. Notice that the monitor and the semaphores from Figure 2.28 are encapsulated in the team.

We are now ready to look at how the collaboration graph can be implemented as a Tempo program.

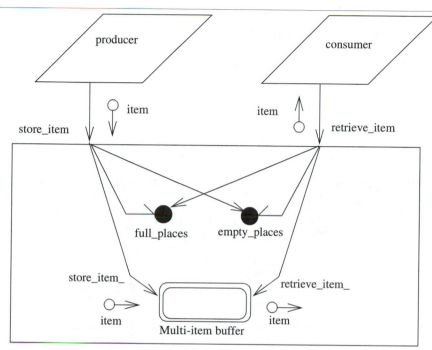

Figure 2.33 Bounded buffer team after initialization: glass box view.

2.4.1 Coding the Bounded Buffer Team

Teams can be implemented using any C++ programming convention that allows us to group code and data into a single unit. In skinny C++, a team is programmed as a C++ compilation unit; that is, a source (`.cpp`) file and its associated header (`.h`) file. Teams differ from processes and semaphores in that they are not created and managed by calling Tempo kernel functions during program execution; in other words, Tempo has no knowledge of the teams in a system. In effect, teams are created during program compilation, in contrast to processes and semaphores, which are created during program execution.

Header file `buffer.h` (Figure 2.34) and source file `buffer.cpp` (Figure 2.35) comprise the bounded buffer team. The header file contains the external declarations for the three interface functions provided by the team.

```
// buffer.h - declarations for the bounded buffer team

void init_buffer();
void store_item(int item);
extern int  retrieve_item();
```

Figure 2.34 Header file for the bounded buffer team.

```
// buffer.cpp - bounded buffer team

#include "tempo.h"
#include <iostream.h>
#include "buffer.h"

// One semaphore keeps track of the number of empty
// places remaining in the buffer; another semaphore
// counts the number of places that have been filled.
Semaphore full_places, empty_places;

// import code for the multi-item buffer object
#include "mbuf.h"

// init_buffer() - initializes the buffer team.
void init_buffer()
{
    full_places = create_semaphore(0);
    empty_places = create_semaphore(SIZE);
    init_buffer_();  // initialize the buffer object
}

// After init_buffer() has been called, the following two
// functions may be called in any order.

// store_item() - enqueues "item" in the buffer object.
void store_item(int item)
{
    wait_semaphore(empty_places);
    store_item_(item);  // store item in the buffer object
    signal_semaphore(full_places);
}

// retrieve_item() - removes and returns the item at the
// head of the buffer object.
int retrieve_item()
{
    int item;

    wait_semaphore(full_places);
    // get item from buffer object
    item = retrieve_item_();
    signal_semaphore(empty_places);
    return item;
}
```

Figure 2.35 The bounded buffer team (interface functions).

Using the collaboration graph in Figure 2.33 as a starting point, coding the buffer team is straightforward (see Figure 2.35). The statement

```
#include "mbuf.h"
```

causes the C++ compiler to include the declarations for the buffer monitor (see Figure 2.25) in the buffer team.

The code for interface functions `init_buffer()`, `store_item()`, and `retrieve_item()` was copied directly from the processes in producer/consumer program in Figure 2.29.

2.4.2 Producer, Consumer, and Main Processes

Figure 2.36 is a version of the producer/consumer program from Figure 2.29 that has been revised so that the processes call the buffer team's interface functions.

```cpp
// ch2ex10.cpp - using the bounded buffer team
#include <iostream.h>
#include "tempo.h"
#include "buffer.h"
void produce(), consume();
void Main()
{
    Process producer, consumer;

    init_buffer();  // initialize the buffer team
    producer = create_process(produce, 0);
    consumer = create_process(consume, 1);
}
// producer
void produce()
{
    for (int i = 0; i < 10; i++) {
        CS(cout << "producer: produced "
                << i << endl);
        store_item(i);
    }
}
// consumer
void consume()
{
    for (int i = 0; i < 10; i++) {
        CS(cout << "consumer: consumed "
                << retrieve_item() << endl);
    }
}
```

Figure 2.36 Producer and consumer processes using the bounded buffer team.

The producer deposits 10 integers in the bounded buffer by calling `store_item()`; the consumer removes these values from the buffer by calling `retrieve_item()`. Notice how the manipulations of the buffer object and the semaphore operations to synchronize the processes are hidden inside the buffer team. The producer and consumer view the buffer team in terms of the services that it provides, but they do not know how the team is organized to provide those services.

The timing diagram in Figure 2.37 illustrates the execution of the bounded buffer program.

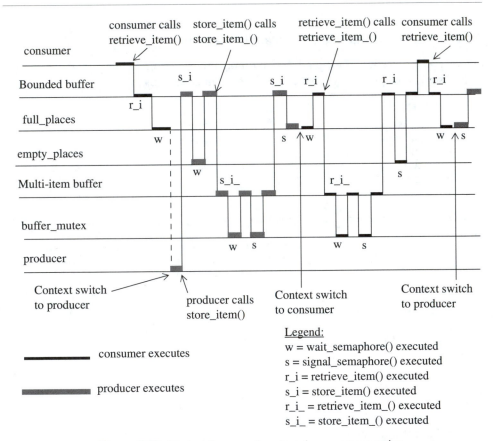

Figure 2.37 Timing diagram of producer/consumer execution.

The consumer process executes first, because it has a higher priority level than the producer, and calls `retrieve_item()`. The buffer object is initially empty, so the `full_places` semaphore has a signal count of 0, causing the consumer to block when it waits on the semaphore. Tempo then switches to the producer process. After storing a new item in the buffer object, the producer signals `full_places`. This causes the consumer process to resume. It retains control of the processor until it again waits on `full_places`. Tempo then performs a context switch to the producer process, which produces another item and stores it in the buffer object.

How would the program execute if the producer had higher priority than the consumer? Drawing the timing diagram for this case is left as an exercise for the reader.

2.5 SUMMARY

In this chapter we have

- Introduced the Tempo real-time kernel for writing multitasking software.
- Examined some fundamental concepts of concurrent programs, including creating processes, scheduling priorities and preemptive process scheduling, and sharing a processor between processes.
- Introduced the semaphore as a mechanism for process synchronization and demonstrated how the semaphore is used to signal events, to synchronize interprocess data transfer, and to enforce mutual exclusion.
- Introduced a *collaboration graph* notation for representing the organization of multitasking programs as systems.

Programming with the Tempo Kernel: Processing Real-Time Events

*I*n the Tempo programs presented so far, processes are the source of all events. Although the programs are multitasking, they are not real time because, by definition, a real-time program responds to events that are received from its environment. This chapter continues our introduction to multitasking programming with Tempo by showing how real-time events enter the picture.

Externally generated events are delivered to a real-time program by a combination of hardware and software. Hardware devices provide the physical interface between a computer system and its environment. *Interrupt service routines* (ISRs) provide the software link between this hardware and processes. When a real-time event occurs (for example, the arrival of a character across a serial communications link), the hardware interface to the link generates a stimulus that *interrupts* the processor, causing it to transfer control from the currently executing process to an ISR. An ISR is similar to a process in that it runs autonomously, but, instead of being scheduled by Tempo, its execution is directly triggered by a real-time event, without any Tempo involvement.

3.1 A REAL-TIME PRODUCER/CONSUMER PROGRAM

As our first example of an interrupt-driven Tempo program, we examine how to arrange for a process to receive a string of characters from an external source. The first item of business is arranging for interrupts to occur when characters arrive.

Most computers are equipped with at least one *serial port* for sending and receiving characters through a cable linked to a corresponding port on a terminal, a modem, a printer, or another computer. Inside the computer, a programmable device—called a *universal asynchronous receiver transmitter* (UART)—provides the software and hardware interface to the serial port. A UART can be programmed to interrupt the processor when it receives a character from the serial port. Figure 3.1 is a block diagram showing how interrupt request signals generated by a UART are passed to a Programmable Interrupt Controller (PIC), which in turn interrupts the processor. (Details about UARTs and interrupt processing in the hardware environment of this book can be found in Appendix C.)

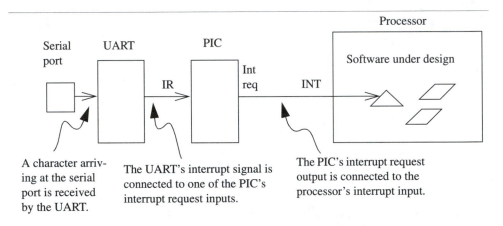

Figure 3.1 Hardware wiring to deliver events to programs via interrupts.

The second item of business is arranging for the software to handle the interrupts and characters. A collaboration graph for a program to do this is provided in Figure 3.2. Real-time events (UART interrupts) are delivered to a Tempo process through an interrupt service routine and a semaphore. Each time a character arrives at the serial port, the UART interrupts the processor, causing the ISR called `rxisr()` to run. This ISR reads the character from the UART, saves it in a shared multicharacter buffer, and signals semaphore `char_avail`, on which the consumer process waits.

Figure 3.2(a) makes it clear that this is a variation of the producer/consumer examples presented in Chapter 2. The ISR acts as the producer (it stores newly received characters in the buffer). The consumer process prints the characters it obtains from the buffer. The shared buffer is implemented as a monitor. For reasons that are explained in Section 3.2.1, the monitor's interface functions provide mutual exclusion by interrupt lockout, not with semaphores. Semaphore `char_avail` counts the number of characters that are in the buffer.

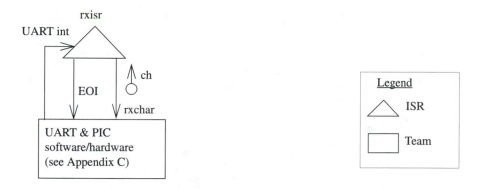

Figure 3.2 UART ISR/process communication (system operation).

Figure 3.2(b) depicts the UART and PIC hardware and the functions that program the hardware as a single box (which, in our design notation, is called a *team*). The connection labeled "UART int" indicates that interrupts generated by the UART/PIC hardware cause rxisr() to run. The connection labeled "rxchar" indicates that calls are made to function rxchar(), which reads a character from the UART. The connection labeled "EOI" corresponds to sending an end-of-interrupt command to the PIC and is explained later in this section.

The components in Figure 3.2(b) are not in the collaboration graph in part (a) because they are usually not required in software design diagrams. Instead, we draw them only when it is necessary to explain details of the interaction between the software and hardware components of a system.

Figure 3.3 shows that the `Main` process is responsible for system initialization. `Main` creates the consumer process and semaphore `char_avail` and calls functions to install `rxisr()` as the new UART ISR (that is, set the UART interrupt vector with the address of `rxisr()`), initialize the UART hardware, and initialize the multicharacter buffer.

Figure 3.3 also shows that the consumer process is responsible for cleanly shutting down the system by restoring the UART interrupt vector to the ISR that was in place before the Tempo program ran. By doing this, the original ISR will handle any spurious UART interrupts that occur after the program finishes.

Initialization/finalization in real-time systems is seldom straightforward, as Figure 3.3 illustrates. There are scattered bits and pieces to be initialized in different ways, resulting in a certain irregularity in the figure. This figure lays the irregularity bare; the case study in later chapters shows how to hide it.

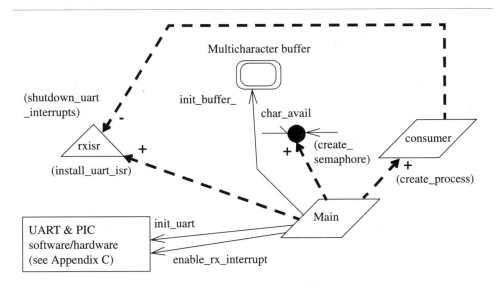

Figure 3.3 UART ISR/process communication (system initialization/shutdown).

The code for this program starts in Figure 3.4. The root function for `consumer`, `consume()`, repeatedly waits on `char_avail` and then removes a character from the buffer and displays it, stopping when a newline or carriage return is received.

```cpp
// ch3ex1.cpp - UART isr/process synchronization

#include <iostream.h>
#include <dos.h>
#include "tempo.h"
#include "char_buf.h"  // see Section 3.2.1
#include "uart.h"       // see Appendix C
// "import" init_uart(), install_uart_isr,
// enable_rx_interrupt(), shutdown_uart_interrupts(),
// rxchar()

Process consumer;
void consume();

void interrupt rxisr(...)

Semaphore char_avail;

void Main()
{
    init_buffer_();
    char_avail = create_semaphore(0);
    consumer = create_process(consume);
    init_uart(); // see Appendix C
    install_uart_isr(rxisr);
    enable_rx_interrupt();
}

void consume()
{
    char ch;

    do {
        wait_semaphore(char_avail);
        ch - retrieve_char_();
        CS(cout << ch);
    } while ((ch != '\n') && (ch != '\r'));
    shutdown_uart_interrupts();
}
```

Figure 3.4 UART ISR/process communication (part 1 of 2).

Figure 3.5 shows the ISR, written as a Borland C++ interrupt function:

```
void interrupt rxisr(...)
```

Interrupt functions are not part of standard C++, but they are convenient way to write ISRs without resorting to assembly language programming, and for our purposes this outweighs any C++ code portability considerations. The three dots in the parameter list are required by the Borland C++ compiler.

```
// destination for EOI command
const int PIC_00 = 0x20;
const int EOI = 0x20;  // end-of-interrupt command

// rxisr() - this isr runs every time a character is
//           received by the uart.
void interrupt rxisr(...)
{
    char ch;

    // send end-of-interrupt command to the PIC
    outportb(PIC_00, EOI);
    ch = rxchar(); // read char from uart (Appendix C)
    if (!buffer_full_()) {
        store_char_(ch); // save char in buffer object
        signal_semaphore(char_avail);
    }
}
```

Figure 3.5 UART ISR/process communication (part 2 of 2).

This interrupt function inputs the newly received character from the UART. If there is room in the buffer, it calls store_char_() to deposit the character in the buffer, then signals the semaphore to inform consumer that another character is available. (Characters are discarded if the buffer is full, for reasons that are explained in Section 3.2.1.)

The first statement in rxisr() is

```
outportb(PIC_00, EOI);
```

In our hardware environment (see Appendix C), when a UART interrupt occurs, the computer's PIC needs a handshake before it can send another UART interrupt. To perform this handshake, the ISR must output an end-of-interrupt (EOI) command to the PIC. Putting the statement that sends EOI at the beginning of the ISR guarantees that the PIC always gets the handshake. This, in turn, guarantees that, however the ISR exits, either by running "off-the-end" and returning to the interrupted process or by calling signal_semaphore() (which may cause a context switch to another process), the

PIC can send more UART interrupts. If `rxisr()` signaled a higher-priority process than the one it interrupted, without first issuing EOI, Tempo would context switch to the higher-priority process and further interrupt requests would not be processed for an indeterminate length of time. Sending the EOI command at the beginning of the ISR ensures that this cannot happen. (This is explained further in Section 3.2.)

The timing diagram in Figure 3.6 illustrates what happens when the program runs. The processor executes the idle process when the consumer process is not eligible to run and when the ISR is not being executed.

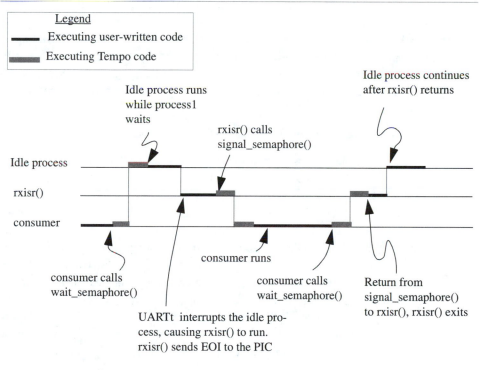

Figure 3.6 Timing diagram: process and UART ISR execution.

3.2 PROCESS EXECUTION AND INTERRUPTS

The interactions between ISRs, processes, and hardware can appear complex to the novice, so it is now time to step back from the details of this example and look at the general properties of interrupt handling in a multitasking environment.

When a process is created, Tempo arranges for it to start running with interrupts enabled. Thereafter, interrupts may be disabled and reenabled for a process for various reasons:

- Figure 3.7(a) shows that the process may disable and enable interrupts itself; for example, to ensure mutual exclusion.
- Figure 3.7(b) shows that when a process is interrupted and an ISR is activated, the processor automatically disables interrupts; that is, an ISR starts with interrupts disabled. The processor will not recognize further interrupt requests from the PIC until interrupts are reenabled. There are three ways this can happen. First, although ISRs normally run with interrupts disabled, the ISR can reenable interrupts by calling Tempo's `enable_ints()` kernel function. Second, interrupts are automatically reenabled when the ISR returns to the interrupted process. Third, an ISR can signal a semaphore (next point).
- Figure 3.7(c) shows that if an ISR signals a semaphore, and if the process waiting on the semaphore has higher priority than the interrupted process, Tempo will immediately perform a context switch to that process, and if this process was running with interrupts enabled when it called `wait_semaphore()`, interrupts will be enabled when it resumes execution.

Figure 3.7 helps us understand the purpose of the EOI handshake:

- In Figure 3.7(b), the ISR issues EOI to the PIC before it returns to the interrupted process. If this did not happen, the PIC would not be aware that the ISR is finished and further interrupt requests would not be handled properly.
- In Figure 3.7(c), the ISR issues an EOI to the PIC before it calls `signal_semaphore()`, causing the waiting Process2 to resume. If this did not happen, the PIC would think that the ISR is still executing after the context switch and further interrupt requests would not be handled properly. When a Tempo kernel function is called by an ISR, Tempo cannot determine whether the end-of-interrupt command has already been issued (in fact, Tempo cannot even determine whether it was called by a process or an ISR) so it cannot issue EOI on behalf of the ISR before the context switch. To ensure that interrupt requests are handled correctly while the process runs, the PIC must have received EOI before the process is scheduled.

To summarize what we've covered so far, here are some important things to remember about processes, ISRs, and the EOI command:

- Every newly created process begins with interrupts enabled.
- If a process that runs with interrupts enabled relinquishes the processor by calling Tempo kernel function, then interrupts will be enabled when the process resumes.

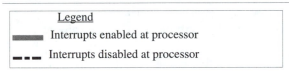

(a) Process 2 disables and enables interrupts

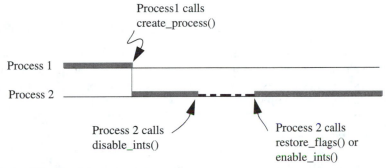

(b) ISR enables and disables interrupts

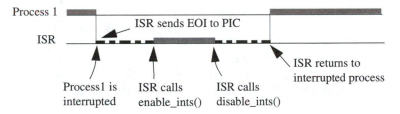

(c) ISR signals a higher priority process via a semaphore

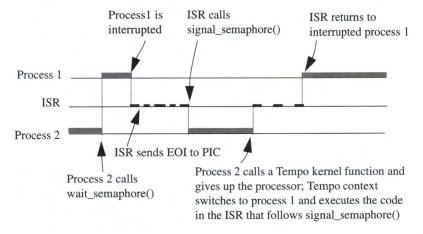

Figure 3.7 Enabling and disabling interrupts.

- If a process that runs with interrupts disabled relinquishes the processor by calling a Tempo kernel function, then interrupts will be disabled when the process resumes.
- Every ISR begins with interrupts disabled; interrupts are automatically reenabled when the ISR returns.
- Every ISR must output an EOI to the PIC before it returns to the interrupted process or signals a semaphore.

3.2.1 Tricky Issues in Communication between Processes and ISRs

Because processes and ISRs may communicate through semaphores and shared objects (for example, as shown in Figure 3.2), it may seem at first glance that communication between ISRs and processes is similar to interprocess communication. To a certain extent it is, but there are many pitfalls for the unwary, as will now be explained.

An ISR must not call any Tempo kernel functions that block. This means that ISRs cannot wait on semaphores. Look again at Figure 3.6, and consider what happens when `consumer` is waiting on `char_avail` and the idle process is running. When a UART interrupt occurs, the idle process is interrupted and `rxisr()` runs. Tempo does not know that an ISR has been activated (remember, ISRs are not scheduled by Tempo) so the kernel thinks the idle process is active even when the ISR is running. This is because *an ISR runs in the context of the interrupted process*. If the ISR calls a Tempo kernel function that blocks, then as far as Tempo is concerned, the idle process is attempting to relinquish the processor. Tempo must perform a context switch from the idle process to another process, but no other processes are eligible to run; otherwise, the idle process would not have been running when the interrupt happened. Tempo aborts the program when it detects this situation.

What happens if a process other than the idle process is interrupted and the ISR calls Tempo to wait on a semaphore? As far as Tempo is concerned, it is the interrupted process, not the ISR, that wants to wait for an event. Remember, Tempo is unaware that an ISR is running; it thinks that the interrupted process called the kernel function. If the process blocks on the semaphore (because the semaphore count is 0), it will wait there until the semaphore is signaled.

We can now explain why `rxisr()` in Figure 3.5 discards the character if the buffer is full. Recall that in the producer/consumer program in Section 2.3.4, the producer process waits on a semaphore until the consumer removes data from the buffer. But as we've just seen, ISRs cannot call any Tempo kernel functions that block, so the ISR cannot wait on a semaphore until there is room for the character. The simplest alternative is to throw away the character.

Mutual exclusion between ISRs and processes must be accomplished by interrupt lockout. ISRs and processes communicate through shared buffer objects, and all operations on those objects by processes and ISRs must be mutually exclusive. We have already seen how to ensure mutual exclusion between processes by means of semaphores, but when the mutual exclusion is between an ISR and a process, semaphores cannot be used, because an ISR cannot wait for a signal. In this case, mutual exclusion must implemented by disabling interrupts prior to accessing the shared data object and reenabling interrupts afterwards.

The code for Figure 3.2's monitor provides an example of mutual exclusion through interrupt lockout (see Figures 3.8 and 3.9). Figure 3.8 contains the definition of the character buffer inside the monitor and the function that initializes it.

```cpp
// char_buf.cpp

#include "tempo.h"
#include "char_buf.h"

// begin character buffer monitor
// a simple ring buffer is used to hold the chars
const int SIZE = 5;    // # chars in buffer

static char buffer[SIZE];
static int in_index, out_index, count;

void init_buffer_()    // initialize the buffer
{
    in_index = 0;      // initially, the buffer is empty
    out_index = 0;
    count = 0;
}
```

Figure 3.8 Monitor for buffering characters between an ISR and a process (part 1 of 2).

Look at the code for the monitor's retrieve_char_() function in Figure 3.9, which is called by consumer to remove characters from the buffer. This function calls two of the functions provided by Tempo to control interrupt lockout. Function disable_ints() disables interrupts at the processor. This function records whether interrupts are currently enabled or disabled before it disables interrupts, and returns that value. Function restore_flags() has one argument, which is usually the value returned by the previous call to disable_ints(). Depending on this value, interrupts are enabled or disabled.

In Figure 3.9, calls to disable_ints() (to disable interrupts at the processor) and restore_flags() (to reenable interrupts) bracket the operations on the buffer. By briefly disabling interrupts, retrieve_char_() guarantees that rxisr() will not run and deposit another character in the buffer while consumer removes a character from the buffer. The monitor's other interface functions, buffer_full_() and store_char_(), use the same technique to enforce mutual exclusion.

```
int buffer_full_()    // return 1 if no room in buffer
{
    short saved_flags;
    int buffer_is_full;

    saved_flags = disable_ints();
    buffer_is_full = (count == SIZE);
    restore_flags(saved_flags);
    return buffer_is_full;
}

void store_char_(char ch)    // store ch in buffer
{
    short saved_flags;

    saved_flags = disable_ints();
    buffer[in_index] = ch;
    in_index = (in_index + 1) % SIZE;
    count++;
    restore_flags(saved_flags);
}

char retrieve_char_(void)    // remove ch from buffer
{
    short saved_flags;
    char ch;

    saved_flags = disable_ints();
    ch = buffer[out_index];
    out_index = (out_index + 1) % SIZE;
    count--;
    restore_flags(saved_flags);
    return ch;
}
// end character buffer monitor
```

Figure 3.9 Monitor for buffering characters between an ISR and a process (part 2 of 2).

Tempo provides a function, enable_ints(), that reenables interrupts at the processor. Why do the monitor's functions use restore_flags() instead of enable_ints() to end mutual exclusion? The answer is: Functions written this way can be called by ISRs (which typically run with interrupts disabled) as well as processes (which typically run with interrupts enabled). These functions will return with interrupts disabled when called by code that is running with interrupts disabled. The same functions will return with interrupts enabled when called by code that is running with interrupts enabled. If Tempo did not provide restore_flags(), the monitor would have to provide two kinds of interface functions: namely, functions that always disable interrupts on entry and enable interrupts on exit (and consequently would only be called by processes) and functions that always return with interrupts disabled (and consequently would only be called by ISRs). In this example, `retrieve_char_()` is only called by the consumer process and `store_char_()` and `buffer_full_()` are only called by `rxisr()`; however, the monitor as coded here can be reused in other programs because any of its interface functions can be called by processes and ISRs.

3.3 SUMMARY

In this chapter we have

- Introduced interrupts and ISRs as a mechanism for delivering real-time events to Tempo processes.
- Shown how semaphores permit ISRs to synchronize and communicate with processes.
- Extended the *collaboration graph* notation to represent hardware and ISRs in systems.
- Explained why and how monitors that are shared by ISRs and processes enforce mutual exclusion by disabling and enabling interrupts.
- Explained the execution of processes and ISRs in an interrupt-driven Tempo program.

Programming with the Tempo Kernel: Advanced IPC

*T*his chapter explains Tempo's more advanced IPC facilities. It introduces event queues as a means for events and data to be transferred directly between processes. This chapter also shows how processes can be organized in dynamic client-server relationships and describes how waiting processes can time out if they do not receive expected events within a specified length of time. We continue to introduce elements of the collaboration graph notation to explain programs as systems.

4.1 EVENT QUEUES AND PROCESS SYNCHRONIZATION

Semaphores are a relatively low-level mechanism for coordinating processes. Sometimes a process must respond to several different events, but the order in which the events will occur cannot be determined ahead of time. Allocating a different semaphore for each event is not the best approach: When a process is waiting on a semaphore for one event, the arrival of a different event at another semaphore will not cause the process to resume execution. For situations like this, the inability of a process to wait on more than one semaphore simultaneously is overly restrictive.

Furthermore, a typical multitasking program will have many more processes and semaphores than the examples presented so far. These programs must be built with care, because a single missing or misplaced signal or wait operation will usually cause the program to operate incorrectly.

Tempo provides a higher-level facility for IPC, called an *event queue*, that does not have these limitations.

In the simplest use, illustrated in this section, event queues provide a means of sending signals directly between processes, instead of indirectly via semaphores. In collaboration graphs, this use is indicated by drawing a signal arrow, like the one we use for a signal to a semaphore, pointing directly at the destination process, as illustrated by Figure 4.1. The signal arrow is given the name of the event queue. Figure 4.1 also suggests the following way of thinking about event queues in relation to semaphores: An event queue is like a private semaphore belonging to a process, because the waiting place is, in effect, inside the process, instead of outside. (Event queues are not literally implemented as internal semaphores, but the effect for signaling purposes is as if they were.) In consequence, while many processes may signal an event queue, only the process that owns it can wait on it.

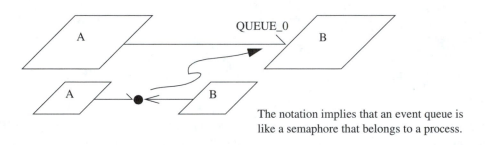

The notation implies that an event queue is like a semaphore that belongs to a process.

Figure 4.1 Notation for signaling an event queue.

4.1.1 Revisiting the UART Example

To illustrate the use of event queues for synchronization in a semaphore-like manner, Figure 4.2 shows how to extend the design of Section 3.1 so that the consumer process runs until either a newline or carriage return character is received by the UART or one minute elapses. Instead of waiting for events at a semaphore, consumer now waits for signals on two of its event queues. The ISR signals the char_avail event queue each time it stores a character in the buffer. Process sleeper sleeps for one minute; when it wakes, it signals the shutdown event queue.

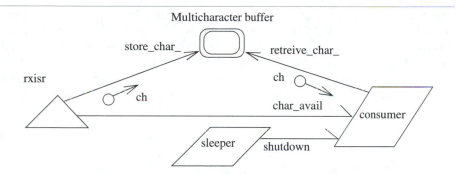

Figure 4.2 Using event queues to wait for events.

The code for this example starts in Figure 4.3. Main() creates the two processes and handles the initialization chores.

```
// ch4ex1.cpp - synchronization with event queues

#include <iostream.h>
#include <dos.h>
#include "tempo.h"
#include "char_buf.h"   // Section 3.2.1
#include "uart.h"        // See Appendix C
// "import" init_uart(), install_uart_isr,
// enable_rx_interrupt(), shutdown_uart_interrupts()

Process consumer, sleeper;
void consume(), sleep_root();

void interrupt rxisr(...);

void Main()
{
    init_buffer_();
    consumer = create_process(consume, 0);
    sleeper = create_process(sleep_root, 1);
    init_uart();
    install_uart_isr(rxisr);
    enable_rx_interrupt();
}
```

Figure 4.3 UART ISR example, using event queues (part 1 of 2).

The root functions for the consumer and sleeper processes and `rxisr()`, shown in Figure 4.4, illustrate synchronization using event queues. Tempo provides each process with a fixed number of event queues, which are identified by integer values (0, 1, 2, etc.). Normally, we associate each event queue with a single event and we assign a symbolic name to the queue, to indicate the event with which it is associated. In this program, `sleeper` sends `consumer` a *shutdown* event, notifying it that a minute has passed, by signaling the consumers's event queue 0. To do this, Tempo's `signal()` kernel function is called with the process and the shutdown queue as arguments:

```
const int shutdown = 0;
...
signal(consumer, shutdown);
```

ISR `rxisr` sends `consumer` a *char_avail* event, notifying it that a character has been placed in the buffer, by signaling the consumers's event queue 1:

```
const int char_avail = 1;
...
signal(consumer, char_avail);
```

The consumer waits on its event queues for *shutdown* and *char_avail* events by calling `wait()`. This function returns an integer value that indicates which queue was signaled:

```
queue = wait();
if (queue == shutdown) {
...
```

`Signal()` and `wait()` have the same semantics as `signal_semaphore()` and `wait_semaphore()`, with one exception: `wait()` allows a process to wait for signals to arrive on any of its event queues. When a process calls `wait()`, it searches all its event queues for a signal; if all the queues are empty, it waits for the first signal to arrive on any of its queues.

4.2 EVENT QUEUES AND MESSAGE PASSING

Tempo's event queues permit data to be transferred directly from one process to another. This kind of interprocess communication is known as *message passing*. A message is sent to a process by depositing the message in one of the process's event queues. Sending a message to an event queue is similar to signaling an event queue, in that neither operation requires the sender to wait. A process retrieves a message by removing it from the queue. Receiving a message from an event queue is similar to waiting for a signal, in that it may cause the process to wait. If there are no messages in the event queues, the receiving process will wait until a message arrives. Thus, event queues provide *asynchronous messaging*.

```
// consumers's event queues
const int shutdown = 0;    // queue 0
const int char_avail = 1;  // queue 1

void consume()
{
    int queue;
    char ch;

    do {
        queue = wait();  // wait for an event
        if (queue == shutdown) {
            break;
        } else if (queue == char_avail) {
            ch = retrieve_char_();
            CS(cout << ch);
    } while ((ch != '\n') && (ch != '\r'));
    shutdown_uart_interrupts();
}

void sleep_root()
{
    const unsigned int NUM_TICKS = 18 * 60;

    process_sleep(NUM_TICKS);
    signal(consumer, shutdown);
}

// destination for EOI command
const int PIC_00 = 0x20;
const int EOI = 0x20;  // end-of-interrupt command

// rxisr() - this isr runs every time a character is
//           received by the uart.

void interrupt rxisr(...)
{
    char ch;

    // send end-of-interrupt command to the PIC
    outportb(PIC_00, EOI);
    ch = rxchar();  // read char from uart
    if (!buffer_full_()) {
        store_char_(ch); // save char in buffer object
        signal(consumer, char_avail);
    }
}
```

Figure 4.4 UART ISR example, using event queues (part 2 of 2).

Figure 4.5 shows the notation for asynchronous messaging between two processes via event queues. Notice that the signal arrow used earlier to represent signaling an event queue is used here to depict sending messages. The two operations are asynchronous, so we use the same notation to represent both, but the parameter symbol beside the arrow indicates that we mean message passing (data transfer) instead of signaling.

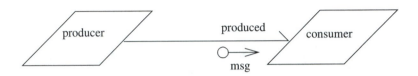

Figure 4.5 Producer and consumer processes communicating by message passing.

The message parameter is actually a pointer to a block of memory that is allocated by the producer, released by the consumer, and used by both processes. Creation of program entities (here, allocation of a memory block), their use in different places, and their eventual destruction (here, release of the memory block), are aspects of *structural dynamics*, meaning some aspects of the structure of the program change over time. This diagram oversimplifies the situation by omitting any depiction of structural dynamics. Such simplification is often useful and possible, but not always. The topic is important enough that we will devote an entire chapter to it (Chapter 9).

Messages are sent to a process by calling Tempo's `send()` function:

```
send(destination, queue, msg, ack_queue);
```

The function's arguments are as follows:

- `destination`—the process identifier of the intended recipient of the message.
- `queue`—the event queue where the message will be deposited.
- `msg`—the message (a pointer to a block of memory. The structure of this memory is irrelevant to Tempo, but is assumed to be understood by both the sending and receiving processes).
- `ack_queue`—the queue where the sending process will expect to receive a reply.

To obtain a message from one of its event queues, a process calls `receive()`:

```
queue = receive(msg, correspondent, ack_queue);
```

This kernel function searches the process's unmasked event queues for a message and removes it from the head of a queue. If all the queues are empty, the process waits until a message arrives in one of the unmasked queues. Four pieces of information are returned by `receive()`:

- queue—the queue from which the message was removed.
- msg—the received message (a pointer to a block of memory).
- correspondent—the process identifier of the *correspondent process* (the process that sent the message).
- ack_queue—the queue where the correspondent process will expect to receive a reply.

To demonstrate the use of event queues for message passing, we present another version of the producer/consumer example (see Figures 4.6 and 4.7).

```cpp
// ch4ex2.cpp - message passing between producer and
//               consumer processes

#include <iostream.h>
#include "tempo.h"

void produce(), consume();
Process producer, consumer;

const int produced = 0; // producer sends data to the
                        // consumer's event queue 0

void Main()
{
    producer = create_process(produce);
    consumer = create_process(consume);
}

// produce - send 10 messages to the consumer process
void produce()
{
    int *msg;

    for (int i = 0; i < 10; i++) {
        CS(msg = new int);
        if (msg == NULL) {
            CS(cout << "producer: new returned NULL"
                    << endl);
            terminate_multitasking();
        }
        *msg = i;
        send(consumer, produced, (message)msg,
             NO_ACK);
        msg = NULL;
    }
}
```

Figure 4.6 Message passing between producer and consumer processes (part 1 of 2).

The code for the producer process is shown in Figure 4.6. The producer no longer updates a shared data object; instead, the process creates a new message by allocating enough space from the system's memory pool to hold one data item (an integer, in this example). The new operator returns a pointer to that memory, which is assigned to the variable msg. After assigning a value to the integer, the producer sends the message to the consumer process's produced queue:

```
send(consumer, produced, (message)msg, NO_ACK);
```

The send() function's third argument is declared to be of type message, so a cast is required to force msg (a pointer to an integer) to the correct type. By passing NO_ACK as the fourth argument, the producer indicates that it does not intend to wait for a reply from the consumer.

Figure 4.7 contains the root function for the consumer process. This process calls receive() to wait for a message from the producer:

```
queue = receive(msg, correspondent, ack_queue);
```

This function removes a message from the consumer's "produced" event queue and stores it in msg. Because a message is a pointer, the consumer first casts the message to the appropriate type (a pointer to an int), then dereferences the pointer to obtain the value that it consumes (prints).

```
// consume - receive 10 messages from the producer process
void consume()
{
    int queue, ack_queue;
    message msg;
    Process correspondent;

    for (int i = 0; i < 10; i++) {
        queue = receive(msg, correspondent, ack_queue);
        CS(cout << "consumer: received message on queue "
                << queue << endl);
        CS(cout << "received " << *(int *)msg << endl);
        CS(delete msg);
    }
}
```

Figure 4.7 Message passing between producer and consumer processes (part 2 of 2).

After the integer has been printed, the consumer uses the delete operator to release the memory where the integer is stored. Although the producer allocates a word of memory to hold each new value that it produces, it cannot return this memory to the system after it sends a message to the consumer—the producer does not know when the consumer is finished with the memory. The consumer and producer must therefore share the responsibility of managing the dynamically allocated storage: The producer allocates memory from the system's memory pool, and the consumer returns it to the system.

The producer/consumer example demonstrates the protocol followed by a pair of Tempo processes when they communicate by message passing. We often refer to blocks of memory as *buffers*. Dynamically allocated buffers are passed from one process to another by sending pointers to the buffers as messages. Careful programming is needed to prevent conflicting accesses to the same buffer by multiple processes. It is important to ensure that a process does not continue to use a buffer after it has passed the buffer to another process. In effect, a process obtains ownership of a buffer when it receives the pointer to it, and the right to use that block of memory is relinquished when the pointer is sent to another process, but this must be enforced by programming conventions.

It is also typical of producer/consumer programs for buffers to be released by processes other than the processes that allocate the memory. Care is required to ensure that buffers are allocated correctly before they are used and returned to the system when they are no longer required. Incorrect use of dynamically allocated memory is a well-known source of bugs in sequential programs, and these flaws are especially difficult to find in multitasking programs.

4.2.1 Event Queues as Bounded Buffers

The behavior of the producer/consumer program in Section 4.2 is similar to the program in Section 2.4.1 that used a bounded buffer team. Notice that the producer and consumer processes do not run in lockstep fashion. Instead, messages sent by the producer are buffered in the consumer's event queue until they are picked up by the consumer, allowing the producer to get ahead of the consumer.

There are additional similarities. The bounded buffer team used a semaphore to enforce mutual exclusion on the buffer; similarly, Tempo's `send()` and `receive()` kernel functions ensure that operations on a event queues are mutually exclusive (although they do not do it with semaphores). Also, recall that the bounded buffer team prevented attempts to place data in a full buffer and remove data from an empty buffer. Tempo's `receive()` function does the same thing; if the event queues are empty, it forces the consumer to wait until a message is available.

Thus, for designs in which two processes have a producer/consumer relationship, the need for a separate buffer team is eliminated if an event queue is used to transfer data between the processes. Can this be extended to cases in which we have multiple producers or consumers?

Figure 4.8 shows two ways of buffering data between multiple producers and one consumer. Figure 4.8(a) uses the bounded buffer team from Chapter 2. Figure 4.8(b) shows that the buffer module can be replaced when message passing is used to transfer data between processes. Here, the producer processes send messages directly to the consumer process's event queue.

(a)

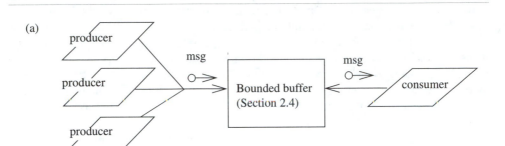

(b)

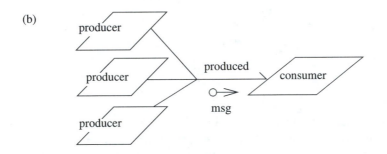

Figure 4.8 Multiple producers, one consumer.

However, Figure 4.9 shows that the two approaches (bounded buffer team and event queues) are not equivalent when we have one producer and several consumers. In Figure 4.9(a), each consumer process obtains data from the bounded buffer when it is ready to do work. The implication is that the producer does not care which process consumes a particular item. As shown in Figure 4.9(b), when we attempt to convert this to a design in which the producer sends messages directly to the consumers, a problem becomes evident. The producer must select a specific process to be the recipient of each message. This may lead to a situation in which one consumer has several pending messages in its event queue while the other consumers sit idle.

4.2.2 Client-Server Process Organizations

A general kind of interprocess relationship is *client-server*. Figure 4.10 gives an example, in which the interaction between a client and a server consists of a pair of message exchanges. The client sends a message to the server, requesting an operation that the server is to perform on behalf of the client. Both processes execute concurrently once the request is received.

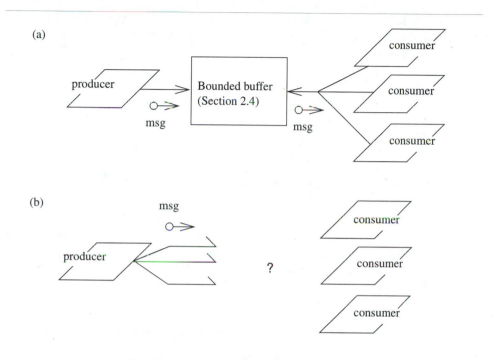

Figure 4.9 One producer, multiple consumers.

Later, the client waits for the server to send it a reply containing the results of the completed request. After the reply is received the client continues (presumably using the information it received from the server) while the server waits for another request.

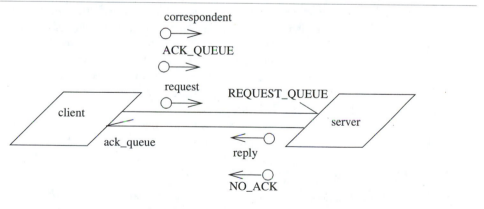

Figure 4.10 Client-server interaction.

Client-server organizations are easily programmed with Tempo. Using `send()`, a client process directs its request to a server, specifying the name of the server process, the event queue where Tempo will deposit the message, and an *acknowledgment queue*—the queue where the server should send a reply:

```
send(server_process, REQUEST_QUEUE, (message)request,
    ACK_QUEUE);
```

The server calls `receive()` to wait for a request to arrive from *any* of its client processes, performs the requested operation, and then prepares the reply. A reply is simply a message sent from the server to the client, but how does the server identify the client?

Tempo's `receive()` kernel function is called with three arguments:

```
queue = receive(msg, correspondent, ack_queue);
```

When the function returns, the second argument contains the identifier of the process that sent the message, also known as the *correspondent process*. The third argument, `ack_queue`, is the queue where the reply message should be sent. These two arguments register the client with the server for a reply. The server can send the reply by calling `send()`:

```
send(correspondent, ack_queue, (message)reply, NO_ACK);
```

(By passing NO_ACK as the last argument, the server informs the client that this is the end of the interchange.)

In general, the relationship between a client process and a server process, such as in Figure 4.10, is a structurally dynamic one. In effect, the client's call to the `send()` kernel function does more than just pass a request from the client to the server; it also registers the client for a reply. In Figure 4.10, the parameters labeled "correspondent" and "ACK_QUEUE" indicate that information about the client is passed to the server via `send()` and `receive()`. This means that the server is not hardwired to work with a single client; instead, it can handle requests from any client. The relationship between the server and a client is established dynamically when the client sends its request. We can show this as a fixed structure, as in Figure 4.10, if we assume that the same processes are always involved and therefore the same relationship is always established by every `send()` call. Chapter 9 presents notations for representing structurally dynamic systems with changing relationships between client-server pairs.

Replies can also be sent using Tempo's `reply()` function, which has the same semantics as `send()`—it sends a message to the specified process and event queue:

```
reply(correspondent, ack_queue, (message)reply);
```

Using both these functions helps us distinguish the messages that are sent as requests and the messages that are sent as replies; however, the recipient cannot tell the difference.

4.3 SELECTIVELY RECEIVING SIGNALS AND MESSAGES

Tempo's `receive()` kernel function can be called instead of `wait()` to wait for signals. For example, we could modify the consumer process in Figure 4.4, replacing the statement

```
queue = wait();
```

with

```
queue = receive(msg, correspondent, ack_queue);
```

To indicate that it has received a signal rather than a message, `receive()` assigns NULL to the `msg`, `correspondent`, and `ack_queue` parameters.

The power of the `receive()` function lies in its ability to wait for both signals and messages. Real-time systems often contain processes that must respond to both types of events, but we can rarely guarantee the order in which messages and signals will arrive (recall that a real-time system must respond to *unpredictable* stimuli). A process that blocks by calling `wait()` will remain blocked until it is signaled, even if messages are deposited in its event queues before a signal arrives. Using `receive()` to wait for both signals and messages helps ensure timely delivery of these events, regardless of how their arrivals are interleaved.

What happens when a process's event queues contain both signals and unreceived messages? Does one type of event take precedence over the other? The answer depends on which of Tempo's kernel functions is called to wait for the events:

- When a process calls `wait()`, it searches the process's unmasked event queues for a signal. Messages are always ignored by `wait()`, and they remain in the queues until they are removed by `receive()`.
- When a process calls `receive()`, it checks the process's unmasked event queues for both signals and messages. Signals are always received before messages; that is, `receive()` will return a message only if there are no signals in any of the unmasked queues. In effect, signals stored in any event queue are deemed to be higher-priority events than any messages stored in the queues (even if the messages were sent first) and are received first.

Exploiting the full capability of `receive()`, by designing processes that wait for signals and messages on the same event queue, can result in root functions that are difficult to understand. Controlled use of `signal()` and `send()` prevents this. We recommend adopting this convention: Signals and messages should not be sent to the same event queue (or set of queues) at the destination process. As each process is designed, select one or more of its event queues for receiving signals, and then select different queues to receive messages.

4.3.1 Waiting on Selected Event Queues

It is often useful for a process to wait on a subset of its event queues, ignoring any signals on the other queues until it is ready to handle them. To do this, each queue may be individually *masked* and *unmasked*. Masked queues are ignored by `wait()`; that is, `wait()` returns after removing a signal from one of the calling process's unmasked event queues. Masked queues are also ignored by `receive()`. This kernel function returns after it removes a signal or a message from an unmasked event queue. If an event queue is signaled or receives a message while it is masked, the signal or message is not lost; instead, the signal or message is stored in the queue and will be received after the queue is unmasked.

The next example illustrates event signaling between processes with different priorities and the effects of masking and unmasking event queues (see Figures 4.11 through 4.14). Two processes (`process1` and `process3`) repeatedly signal `process2`. The labels in the collaboration graph indicate that both processes signal `QUEUE_0` and `QUEUE_1`. For each signal it receives, `process2` prints the queue number returned by `wait()`.

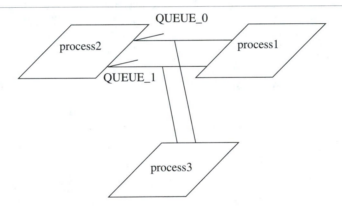

Figure 4.11 Waiting on selected event queues.

Because `process1` has the highest priority, it signals `process2` three times and terminates. When `process2` runs, it will have two pending signals on `QUEUE_0` and one pending signal on `QUEUE_1`. The first three calls to `wait()` in `process2root()` remove these signals from the queues.

After handling these events, `process2` waits to be signaled by `process3`. For the first two signals, the execution of `process2` and `process3` is interleaved—`process3` has lower priority than `process2`, so Tempo performs a context switch to `process2` when `process3` calls `signal()`. The remaining code in `process2root()` illustrates the use of `mask_queue()` and `unmask_queue()` prior to waiting for a signal. Although `process3` signals QUEUE_0 before signaling

QUEUE_1, the signals are received by process2 in the reverse order. After masking QUEUE_0, process2 waits until it receives the signal from QUEUE_1.

```
// ch4ex3.cpp

#include <iostream.h>
#include "tempo.h"

#define QUEUE_0 0
#define QUEUE_1 1

void process1root(), process2root(), process3root();
Process process1, process2, process3;

void Main()
{
    process1 = create_process(process1root,2);
    process2 = create_process(process2root,1);
    process3 = create_process(process3root,0);
}

// process1 has higher priority than process2, so will run
// to completion before process2 starts to run. When
// process1 finishes, process2 will have two pending
// signals on QUEUE_0, and one pending signal on QUEUE_1.

void process1root()
{
    CS(cout << "process1: signaling queue 0" << endl);
    signal(process2, QUEUE_0);

    CS(cout << "process1: signaling queue 1" << endl);
    signal(process2, QUEUE_1);

    CS(cout << "process1: signaling queue 0" << endl);
    signal(process2, QUEUE_0);
}
```

Figure 4.12 Waiting on selected event queues (part 1 of 3).

```
// process2 receives 3 signals from process1, followed by 4
// signals from process3.

void process2root()
{
    int event;

    CS(cout << "process2: all queues unmasked" << endl);
    event = wait();
    CS(cout << "process2: queue " << event
        << " signaled" << endl);

    CS(cout << "process2: all queues unmasked" << endl);
    event = wait();
    CS(cout << "process2: queue " << event <<
        " signaled" << endl);

    CS(cout << "process2: all queues unmasked" << endl);
    event = wait();
    CS(cout << "process2: queue " << event
        << " signaled" << endl);

    CS(cout << endl);

    CS(cout << "process2: all queues unmasked" << endl);
    event = wait();
    CS(cout << "process2: queue " << event
        << " signaled" << endl);

    CS(cout << "process2: all queues unmasked" << endl);
    event = wait();
    CS(cout << "process2: queue " << event
        << " signaled" << endl);

    CS(cout << "process2: masking queue 0" << endl);
    mask_queue(QUEUE_0);
    event = wait();
    CS(cout << "process2: queue " << event
        << " signaled" << endl);

    CS(cout << "process2: unmasking queue 0" << endl);
    unmask_queue(QUEUE_0);
    event = wait();
    CS(cout << "process2: queue " << event
        << " signaled" << endl);
}
```

Figure 4.13 Waiting on selected event queues (part 2 of 3).

```
// process3 has lower priority than process2.  Each time
// it signals one of process2's unmasked queues, process2
// runs. When process3 signals a masked queue, the pending
// signal is saved until the queue is unmasked by
// process2.

void process3root()
{
    CS(cout << "process3: signaling queue 0" << endl);
    signal(process2, QUEUE_0);

    CS(cout << "process3: signaling queue 1" << endl);
    signal(process2, QUEUE_1);

    CS(cout << "process3: signaling queue 0" << endl);
    signal(process2, QUEUE_0);

    CS(cout << "process3: signaling queue 1" << endl);
    signal(process2, QUEUE_1);
}
```

Figure 4.14 Waiting on selected event queues (part 3 of 3).

4.4 TIMEOUTS

Real-time systems operate in an unreliable world: sensors may be triggered by spurious glitches or fail to operate, and noise may garble communications lines. In addition to correctly responding to expected events and dealing with unanticipated events, real-time programs must be able to cope *when expected events fail to occur.*

We've seen several examples illustrating how processes wait for events to arrive at semaphores or event queues. But because a waiting process remains blocked until an event happens, it will wait forever if the anticipated event never occurs. To avoid this, Tempo provides *timeouts*. As before, processes must wait for events to occur, but if a waiting process does not receive an event before a specified length of time has elapsed, it is unblocked with an indication that a timeout happened. The process can then take whatever steps are appropriate to recover.

The collaboration graph notation allows us to distinguish between waiting indefinitely for event arrivals and waiting with timeout. Figure 4.15 introduces the *timer* symbol—reminiscent of an analog clock face—for indicating waiting with timeout. By placing a timer along one edge of a process, we denote that the process can time out while waiting for the arrival of signals or messages. We can also represent the possibility of timeout while waiting on a semaphore: The timer symbol replaces the solid waiting place circle in the semaphore symbol.

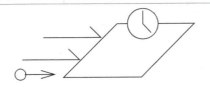

The process waits until (1) one of its event queues receives a signal or a message or (2) a fixed amount of time elapses.

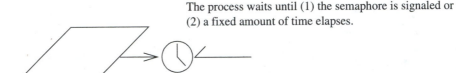

The process waits until (1) the semaphore is signaled or (2) a fixed amount of time elapses.

Figure 4.15 Waiting for event arrivals, with timeouts.

Tempo provides versions of its `receive()` and `wait()` kernel functions with a timeout parameter that allows the calling process to specify the maximum number of ticks of the system clock that it should wait before timing out:

```
queue = wait(timeout);

queue = receive(msg, correspondent, ack_queue, timeout);
```

If the awaited events do not occur within the selected length of time, these functions return the value `TIMED_OUT` (defined in `tempo.h`); otherwise, they return the queue where the signal or message was found. By checking this return value, the process can determine whether a timeout happened or an event arrived.

Timed waiting on a semaphore is similar:

```
result = wait_semaphore(semaphore, timeout);
```

If `wait_semaphore()` returns before the specified timeout elapses, the value 0 is returned; `TIMED_OUT` is returned if the function times out.

In effect, every Tempo semaphore and process may have its own timer. A semaphore's timer is set when `wait_semaphore()` is called with a timeout parameter, and a process's timer is set when `wait()` or `receive()` is called with a timeout parameter. The timer is turned off when the corresponding function call times out or when an event arrives (the semaphore is signaled, a signal or message arrives at the event queue). In other words, regardless of whether a timeout or an event arrival causes a timed call to `wait_semaphore()`, `wait()`, or `receive()` to return, there is no need to cancel the semaphore or process timer. The timer remains off until the next timed call sets it.

4.5 SUMMARY

In this chapter we have

- Introduced event queues and compared them with semaphores as a mechanism for process synchronization.
- Shown how event queues support asynchronous message passing, in which data are transferred directly from one process to another.
- Described how event queues are used to implement structurally dynamic client-server process relationships.
- Explained why processes in a real-time system may need to time out while waiting for events to arrive, and described how Tempo semaphores and event queues support timeouts.

Basic Design Notations

*T*his chapter stands back from programming to focus on design notations. The emphasis of these notations is on helping you to think about the essence of a real-time system under design as a system, not to draw pictures of programs. Therefore, the notations are presented in a code-independent manner. The notations are, at their core, either compatible with, or supplementary to, emerging standard software design notations. They are not completely standard for reasons of both expressiveness about the issues with which this book is primarily concerned and timing (at the time this is being written, standards for real-time system notations have not yet emerged).

This chapter gives the basics of three design notations: *components* (Section 5.1), *collaboration graphs (CGs)* (Section 5.2), and *use case maps (UCMs)* (Section 5.3). CGs and UCMs are, respectively, the *wiring diagrams* and *path diagrams* of Chapter 1 (the latter two terms will continue to be used from time to time). The same component notation is needed for both and so is presented as a separate notation. Chapters 2 through 4 provided some examples of CGs, but not of UCMs.

This chapter assumes that systems may be conceptualized as having fixed structure. The key word is *conceptualized*. Components that are conceptualized as fixed may be created dynamically during initialization (for example, processes). Relationships that are conceptualized as fixed may be established dynamically while the program is running (for example, IPC connections). Conceptualizing such relationships as fixed (for example, fixed IPC connections between processes) is a good abstraction in many cases, but not all. We call systems that cannot be satisfactorily conceptualized as fixed, *structurally dynamic*. Chapter 9 extends the notations of this chapter to such systems. The extensions are relatively minor, but the issues are sufficiently deep that introducing the notations this early in the book could confuse rather than enlighten. By deferring structural dynamics in this way, we are not ignoring that fact that *programs* are often structurally dynamic in a pervasive way, but simply abstracting away from this fact to get a system view.

UCMs come into the notation picture because CGs have some drawbacks from a high-level design perspective: They require so many detailed commitments that the effort required to create them discourages the exploration of design alternatives; and design magic is required to produce good design solutions with CGs, starting from a blank sheet. The reason design magic is required is that CGs tend not to give a good view of stimulus-response paths that may propagate through a set of processes (the issue is not restricted to processes, but they provide the interesting cases in this book). There is something more fundamental about such sequences than the processes and IPC that realize them; they are really properties of the problem, not of the solution with processes and IPC. UCMs enter the picture to overcome these drawbacks; they replace the mental model of such sequences with actual paths that can be drawn in design diagrams at a level above IPC connections. Thus, they provide a means of reasoning from requirements (in terms of paths) to processes. The notation is a lightweight one, easy to learn, and the insight it gives makes the small effort of learning it worthwhile.

UCMs, CGs, and code form a sequence of progressively lower levels of abstraction. Chapters 6 through 8 present a case study in which these form a sequence of development steps. However, do *not* conclude that we are attempting to prescribe a rigid sequence of development steps that must be followed in this order, with complete high-level designs done first with UCMs, followed by complete detailed designs with CGs, and then code. We encourage viewing the notations primarily as aids to thinking and only secondarily as work products of development steps. While in the thinking stage, designers may jump around in the levels of abstraction, opportunistically, as something in one level triggers a thought about something in another that should be checked out or noted immediately. Designers may also develop the levels of abstraction in reverse order, starting from code, to discover designs—this is called reverse engineering, and we did it in Chapters 2 through 4 to introduce CGs.

This chapter aims to give a sufficient introduction to the notations to understand the rest of the book, but not necessarily to become expert. A reference manual on CGs is provided in Appendix B that summarizes the notation, cross-references it to code, discusses its nuances, and presents helpful hints for using it. There is no separate reference manual for the component notation because it is included as part of CG notation in Appendix B. There is no reference manual for the UCM notation, because sufficient information for the purposes of this book is provided in this chapter and Chapters 6, 7, and 9, and other publications are available for those who want to dig deeper (see the Preface and Appendix D).

5.1 COMPONENTS

Figure 5.1 identifies four basic types of *operational* components and summarizes their relationship to code. Assumptions of the component notation are summarized in Section 5.1.1. Implementation-independent characterizations of the basic component types are given in Section 5.1.2. Nuances are added in Section 5.1.3 and Chapter 9.

Teams are design abstractions of compound operational units, the internal organization of which will be shown in a nested fashion. They have nothing in particular to do with multitasking. They are committed as implementation units (modules) only if they are given interfaces in collaboration graphs. Modules may be coded in many ways (commented groupings, instances of classes, files).

Processes implement multitasking. They are coded as ordinary functions (*root* functions) with some special conventions and then made known to Tempo through create calls.

Objects are abstractions that have nothing to do with multitasking and not necessarily anything to do with object-oriented (OO) programming. They are the minimal *diagrammatic* representation of raw data and raw procedure. For C/skinny-C++, they represent related sets of (optionally) raw data and functions; for C++, they represent literal objects (or abstractions of sets of them). Diagrammed objects are primitive visual entities (never decomposed visually).

Nesting of components inside other components is an operational abstraction that helps system understanding even though it may not describe the organization of the code accurately (for example, nothing is literally nested in process code except raw data).

ISRs (interrupt service routines) link hardware to processes outside the kernel. They are coded as ordinary functions with some special conventions. Except for one ISR of its own to handle timer interrupts, the kernel is unaware of the existence of ISRs.

Figure 5.1 Four basic component types.

This figure is more than just a catalog of component types; it is also an example of a *component context diagram* that positions components relative to each other, either as peers or nested. Component context diagrams form the background of both CGs and UCMs. Component context diagrams like this are intended to be fixed, meaning not only that the components have fixed relationships with each other, but also that the general visual form of the diagram (the relative positioning of the components) remains fixed in all appearances of the diagram, whether the diagram stands alone or forms the background for a CG or UCM. This aids system understanding by providing a fixed mental context for understanding the behavior implied by the other notations.

5.1.1 Component Notation: Assumptions

Although the notation seems very simple at first glance, there is a strong set of assumptions underlying it that you need to understand to use it effectively. In the conceptual world of this notation, the components are seen as machines, in other words artifacts that can act and react (we often use the term *operational component* to imply this). Collaborating groups of such components are viewed as forming systems of machines; these systems are themselves machines, and so forth.

The diagrams drawn with the component notation are not pictures of programs for several reasons:

- *Component diagrams explicitly show only elements of programs that are machine-like.* Examples are processes and collaborating teams of them.
- *Component diagrams push down as detail elements of programs that are needed during operation but that are not themselves machinelike.* Examples are pieces of raw data, such as constants, variables, and structures in languages like C. Such pieces do not, by themselves, have a machinelike nature. In a conceptual world of machines, pieces of raw data fulfil a supporting role *inside* machines, but they never appear *on their own* at a peer level with other machines. There is deliberately no way of defining their existence or structure with the component notation, except by means of textual comments. See Section 5.1.3 for a discussion of how this relates to data objects in object-oriented programs.
- *Component diagrams do not necessarily show all machinelike program elements, because some may be too detailed to be helpful at the scale of interest.* An example is smallish data objects in object-oriented programs, which could swamp us in detail if we tried to represent them all as machines at the system level (see the discussion in Section 5.1.3).
- *Component diagrams omit elements of programs that do not have an operational character.* Examples are types and classes. Types and classes are regarded as having the character of manufacturing instructions. Creation, initialization, and destruction of *instances* of types and classes belong in the world of machines, but are treated in a way that does not model the types and classes themselves as machines.
- *Component diagrams treat some elements of programs that you might imagine are machinelike as attributes of machines, not as machines in themselves.* Examples are functions and process mainlines (in this book, the process mainline is the executable body of the root function that defines the process). The code that drives the internal behavior of machines—the kind of thing that might be represented with control flow

charts, state machines, or pseudocode—is assumed to be an implicit part of machines, not a machine itself. There is no separate notation for the mainline of a process; the process symbol implies there must be such a mainline, but the details are left to code. Program elements like functions are not normally viewed as machines by themselves but are bundled into interfaces and connections (except for root functions of processes, which are bundled into processes). Isolated functions would either be swept under the carpet as assumed parts of the components that call them or bundled into the interface of some machinelike component if they must be made visible in design diagrams.

- *Component diagrams treat some elements of programs that are machinelike as supporting layers rather than as peer machines.* Examples are the kernel and the language runtime system. These elements could be viewed as peer machines, but to do so could be counterproductive because resulting CGs would become black with connections from everywhere to these elements, overwhelming us with uninteresting detail.

5.1.2 Component Notation: Types of Components

Objects

For design purposes, an object is a component that supports data and/or procedural abstractions through an interface. *Supporting a data abstraction* means that the interface provides operators (functions in C/C++) to access internal pieces of data that are otherwise hidden from callers. *Supporting a procedure abstraction* means that the interface provides a set of related operators that hide detailed procedural sequences, such as sequences of interactions with other components. Note that interfaces of objects are not shown in component context diagrams and may not necessarily even be known when component context diagrams are drawn. However, the fact that there will be interfaces must be kept in mind.

The term *object* does not necessarily imply object-oriented implementation, the use of classes, or anything other than what has just been said. Procedure or data abstractions are easily implemented in either object-oriented or non-object-oriented programming languages (see Section 5.1.3 for more on the issue of object orientation). In languages like C or skinny C++ that have no explicit objects in the sense of this design notation, an object in a design diagram is implemented as a set of functions and, if appropriate, shared data, the whole of which is treated as a unit by comments and usage conventions.

The model of object behavior is that objects have interface operators to perform their own responsibilities but do not have ultimate control of *when* they perform them; the operators provide the means for other components to exercise control over "when" by invoking the operators. Ultimately, this control comes from processes or ISRs, although it may come indirectly through other nonprocess components such as teams or other objects.

Objects are viewed as primitive components from a design-diagram perspective, meaning not further decomposable in diagrammatic form. This provides an explicit identi-

fication of the scale of the design diagram. Anything shown as an object will not be further refined diagrammatically at this scale, but left to code. Objects may have internal state, but the data structures that define this state are not defined diagrammatically: the only visibility of them is through interface operators that implicitly access the state. In general, a data object might be a composite abstraction for many data constants, data variables, and data structures that we wish to view as a unit from a system perspective. For example, an entire data base might be shown as a single object if the internal details of the data base are not of interest at the scale of the diagram.

If an abstraction is needed for a multiobject component, use a team.

Teams

Teams represent operational groupings of components, including other teams. A team may be drawn as a black box (an outline with nothing inside it) or opened up as a glass box (next diagram).

Showing a team in a design diagram does not necessarily make a commitment to having a distinct implementation unit for the team box itself in the software (for example, a distinct source file that packages interface functions and team members in one place). A team in a high-level design diagram may only be a useful abstraction to aid understanding. Commitment is made to an implementation unit when an interface is defined for a team (for example, a set of interface functions). A team with a defined interface that is intended to be an implementation unit is sometimes referred to as a *module* in this book, although we shall often stick with the term *team* where the intent is clear from the context.

In languages like C or skinny C++, a module will be implemented as a set of interface functions and member components, the whole of which is treated as a unit by comments and usage conventions. In languages like full C++, a module will be implemented as a container class. In either case, the difference between the teams and objects of our design diagrams may sometimes be hard to distinguish in the implementation, except by comments. The distinction lies in how we think about them in our conceptual world of machines; we reserve teams for components that are decomposable in diagrammatic form at the scale of the diagram in which they appear. Remember that the main aim of this nota-

tion is not to show pictures of programs but to assist in understanding systems. See
Section 5.1.3 for more on these issues.

A team is said to be *passive* if it contains no processes or interrupt service routines
(at any level of recursive decomposition of its members) and to be *active* otherwise.

A team box is also used as a neutral representation of a component of a type not yet
committed, on the principle that anything may be inside a team.

Processes

A process is an autonomous, self-directed component that may operate concurrently with other processes. For Tempo design, the internal logic of processes is assumed
to be sequential; in other words, there are no processes inside processes (see Section 5.1.3
for a discussion of more general cases).

For most design purposes (except evaluating performance) we imagine processes as
fully concurrent. Software processes are pseudo-concurrent when many of them share a
single processor, but the pseudo-concurrency is hidden from the programmer. In design
diagrams, we use the same notation for fully concurrent and pseudo-concurrent processes,
leaving the two cases to be distinguished by context .

Processes have a special relationship to the terms *perform* and *control*. All components *perform* their own responsibilities. Processes (and ISRs) perform them spontaneously and objects and passive teams when their interface operators are invoked. However,
only processes (and ISRs) are ultimate sources of *control*. This means that all invocations
of objects or passive teams must ultimately come from processes (or ISRs) either directly
or through chains of invocations that pass through other objects or passive teams. The
consequence for design diagrams is that there must be—somewhere in a set of design diagrams for a system—at least one controlling process (or ISR) for every object or passive
team. The relationship may be one to many in either direction; for example, one process
may control many objects and passive teams exclusively, or many processes may control
one shared object or one shared passive team (in the latter case, control must be properly
synchronized). By itself, the positioning of processes in component context diagrams does
not indicate which components they control (except for one case that we will get to
shortly—components nested operationally inside processes); control is indicated explicitly by CGs and implicitly by UCMs.

In principle, the design model of a *sequential* program is one controlling process
(corresponding to the main program) causing the action to unfold through chains of invocations. However, care must be required not to interpret this model too literally in some
cases. For example, although we may, in principle, view a sequential program running
under DOS as a process (thus viewing DOS as a limited kind of operating system that runs
only one process at a time), DOS does not see the program as a process. When the program running under DOS is a Tempo program, the only actual processes are the ones supported by Tempo. If a Tempo program was running under an operating system that

supported processes, there would be two levels of processes, one supported by the operating system and the other supported by Tempo (see Section 5.1.3 for a discussion of how to use the design notation in such cases).

The situation often occurs that a process interacts with objects and passive teams that are essentially private to the process, because no other processes interact with them. In such cases, the objects and passive teams should be shown within the process outline. This does not imply code-level nesting, only operational grouping. For example, in the Tempo

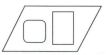

world, a process that calls some functions that no other process calls may have these functions represented as interface operators of an internal object, even though the functions are actually not nested in the root function that defines the process and there may be no actual "object" in code. By definition, the process controls the nested components.

Interrupt Service Routines (ISRs)

An ISR is a component that acts as a link between hardware devices and the process level of software. It is activated by a stimulus called an interrupt that arrives from hardware. Our design model is that ISRs are triggered directly *only* from hardware. This may be shown diagrammatically by showing hardware boxes invoking ISRs (Section 5.2). However, software may also trigger ISRs indirectly by issuing commands to force hardware to generate interrupts. This may shown diagrammatically by showing software boxes invoking hardware boxes (Section 5.2).

An ISR may perform responsibilities over a series of interrupts before communicating with the process level.

An ISR is half like a process and half not (the triangle shape symbolizes this—a triangle is half a parallelogram). The half that *is* like a process has the following characteristic: ISRs run autonomously and therefore are autonomous sources of control, just like processes; ISRs may have teamlike character in the same sense as processes, meaning that objects and passive teams may exist that are operationally private to an ISR and that may be shown inside the triangular ISR box. The half that *is not* like a process has the follow-

ing characteristics: ISR-to-process communication is possible only by means of shared data and/or asynchronous interactions; process-to-ISR communication is not possible through software; ISR-to-ISR communication is possible only through shared data.

Typically, an ISR runs in a short burst that steals cycles and stack space from the currently running process, although this is a detail, like process pseudo-concurrency, that is not in focus at the diagram level (except for performance and memory implications).

5.1.3 Component Notation: Advanced Issues

All but the first topic of this section may be skipped without loss of continuity.

Monitors

A monitor is a component that provides services to processes in a serially reusable fashion. To do this, it provides its own mutual-exclusion protection for all interactions through its interface. The protection is to prevent many processes (or ISRs) from accessing the internal state of the monitor at the same time. The concept of a monitor is a well-known concept from the field of operating systems that was adapted under another name by Ada (protected units) and is used directly under its own name in Java. Tempo does not support the concept directly, but it is easily implemented in Tempo programs.

The notation for a monitor used in this book (next diagram) is a box of the appropriate shape with a double outline (think of the double outline as symbolizing a *heavyweight* component that provides *protection*). When drawing diagrams by hand or with a drawing tool that does not understand the notation, careful spacing or positioning conventions must be used to distinguish double outlines from nested boxes. The notation indicates a protected interface without requiring identification of the interface operators, so it may be used at a high-level of design, before interface operators have been identified.

Sometimes components are partial monitors, indicated by a partial double outline. This signifies that part of the interface provides protection and part does not.

The meaning of *protected* in a Tempo context is that the monitor's interface functions are protected by a mutual-exclusion (mutex) semaphore, if only processes use the monitor, or by disabling interrupts, if ISRs also use the monitor. This must be programmed into the monitor's interface functions because user-programmable monitors are not directly supported by Tempo (see Section 5.2.3 for more). All of this is implied by the double outline and requires no further notation, for example, to show mutex semaphores.

If the services provided by a monitor are always available, apart from the monitor sometimes being busy, then that is all there is to monitors. However, sometimes there is more to them. The availability of services may depend on the internal state of a monitor, which in turn may depend on interactions with other processes. Thus a process that calls a monitor to get service may have to wait, even if the monitor is not busy, until some other process comes along to change the state of the monitor to one in which the service can be provided. This kind of thing is easily accomplished by associating additional semaphores with the monitor in a manner described in Section 5.2.3.

Tempo is itself, in effect, a large-scale monitor that offers services to processes. It provides mutual exclusion through the uninterruptibility of its interface functions and supports delayed services by its own internal means. However, we do not recommend showing it as an explicit component in design diagrams of multitasking programs because it provides fixed infrastructure that is used everywhere. For design purposes it is best viewed as an implicit layer.

Tempo semaphores are themselves, in effect, small-scale monitors in which mutual exclusion and waiting for service are implemented internally in Tempo. They are closer than the Tempo kernel to being components that might be usefully shown explicitly in design diagrams of multitasking programs because, although they are not themselves user-programmable, their *existence* is. If we wanted to show them as explicit components in design diagrams, we would show them as monitor objects with special connection arrows to distinguish wait and signal operators (see Section 5.2.3). However, we have found that doing so clutters design diagrams without adding insight and that, for most design purposes, semaphores are best viewed as special IPC connections implicitly supported by Tempo (see Section 5.2).

Heavyweight Processes and Threads

Although not needed for the examples of this book, multiple levels of processes are becoming increasingly popular in practice for distributed systems. For example, one level might be supplied by a conventional operating system (*heavyweight processes*) and another level by *threads* (*lightweight processes*) running within operating system processes. In this view, Tempo processes are like threads, even though the operating system in which we normally run Tempo programs, DOS, does not support processes of its own.

For the sake only of completeness (heavyweight processes will not appear again in this book), we observe that the component notation could be generalized to include heavyweight processes by taking a cue from the monitor notation—use double outlines to symbolize *heavyweight*. For example, the following diagram could be interpreted as showing two lightweight processes (threads) nested inside one heavyweight process. The question

mark indicates this may be overkill; in other contexts, we have sometimes found it convenient to use simple rectangular boxes for heavyweight processes, distinguishing them from teams by naming conventions. While we do not necessarily recommend the foregoing notation, it is *not* inconsistent with the use of the same notation for monitors. Interpreting the double outline for processes as meaning mutual exclusion would be obviously incorrect because all processes provide their own mutual exclusion, by definition (only they can access their own internal state, meaning their own programmer-defined local variables).

Objects and Object Orientation

Although this book is not about object-oriented programming, some comments on the relationship between the objects of the component notation and the objects of object-oriented programming will be helpful for readers with experience in the latter area. The component notation and object-oriented programming (for example, C++) overload the term *object*. From the notation's perspective an object is a design concept, not necessarily an implementation one (for example, it may simply identify a set of more detailed objects in the implementation that are grouped together as a conceptual unit, without any object existing in the program to represent the unit); however, in object-oriented programming, an object is always an implementation unit. The reason for sticking with the term *object* in the component notation, in spite of possible confusion, is that the objects of the notation are candidates for implementation as implementation objects.

For clarity, let us refer—in the rest of this section only—to the objects of the design notation as *design objects* and the objects of object-oriented programming as *programming objects*.

Programming objects are either not supported at all in programming languages (for example, C, skinny C++) or they are and everything (or almost everything) is a programming object (for example, C++). Programming objects are satisfyingly machinelike, so there is no problem fitting them into our conceptual world of machines. The problem is the sheer number of them. Because programming objects may be used for everything from small data stores to large subsystems, the world of machines could be populated by so many programming objects at all scales that we could be overwhelmed.

The philosophy that everything is an object is useful for programming, where it provides a fractal-like self-similarity at different scales that fosters uniform programming paradigms. However, it is not useful for system design, where we want to focus on particular scales (for example, the scale of a system as a whole). The bottom line is that we may have to perform some conceptual chunking of programming objects (or potential programming objects if the code has not yet been written) to come up with suitable design objects at the scale of interest. This is really no different from the conceptual chunking of ordinary data constants, data variables, and data structures recommended earlier, because programming objects are used to implement these things in object-oriented programs.

In other words, in our conceptual world of machines, whether details are implemented with programming objects or some other way, we may regard them as hidden in design objects that are as large scale as necessary to understand the big picture. Obviously, there is some creative license here, but we are talking about design, so this is only to be expected.

5.1.4 Component Notation: Layering

Figure 5.2 sets the stage for discussing layering in relation to the design notation (this diagram is topologically identical to the layer diagram of Tempo programs in Chapter 2, but the layout is slightly different to pave the way for indicating where layer boundaries are positioned in multitasking design diagrams). The Tempo kernel is shown as a monitor team because it acts as a monitor in relation to processes in the user code; this highlights the fact that the language runtime system and the operating system do not act as monitors from the perspective of Tempo processes.

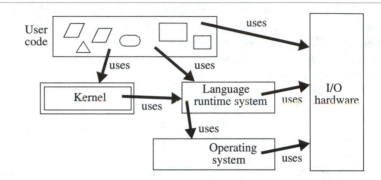

Figure 5.2 Uses relationships among components of Tempo-style systems.

Figure 5.3 shows how the system is layered from the perspective of the component notation. The components realized in the user code and any I/O hardware directly handled by them are above the layer boundary. For example, the communications software of the case study of Chapters 6-8 directly accesses a communication device (a UART) that may be viewed as being above the layer boundary. The kernel, the language runtime system, and all I/O hardware that is not directly handled by the user code are below the layer boundary.

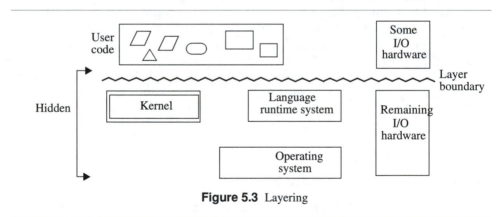

Figure 5.3 Layering

5.2 COLLABORATION GRAPHS (CGs)

CGs are analogous to wiring diagrams for digital logic, in the sense that they show components and connections. We use the term *wiring diagram* to carry forward the theme stated in the introduction to this chapter that the notations of the chapter are for systems that can be conceptualized as having fixed structures, regardless of how the structures are established in code (wiring diagrams are nothing if not fixed). However, for software, the connections that the term *wiring diagram* implies are mostly in our minds. Not only are they not explicit in the code, but the very concept of them being fixed is contradicted by the fact the corresponding relationships are often established dynamically in the code at the moment they are needed (for example, IPC connections implemented with Tempo). None of this stops the notation from being useful. It is useful precisely because it describes concepts embodied in code, not the code itself.

Consider the relationship between code and CGs for IPC. In the code, all we see are calls to kernel functions. We could show IPC in CGs the way it actually occurs in code (next diagram), but this would add diagrammatic clutter without adding insight (the diagram would be black with arrows from everywhere to one box and would give no sense of relationships between processes).

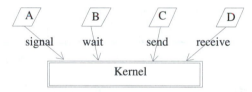

So we push the kernel out of sight, as a layer, and use some special notations that give us insight into IPC (next diagram).

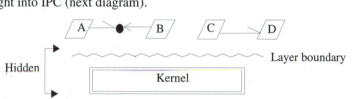

When we find we cannot avoid showing a call to an underlying layer in a diagram in which the layer is intended to be hidden (like the kernel in the previous diagram), we use the following notation, in which the arrow labeled f identifies a function in the layer and

the wiggly line labeled L indicates the existence of the layer. In this way, we may bring important functions of a lower layer into diagrams of higher layers without being committed to creating the kind of cluttered diagram criticized earlier.

The basic collaboration-graph notation has two aspects: operation and initialization/finalization. The operational notation is explained in Sections 5.2.1 through 5.2.5. Initialization/finalization for structurally static systems is covered in Section 5.2.6. The notation is more general than Tempo, but readers interested only in Tempo designs may safely skip the parts that are not supported by Tempo (these parts are clearly identified).

5.2.1 Basic Notation

The operational notation uses the component symbols already explained and the following connection symbols:

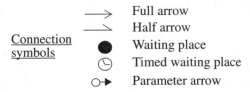

To explain the notation in an implementation-independent manner, components at the ends of connections are referred to as *initiators* and *responders* (these terms are introduced to avoid confusion with terms like *caller*, *sender*, and *receiver*, which have more specific and implementation-dependent meanings). An initiator (labeled I in the following diagrams) is the component that *starts* any interaction over a connection (for example, makes a call, sends a signal). A *responder* (labeled R in the following diagrams) is the component at the other end of the connection from the initiator. The direction from initiator to responder is referred to as the *control* direction. When we speak of initiators and responders here, we are *not* referring to functions or semaphores (which are viewed as implied by the connection symbology) but only to components represented explicitly in the component notation, namely processes, ISRs, objects, and teams (including monitor versions of objects and teams).

The following are explanations of the various connection types with a standard list of description items for each. The item labeled "queueing" is *not* concerned with ready-to-run queues, because a process in a ready-to-run queue is regarded, in principle, as running, but only with other process queues of the kernel, such as event queues and semaphore queues.

Call Connections

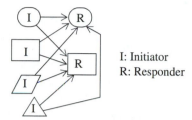

I: Initiator
R: Responder

- **Connection type:** Call.
- **Meaning:** Indicates a path for making an ordinary function call. The return occurs in the reverse direction of the arrow and may indicate anything from an implicit *got it* to the provision of data (in which case a parameter arrow is needed in the reverse direction).
- **Relationship to code:** The connection identifies an interface function of the responder. Call connections are supported by the runtime system of the programming language, not by Tempo.
- **Naming conventions:** The name of the arrow should be the name of the corresponding function.
- **Initiator:** The initiator is the caller.
- **Responder:** The responder is the component of which the called function is an interface element, not the function itself.
- **Initiator-responder synchronization:** While it is tempting to think of a call connection as synchronous because the caller does not return until the called function has completed execution, this is misleading. First, the responder is not the function. Second, a plain ordinary responder has no control over acceptance of calls to its interface functions. Thus initiators and responders are unsynchronized relative to each other over call connections.
- **Initiator-initiator synchronization:** Calls from many initiator processes are not synchronized at the responder and therefore may be unsafe in general, although perhaps safe in a particular application where the calls cannot overlap (remember that calls may come from processes indirectly through intermediate objects or passive teams, so the simple fact that there are no direct connections from many processes does not necessarily guarantee safety). When connections come from multiple processes, interface functions should be reentrant for parameter safety and the object. or team may be changed into a monitor for general safety.
- **Queueing:** There is no queuing of either initiators or responders.
- **Parameters:** Parameter arrows, labeled to indicate the nature of the parameter, are

needed if data items are transferred in either direction (labelling is not shown).

- **Symbology:** Think of the double-sided arrowhead as symbolizing call-return. This arrow only indicates a call connection in an appropriate context—one in which it points at a component that has interface functions that can be called. The same arrow pointing at processes means something different.
- **Special notes:** Processes (or ISRs) that use private objects or teams (ones not shared with other processes) should have the calls to these depicted in the style of the next diagram (the meaning is that the mainline of this process only makes the calls). Call connections pointing outward from processes should be used only for peer components that are shared.

- **Alternative notation:** There is no alternative notation.

Send Connections

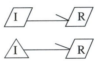

- **Connection type:** Send.
- **Meaning:** A *send* connection identifies a path for sending a signal or message asynchronously from one process (or ISR) to another.
- **Relationship to code:** For Tempo design, each send connection (or fanned-in set of *send* connections from more than one initiator) implicitly indicates the existence of an event queue in the responder process.
- **Naming conventions:** For Tempo design, the name of the connection should identify the event queue, not the kernel function to be called (the kernel function is an implied programming detail).
- **Initiator:** The initiator is the sending process.
- **Responder:** The responder is the receiving process, not the Tempo kernel function that implements the send operation.
- **Initiator-responder synchronization:** The connection is asynchronous, meaning the initiator does not wait for the responder to get a sent message or signal. The initiator simply assumes the responder will eventually get it.
- **Initiator-initiator synchronization:** Multiple initiators are synchronized relative to each other only to the extent that the send operation itself is uninterruptible. This

does not require process queueing because no other process can be executing while a *send* call is being processed by Tempo.

- **Queueing:** There is implicitly a single-process event queue at the responder end where the responder may receive (and possibly have to wait for) events. In Tempo, the responder normally waits for the first event to arrive at any event queue, not a specifically selected one (although ones that are not of interest at the moment may be masked out). The initiator never queues.
- **Parameters:** For Tempo design, parameter arrows are not normally needed for send connections because Tempo has so few options that they can usually be made obvious by the connection name. When parameters are shown, they go in the direction of the arrow only. Values returned by the Tempo function that implements *send* are not connection parameters because they are not the result of initiator-responder interaction (neither the *send* function nor Tempo is the responder).

- **Symbology:** Think of the half arrow as symbolizing half communication (in other words, going only in the arrow direction).
- **Special notes:** There is no notation for indicating event-queue masking; for system understanding, masking may be indicated by textual annotation (associating waiting places with send connections for this purpose would be incorrect, because waiting places imply processes wait and the initiator never waits on a send connection).
- **Alternative notation:** There is no alternative notation.

Semaphore Connections

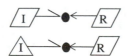

- **Connection type:** Semaphore.
- **Meaning:** A *semaphore* connection indicates a path for sending signals asynchronously to the responder via an implied semaphore.
- **Relationship to code:** The idea of a semaphore connection is a design abstraction. Semaphores are actually primitive components supported by Tempo. However, the abstraction is useful because it simplifies diagrams while conveying the essential meaning.
- **Naming conventions:** The name of the connection should be the name of the semaphore, which in turn should be named to identify the event that is signaled through it.

- **Initiator:** The initiator is the signaling process.
- **Responder:** The responder is the process that receives the signal, not the semaphore.
- **Initiator-responder synchronization:** Like send connections, semaphore connections are asynchronous between initiator and responder.
- **Initiator-initiator synchronization:** There is no synchronization, apart from mutual exclusion enforced by Tempo on execution of its semaphore functions.
- **Queueing:** There is a multiprocess queue at the waiting place where responder processes wait for signals when there are none. Responders queue for a specific semaphore and, while queued there, may miss other events arriving elsewhere (for example, at other semaphores or at the responder's own event queues).
- **Parameters:** For Tempo, a parameter to indicate a data item for the signal would be incorrect; the flow of signals is implied by the connection notation.
- **Symbology:** The waiting place marker symbolizes the existence of the semaphore without showing it as a component. The half arrow symbolizes the signal operation. The full arrow symbolizes the wait operation. The direction of the connection as a whole is the signal direction.
- **Special notes:** A signal connection with a parameter would indicate a *mailbox* mechanism not supported by Tempo.
- **Alternative notation:** See Section 5.2.3.

Callwait Connections

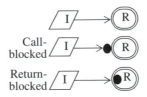

- **Connection type:** Callwait.
- **Meaning:** A *callwait* connection identifies a path for calling a monitor (monitors may be objects or teams, but only objects are illustrated). The return occurs in the same interaction in the reverse direction of the arrow and may indicate anything from an implicit *got it* to the provision of data (for which parameter arrows are needed).
- **Relationship to code:** Tempo does not directly support callwait connections, they must be explicitly programmed by using a combination of ordinary functions and semaphores or interrupt enabling/disabling (see Section 5.2.3 for more).

- **Naming conventions:** Same as for call connections.
- **Initiator:** The caller.
- **Responder:** The monitor.
- **Initiator-responder synchronization:** Callwait connections are *synchronous*, meaning, in this context, that each initiator process is synchronized with the responder (the monitor), one at a time. In other words, they can only be exercised in a mutually exclusive fashion by different processes.
- **Initiator-initiator synchronization:** Initiators are indirectly synchronized relative to each other by the queueing mechanism that supports mutual exclusion. When a call is made, the initiator must be prepared to wait for a return until all callers before it have finished.
- **Queueing:** If the monitor is busy, initiators go into the wait queue of the mutex semaphore from which they emerge one at a time in first-in-first-out (FIFO) order.
- **Parameters:** Parameters have the same meaning as for call connections.
- **Symbology:** The notation is the same as for a call connection, but the context implies an additional property: The responder (the monitor) may defer accepting or completing the call, thus forcing the initiator to wait.
- **Special notes:** Call-blocked and return-blocked connections with waiting places indicate cases where the ability to respond depends on the internal state of the monitor, not just the fact that it is currently busy.
- **Alternative notation:** None.

Sendwait Connections

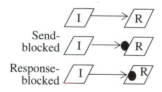

- **Connection type:** Sendwait.
- **Meaning:** A *sendwait* connection identifies a path for sending a message or signal synchronously from one process to another (but never from an ISR to a process). The plain sendwait notation indicates that the responder's ability to receive a request or send a response does not depend on its internal state (as represented by values of variables local to the root function, not the state maintained by Tempo).
- **Relationship to code:** Tempo does not directly support sendwait connections at the time this is being written (although we expect it will in the future) but, for the present, the notation can be used to express desired patterns to be implemented with Tempo send connections. See Section 5.2.4 for more.

- **Naming conventions:** The connection should be named for the service it supports, not the function calls that must be made to implement the service with Tempo.
- **Initiator:** The initiator is the sending process.
- **Responder:** The responder is the receiving process.
- **Initiator-responder synchronization:** Initiators are synchronized with responders, one at a time.
- **Initiator-initiator synchronization:** Initiators are implicitly synchronized with each other by the queuing mechanism that delays responders while they wait for responses. When a message is sent, the initiator must be prepared to wait for a response until all senders before it have finished.
- **Queueing:** Many initiators for a single connection queue, in principle, in a common FIFO queue at the responder. There is, in principle, a one-process queue for the responder to wait for any interaction over any connection.
- **Parameters:** Parameter arrows in both directions may be needed.
- **Symbology:** The arrow notation is the same as for call and callwait connections because all have the means to deliver a response at the end of an interaction.
- **Special notes:** Send-blocked and response-blocked connections with waiting places indicate situations in which the ability to respond depends on the internal state of the responder process (as represented by values of variables local to the root function, not the state maintained by Tempo), not just the fact that it is currently busy.
- **Alternative notation:** See Section 5.2.4.

Connection Timeout

- **Connection type:** Semaphore, callwait, sendwait.
- **Meaning:** In all cases, the meaning is that the waiting condition has some time limit on it, after which waiting will be abandoned. The implication is that the timer is started when normal waiting begins and is canceled if the waited-for event occurs before timeout.
- **Relationship to code:** Tempo only supports this form of timeout on semaphore connections (it does not support callwait or sendwait connection timeout, because it does not support those types of connections). Tempo has an internal clock ISR to handle all timeouts.
- **Naming conventions:** An additional name is required for the timeout period.
- **Initiator:** Timeout on a *callwait* or *sendwait* connection means the *initiator* times out.
- **Responder:** Timeout on a semaphore connection means the *responder* times out.

The difference is because semaphore connections are a shorthand for a more complicated situation that we choose not to represent diagrammatically.

- **Initiator-responder synchronization:** Nothing new is added by timeouts.
- **Initiator-initiator synchronization:** Nothing new is added by timeouts.
- **Queueing:** Nothing new is added by timeouts.
- **Parameters:** Nothing new is added by timeouts.
- **Symbology:** The clock symbol is intended to give a visual indication at a glance of where timeout occurs. No additional notation is required to indicate starting or canceling the timer (the call starts it and the normal termination of the wait condition cancels it).
- **Special notes:** Connection timeout is selective, meaning that it is associated with a selected connection.
- **Alternative notation:** None.

Process Timeout

- **Meaning:** A process times out on nonselective waiting for any event arriving at the process via any connection.
- **Relationship to code:** This form of timeout is supported by means of a generalized wait or receive function with a timeout parameter. As said earlier, Tempo has an internal clock ISR to handle all timeouts.
- **Symbology:** The clock symbol is positioned on the process symbol edge to give a visual indication that timeout applies to all connections of the process.
- **Special notes:** Any event will cancel the timer. If the timer was set for a specific event, different from the one that canceled it, then the a new timeout period needs to be set by subtracting from the original one the interval between setting the timer and the canceling event occurring. However, Tempo does not provide a function to read the time. A workaround is to use the same timeout period on every wait and deem timeout to have occurred after some set number of repetitions. Another workaround is to reduce the timeout period by some arbitrary amount on every wait. The workarounds are acceptable for situations in which the timeout period is not required to be precise (often the case in practice, and certainly good enough for most student exercises). Improving Tempo's timeout capability is on our wish list.
- **Alternative notation:** None.

The meaning of the term *connection* is context dependent when connections fan in from many initiators to the same point on a single responder. For example (next diagram), connections from more than one initiator fan in to the same point on a single responder,

meaning in this case to a single interface function f (this diagram illustrates a recommended convention of drawing fanned-in connections offset to avoid overlapping arrowheads). From a *system* perspective (shown on the left of the previous diagram), there are multiple connections. However, from the *responder's* perspective (shown on the right of the previous diagram), there is only one connection, namely f. We shall use the same term *connection* in both cases, relying on context to make the meaning clear. This ambiguity does not arise with connections that fan out from an initiator to many responders because the shared part of the connection before the fan-out point is only a drawing convenience; the same number of connections exists from both the system perspective and the initiator's perspective.

The following situation may occur in practice: Connections may fan in to a single responder from a number of operationally identical initiators, or fan out to many operationally identical responders from a single initiator. In this situation, diagrammatic clutter is reduced by showing the responders of the fan-out (at the head of the f connection in the next diagram) or the initiators of the fan-in (at the tail of the g connection in the next diagram) as a stack of identical components, with fan-in and fan-out symbolized by single connections (f and g here). This is only a drawing convenience, there is no new meaning—interpret the f connection as implying that any component in the stack may act as a responder on its own f, and the g connection as implying that any component in the stack may act as an initiator on a common g.

5.2.2 Relationships to the Current Version of Tempo

Figure 5.4 summarizes the main relationships of the CG notation to the current version of Tempo. Numbers in the CGs refer to the numbered list of Tempo functions at the bottom. Placement of the numbers in these CGs indicates where calls to Tempo functions are made to perform interactions over the connection. Only *send* and *semaphore* connections are shown because these are the only ones directly supported by the current version of Tempo (*call* connections are supported by the language's runtime system and *callwait* and *send-wait* connections are treated in Section 5.2.3 and Section 5.2.4, respectively). Not all function numbers are shown in the CGs at the top of this figure (ones that are not will be treated later).

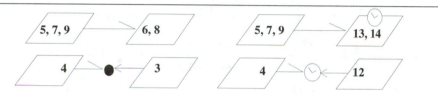

List of Tempo Functions

1. create_process(void (*root_fn_ptr)(), int priority = 0)
2. create_semaphore(int initial_count = 0)
3. wait_semaphore(Semaphore semaphore)
4. signal_semaphore(Semaphore semaphore)
5. void signal(Process process_id, int queue)
6. wait()
7. send(Process destination, int queue, message msg, int ack_queue)
8. receive(message &msg, Process &correspondent, int &ack_queue)
9. reply(Process correspondent, int queue, message reply)
10. mask_queue(int queue)
11. unmask_queue(int queue)
12. wait_semaphore(Semaphore semaphore, int timeout)
13. wait(int timeout)
14. receive(message &msg, Process &correspondent, int &ack_queue, int timeout)
15. disable_ints()
16. enable_ints() (an additional restore_flags functions used with this is not listed he)
17. terminate_multitasking

Figure 5.4 Relationship between IPC connections and the current version of Tempo.

It is important to recognize that Tempo supports the connections in this figure only in a conceptual sense. It has no independent representation of the concept of a connection. The fixed connections represented here are actually established dynamically by using semaphore and process identifiers as parameters of calls to Tempo. Conceptualizing the existence of fixed connections is a mental trick to get a better system view. The trick works as long as we do not write programs that are so dynamic that we cannot draw sensible fixed connection structures for them (otherwise, see Chapter 9).

5.2.3 Callwait Connections and Monitors

Callwait connections and monitors are not supported directly by Tempo. The simplest interpretation is shown in the next diagram. As before, the numbers refer to the Tempo functions of Figure 5.4 and are positioned to indicate where they are used to implement the monitor concept. Note that the numbers are not positioned in the bodies of components as before, but adjacent to connections, because the Tempo functions are called from ordinary functions that implement the connections, not directly from the bodies of the processes or ISRs. These connections form the monitor interface; thus the monitor provides protection through its interface instead of leaving it up to the processes or ISRs.

Implemented by
ordinary interface function with code bodies
bracketed by calls to wait/signal

Implemented by
ordinary interface functions with code bodies
bracketed by enable/disable

Call-blocked and return-blocked variants of *callwait* connections use waiting places to indicate cases where monitors may defer accepting calls or returning from calls until some suitable internal state is achieved as the result of other interactions. To illustrate these, an example is helpful. We shall use an example suggestive of the bounded buffer of Chapter 2, except that, for brevity, we shall use put and get as the operators instead of store_item and retrieve_item, and show delayed service only on get, not put (this would imply the buffer is unbounded for put, but the purpose here is only to illustrate notation, not to illustrate solution of the bounded buffer problem).

With these changes and some details omitted, the next diagram shows the style of solution in Chapter 2. The buffer object as an ordinary monitor. The delayed service on get is implemented using a full_places semaphore outside the monitor in the enclosing team. There is nothing new in this use of semaphores, so Figure 5.4 suffices to indicate how to implement this with Tempo. This solution has the property that only the buffer object is protected, allowing many processes to be active in the team concurrently. This might be desirable for performance reasons in some general case where the team has other responsibilities to perform (not shown here) that do not require mutual exclusion.

Here is a different diagram that implies somewhat different general properties. The

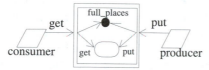

entire team is a monitor with the `full_places` semaphore inside. The implication is that the mutual exclusion protection is in the interface operators of the team, not the internal object. This might be desirable if there was a requirement to guarantee exclusion of all processes from any concurrent activity within the bounds of the team. There is nothing new in this use of semaphores except that implementing this design will result in operations on the implicit `mutex` semaphore and the explicit `full_places` semaphore being performed in the *same* interface function. Care must be taken to ensure that these operations do not occur in an order that would cause deadlock; for example, calling wait on `mutex` before wait on `full_places` would cause deadlock (why?). This was not a problem with the previous design because the semaphore operations are performed in different functions that are themselves called in safe order.

A less committed design would show the whole thing as a single monitor object with, say, a return-blocked connection for *get*, to indicate the possibility of delayed service there. Objects not being decomposable diagrammatically, the rest would be left to code.

The difference between return-blocked and call-blocked connections is only important when multiple consumers with variant requests fan in to a single request point, such as *get*. This does not occur with this example, so the choice of a return-blocked connection instead of a call-blocked one has no significance for this example. In either case, the delayed response is implemented by waiting on the `full_places` semaphore in the same way. A return-blocked connection in the more general case implies that request parameters should be read before deciding whether or not to wait. This is more flexible because it enables the monitor to distinguish variant requests.

Let us now leave this example and turn to an observation we made earlier that the semaphore connection notation could be viewed as a shorthand. The following figure shows this explicitly. A semaphore is represented on the right as a monitor object with two

callwait connections representing Tempo's wait and signal functions. Although semaphores are supported internally in Tempo, viewing them as system components outside Tempo is logically consistent with the treatment of processes (the main difference is that process code is defined by Tempo users outside the kernel and semaphore code is defined inside Tempo, but the system perspective is that they are both system components). However, the full notation on the right is too cluttered for most purposes, so we recommend using the shorthand notation on the left. We introduced this notation earlier as a connection, but it could equally well be regarded as a shorthand for a semaphore component, in which special arrow types represent the two interface functions. Note that in the representation on the right, the *signal* and *wait* arrows now represent separate IPC connections for both of which the semaphore is a responder, but in the shorthand notation, the semaphore is viewed as part of a single IPC connection for which the signaled process is the responder. It is all a matter of point of view.

5.2.4 Sendwait Connections and Processes

Sendwait connections are not supported directly by Tempo (at least in its current incarnation). Here we simply relate them to *send* connections that *are* supported (refer back to Figure 5.4).

The next diagram indicates how the effect of *sendwait* connections may be achieved

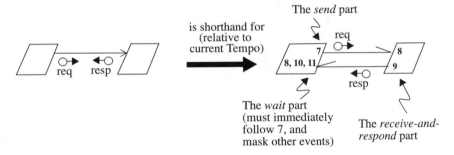

with Tempo by pairs of *send* connections. The equivalence is exact if the following assumptions are satisfied: (1) The *sendwait* initiator does nothing else between sending the request and waiting for the response, including processing its own events (its response event queue should not be shared with other processes and its other event queues should be masked while specifically waiting for the response and then unmasked when the response is received); and (2) there is no possibility of failure of the request-response cycle due to its being split into two parts.

General send-reply patterns like the one on the right in the previous diagram—but *without* the constraint of immediate waiting by the initiator—tend to be very common in practical systems. Because the *sendwait* notation is too restrictive to represent them, a different notation for them can be useful (next diagram). Note that the response is still conceptualized as coming back via a fixed send connection.

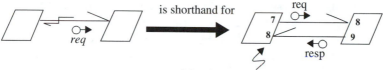

is shorthand for

May do other things after sending the request

The send-blocked and response-blocked variants of *sendwait* connections are useful for indicating cases where the responder may defer receiving messages or returning responses until some suitable internal state (as represented by values of variables local to the root function, not the state maintained by Tempo) is achieved as the result of other interactions. The difference between send-blocked and response-blocked connections is significant only when there are many initiators for the same responder on the same connection.

Send-blocked means the responder ignores all initiators on the connection while some condition on the responder's internal state is false. Thus the responder cannot distinguish variant requests from different initiators, so some can be processed and others deferred; a different interface connection is required for each variant that must be distinguished. The same Tempo-compatible CG with some additional textual annotation indicates the implementation.

is shorthand for
(relative to
current Tempo)

Send-block
by masking events

Response-blocked means the responder accepts initiators but may defer responses. Response-blocked connections are more flexible because the ability of the responder to process the interaction partially without immediately completing it allows variant requests from different initiators to be handled by a single connection (the variants can be determined by reading parameters). The same Tempo-compatible CG with different textual annotation indicates the implementation.

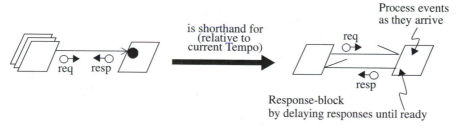

is shorthand for
(relative to
current Tempo)

Process events
as they arrive

Response-block
by delaying responses until ready

5.2.5 Interaction of Software with Physical Components

If all we want to show is that some hardware device can be accessed from software, without showing details at the level of interrupt processing, we may draw diagrams like the next one. There is no need for special notations for hardware devices or hardware-software connections. The existing notations do the job, with appropriate conventions.

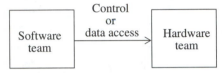

For example, suppose we add explicit printing to the simplified bounded buffer system of Section 5.2.3 by requiring the buffer object to print out trace information on each call of its interface functions (following the pattern of the more complete example in Chapter 2). Then we might show this as in the next diagram. The printer box is, conceptu-

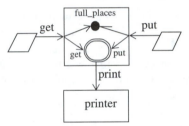

ally, a hardware box, although showing a `print` connection to it as a call connection implies the existence of a `print` function to interact with the printer (when C++ I/O streams are used, there are no explicit `print` calls in the code, but this is a detail below the level of a diagram like this). The `print` function is, of course not a literal part of the print hardware, but showing it this way gives a useful system view without cluttering the diagram with details of software support layers. Observe that the causal connection between calling `get` or `put` and performing `print` is missing from this diagram, but it can be added by using sequence numbering (see Appendix B).

A general way of indicating interactions with physical components is shown in the next diagram (the previous diagram is a simplification). In a diagram like this, the teams

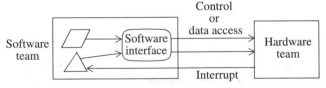

will both be active, the hardware team because that is the nature of hardware and the software team because it has internal processes and ISRs.

The connections have the following meanings. A control interaction causes the hardware to start doing something. A data-access interaction transfers data from or to the hardware. The software interface object is an example of a procedure-abstraction object; this particular object identifies the existence of interface functions that virtualize the hardware by hiding messy hardware details associated with control and data access. An interrupt interaction causes a software ISR to run. This is shown with a call arrow because it is often useful to think of ISR execution as like a function call from hardware. Nuances of interrupt processing beyond this are not intended to be represented by this notation.

A useful shorthand notation is achieved by pushing the software interface object down as a detail (next diagram). Drawing control and data access arrows as call arrows like this directly to hardware boxes is assumed to imply the existence of functions in the software that hide messy hardware details. Leaving out the ISR gives us a diagram of the type with which we opened this section.

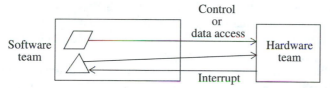

Now let us add ISR-process interactions to the picture. The connection types available for this purpose are constrained to the asynchronous ones (next diagram). This is

because, although ISRs are somewhat like processes in being autonomous, they are not processes and user-written ISRs are invisible to Tempo. When Tempo is called, it assumes the call comes from the currently running process. This includes calls from ISRs. If ISR-to-process connections are other than asynchronous, the interrupted process will be blocked and the ISR itself will not complete until the process runs again. The interrupted process does not have anything to do with the ISR, so blocking it does not make sense. Many system problems can result from holding up ISR completion, ranging from slow response to deadlock.

We can now put together a picture of how a process and an ISR might cooperate to print a chunk of text a character at a time, via a shared buffer object that exists only to hold the chunk while its characters are being printed (for simplicity, parameters are omitted from this diagram). The pattern of this diagram is a general one for interrupt-driven output of any kind, such as sending packets over a communication line. The *kickstart* connection

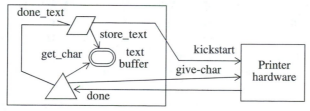

is used to trigger the first *done* interrupt (this may be accomplished by actually printing the first character or by invoking some hardware control magic that generates a done interrupt without any printing having occurred yet). The kickstart connection is, in effect, a form of process-to-ISR communication that tells the ISR to get started. After that the ISR takes over and the process is not involved again until the entire chunk of text has been transmitted. The give_char connection is used to hand over a character for printing. As said earlier, connections like kickstart and give_char imply the existence of software functions that hide hardware details.

5.2.6 Initialization/Finalization of Structurally Static Systems

Fixed program organizations may be set up and torn down dynamically during system initialization and finalization by creating and destroying components and passing their identifiers to other components. For fixed organizations, this occurs only during initialization/finalization, not normal operation (see Chapter 9 for a treatment of dynamic organizations, for which this also occurs during normal operation).

Being able to show such initialization/finalization in design diagrams can be useful. For this purpose, dashed arrows are used between fixed components (ones that are conceptualized as fixed during normal operation). These arrows are not *connections*, in the sense we have been using the term, because they are not paths for interaction between the joined components. They are really *assertions* about things that must be done by means of implied interactions with hidden support layers. The assertion notation is as follows.

Create a fixed component in the place shown (an assertion, not a call). The head of the arrow points to the desired fixed component. The tail of the arrow indicates the component that must implement the assertion. A create arrow asserts that (1) some underlying factory layer must be invoked to create the desired component and (2) the component must be made visible in the desired position. A create arrow does *not* imply communication with the component itself, because there is no component in the position shown until the sequence of actions implied by the create assertion is completed. The component at the tail of the arrow is implicitly assumed to get back an identifier for the created component (such identifiers may then be passed around as ordinary parameters to complete the initialization).

Destroy a fixed component in place (an assertion, not a call). A destroy arrow asserts that (1) the component is no longer visible in the place shown and (2) the component is returned to the factory layer from whence it came, for destruction. The arrow does *not* imply communication with the component to ask it to terminate itself (an ordinary connection suffices for that, if it is a type of component that can terminate itself, such as a Tempo process).

Examples of factory services that support *create* assertions are C++ constructors, malloc in ordinary C, and create_process and create_semaphore in Tempo. Tempo has no services to implement *destroy* for individual processes and semaphores.

Processes can destroy themselves by returning from their root functions, or everything can be destroyed by invoking `terminate_multitasking`.

For example, the following diagram shows how we might indicate initialization for the simplified bounded buffer example of Section 5.2.3. The `Main` process initializes the buffer team by calling its `init` interface function and then creates the producer and consumer processes (the order is not shown by the figure but could be indicated by sequence numbering—see Appendix B). The outermost `init` function creates the `full_places` semaphore. This `init` function also calls a second `init` function to initialize the monitor object. The assumption is that this initialization will create the implied `mutex` semaphore inside the object as well as initializing any data structures required to store data.

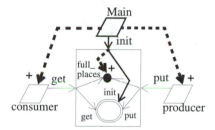

Except in the simplest cases, initialization diagrams should be shown separately from normal operation ones to avoid diagrammatic clutter (next diagram).

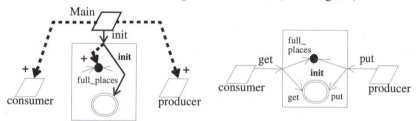

Tempo does not directly support individual process destruction from outside the process because this can leave a system in an inconsistent state (in multitasking systems that do support such destruction, it is well known to be dangerous although sometimes useful in emergencies). The only way for a *specific* Tempo process to be destroyed is to have it exit its root function.

However, before worrying about how to force this, remember that it is normally adequate for systems with fixed structure to program all processes except one as infinite loops and leave it to that one to call `terminate_multitasking` upon receipt of some event (for example, a timeout event or a special keystroke). Tempo then performs all the necessary finalization, including release of all allocated memory. The only finalization action Tempo does not perform is resetting of interrupt vectors that were changed by user code. Therefore, the process charged with calling `terminate_multitasking` must also first call a `finalize` function in any team that revectored interrupts (`finalize` is assumed to undo some `init` operation that changed the interrupt vectors in the first place). Otherwise, the operating system's interrupts would not be restored.

How can we indicate in a design diagram that a selected process must call Tempo's `terminate_multitasking` function when we do not show Tempo itself in our normal design diagrams? This is an example of a more general question: How do we indicate calls to important layer services when we do not show the layer itself? The general form of the answer is illustrated by a Tempo-specific solution to the finalization problem (next diagram). The `terminate_multitasking` connection is shown as an ordinary call connection that terminates on a wiggly line symbolizing the existence of an invisible layer (in this case, Tempo). This approach is also useful for indicating calls to create/destroy services of factory layers in structurally dynamic systems (see Chapter 9).

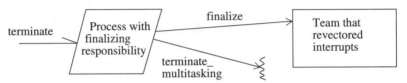

Kill messages are useful for programs that may require dynamic reconfiguration

during normal operation (for example, to start a new operating mode that requires different processes than the ones currently in operation). Using this notation in the context of fixed system structures implies that different fixed diagrams are used to show the different operating modes (otherwise, see Chapter 9). Receiving processes must give `kill` messages first priority. When a `kill` message is received, the process cleans up anything that would result in the system being left in an inconsistent state and then returns from executing its root function, resulting in its automatic destruction by Tempo.

5.3 USE CASE MAPS (UCMs)

UCMs are diagrams to aid human communication about how a system behaves (or is intended to behave) as a whole. In this book, they are used in examples to reason systematically from application requirements to processes and process architectures. This section describes the principles of UCMs and summarizes their basic elements. Additional elements are explained in Chapter 9.

5.3.1 CGs and Stimulus-Response Sequences

Recall that, in the introduction to this chapter, we said that UCMs help us understand stimulus-response sequences that propagate through sets of processes. To understand why a notation different from CGs is useful for this purpose, let us analyze how such sequences would (or would not) be revealed to us by CGs, using the following diagram as an example. The configuration of three processes in a line shown in this diagram (with four differ-

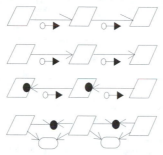

ent IPC arrangements) might arise because the two outer processes handle interactions with the physical environment, the middle process handles intermediate processing, and stimuli propagate from left to right from a process that handles input, through the middle process, to a process that handles output. In other words, stimuli propagate through a pipeline of processes. The four different IPC arrangements (which are only a few of many possibilities) are all capable of making this happen.

The previous diagram emphasizes the IPC differences and obscures the underlying commonality of the stimulus-response sequences. Of course, we may guess that a stimulus-response sequence is implied from the linear form of these CGs, but things may not be so neat in practical systems.

For example, individual processes along one path may also participate in other path that cut across them in some manner, so that the stimulus-response sequences we may read into the chains of IPC connections in a linear diagram like the previous one, are lost, and we must consult the internal details of processes to figure them out. The next diagram combines different stimulus-response paths in a single IPC style (the style of the second example in the previous diagram). Such a combination might come about because there is commonality in the management that must be performed by the middle process or because there is actual coupling between paths.

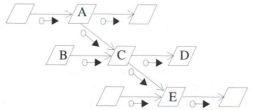

The issue is that the visibility of stimulus-response paths is lost. Does ACD identify a path? Does ACE? Does BCD? Does BCE? Does AC followed by CD and CE in parallel identify a path that splits into parallel paths? And so forth. The diagram does not give us answers. We might try numbering the connections in sequence to indicate stimulus-response sequences along paths, but the diagram would rapidly become cluttered with numbers and would probably have to be split into several diagrams.

These simple diagrams, questions, and issues are enough to give a sense of the difficulty of seeing the forest for the trees with CGs.

5.3.2 The Essence of UCMs

UCMs give a high-level view of causal sequences. The essence of UCMs is summarized by Figure 5.5.

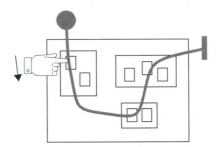

Imagine tracing a path with your finger on top of a diagram of the structure of a system, to explain various causal sequences of events that might occur. Then a use case map is basically a record of paths traced by one or more such finger-pointing sequences (called "scenarios").

Figure 5.5 The essence of UCMs.

As you proceed through later examples using UCMs, keep this simple essence constantly in mind. The maps, as used in this book, have no inner meaning beyond the one in Figure 5.5. If the notation is starting to look deeper than this, you are trying to assign more meaning to it than you should. If you can read a road map, or sketch a map showing a friend how to get to your home by car, then you can work easily with UCMs. No matter how complex a road map may look, its essential nature is simple, and the same is true of UCMs.

UCMs deliberately push the following system details down to a lower level of abstraction: all quantities flowing between components, such as messages or data parameters; interfaces and operators of components; interaction sequences between components (notice that this says "interaction sequences" not "causal sequences"); transfer of control in a programming sense between components; and states of components. They do so in order to focus on the big picture in a way that is free of commitment to details.

The basic assumption of UCMs is that stimulus-response behavior described by scenarios can be traced through the components of a system by means of continuous paths. This is a very common characteristic of real-time systems, so UCMs are widely applicable to such systems. In UCM diagrams, the boxes that represent system components (which may be peers at the same level, or nested) are positioned in fixed relative relationships to each other, thus providing a fixed *component substrate* that gives shape to the paths.

UCMs may show all levels of component decomposition in a single diagram, as in Figure 5.5, or in separate diagrams. The view of Figure 5.5 is often called a *glass-box* view. A view in which internal components were hidden would be called a *black-box* view.

Drawing a UCM is a lot like playing the child's game of *connect the dots*. The underlying concept is of a set of labeled dots on a blank sheet of paper, each of which rep-

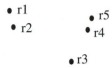

resents some action to be performed by the system at some time. The labels for the dots are called *responsibilities* and are described off the diagram by active natural language phrases, e.g., "r2: prepare a data packet for transmission"). To begin the UCM version of connect the dots, all we need are sufficient dots for one path. We may be guided in positioning the dots initially by a sense of the geography of the eventual component substrate and of the likely disposition of the dots in relation to the components (even if we do not have this sense initially, we must have it eventually).

Paths may now be drawn linking the dots to show causal order of execution of the responsibilities in individual scenarios. The concept is that a scenario progresses along the path, causing responsibilities to be performed in path order. We say that the paths are *causal* paths. Observe that causality is a property of the paths, is defined by a person, and is not a property of the responsibilities.

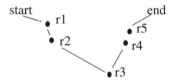

Fairing the dots into a continuous curve with special start and end symbols yields a path in UCM notation (next diagram). The dots have disappeared into the path (thus avoiding notational clutter by avoiding special symbols for responsibilities, which are identified only by labels).

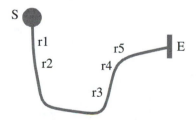

Another way of playing the UCM version of connect the dots is to fill in the component substrate and bind the dots to component boxes by positioning them on top (next diagram). Note that doing this gives the components no knowledge of causality in relation to the paths that will be drawn on top of such a diagram, because causality is not a property of the responsibilities. Earlier, when we positioned the dots against an empty background, we were anticipating the substrate of this diagram (such anticipation is not necessary, but it certainly helps).

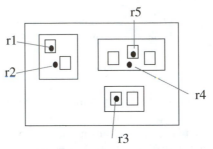

Now we can connect the dots to get a UCM with one path (next diagram). This is the same UCM as the one that opened this section, except that the responsibility dots are now explicitly indicated by labels associated with the path (in general, the labels may be offset from the path, as here, or positioned directly adjacent to it, as in the previous diagram). The opening diagram without any labels illustrated that UCMs may be usefully presented as abstract shapes, without responsibility labels, to get a quick overview.

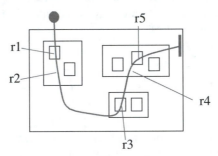

After completing a number of paths, the result is a diagram in which paths may cross many components and components may have many paths crossing them, each path connecting the dots in different ways (next diagram).

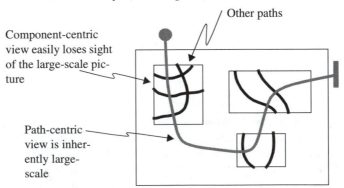

A path traversing a set of components gives us information about the system; think of this as a path-centric view. As path-centric descriptions, UCMs push down details to give us a bird's eye view of a system as a whole. A segment of a path that crosses a component tells us that the component must perform the responsibilities associated with the dots along the segment within the component boundaries, but not how the component will discover or be told that it must do this. A segment of a path that joins dots on two different components tells us that the components must collaborate (directly or indirectly) to achieve the causal sequence represented by the joined dots, but not how they will collaborate. The simplest way would be for the first component to send a message to the second one (in the direction of the path). However, many other possibilities exist, such as exchanging a series of messages, starting with either component, or interacting through some underlying layer not shown.

A set of path segments traversing a component gives us information about the component; think of this as a component-centric view. As component-centric descriptions, UCMs provide too little detail to implement components from them, because they leave out important information. However, UCMs provide a starting point for discovering the details, and a high-level way of relating them to the system as a whole. If the component is primitive (not decomposed into internal components at the UCM level), then a component-centric view of it is a starting point for detailed design. Otherwise, the component may be opened up as a glass box, with the same paths traversing the internal components of the box (responsibilities must have first been identified along these paths that can be bound to the internal components). A separate UCM for this glass-box view may be created by factoring (cutting and terminating the traversing paths, outside the glass box).

This description does not include the possibility of responsibilities themselves being decomposed. There is a technique for doing this with a generalized form of responsibilities call *stubs*, but component-based UCM decomposition is sufficient for the purposes of this book.

Of course, each path is only an example, and a set of examples cannot, in general, no matter how carefully chosen, provide a complete specification for a system. However, examples give insight. With care, system paths can be selected that will exercise all the important paths in the component-centric view of each component of a system. Although the result may not be a complete specification of the system, it is a good starting point for a complete specification of its components, with the added advantage of being tied directly into a system-level description. This is good design information, as well as being helpful for system understanding.

Just as with the child's game, a UCM may contain meaningful shapes created by connecting the dots. However, the shapes characterize not concrete objects a child might recognize, but shapes of scenario paths in a system that an engineer familiar with the system might recognize. When shapes are recognizable in this way, responsibility labels may often be left off to give an uncluttered overview.

UCMs with many paths may sometimes have shared path segments (meaning different scenarios share causal subsequences). Visual ambiguity then exists at apparent forks and joins, called OR-forks and OR-joins because a scenario takes one *or* the other of the entering or exiting path segments. Such UCMs may be disambiguated by giving different end-to-end paths (routes) different coloring or shading (next diagram). The routes identify the scenarios from which the UCM was composed. Unidentified routes are presumed to be forbidden.

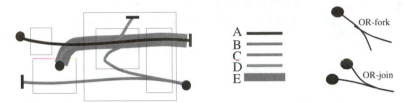

When multipath UCMs become too complicated for a person easily to separate the routes by eye, a useful technique is to show different routes in different *presentation diagrams*, against a background of the same substrate, with all the other paths shown lightly to provide context (next diagram). When UCMs become too complicated to show all paths on a single diagram, different aspects of operation—for example, initialization/finalization, error discovery/recovery, normal operation in different modes—may be shown in different diagrams, but still against a background of the same substrate. Large-scale, complex systems will require use of other techniques as well, such as factoring, path stubbing, and layering. Factoring and layering are treated, in passing, in various examples in this book. Path stubbing is outside the scope of this book.

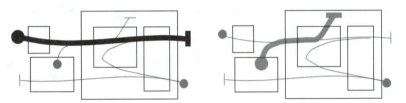

Underlying any presentation scheme for displaying routes in an understandable way must be map documentation that associates route identifiers with each path segment (in the way numbers for highways are posted on a city street to show all the highways that share the street). Such documentation is the UCM way of specifying what should happen at OR-forks and OR-joins because UCMs do not contain data or state information on which decision logic at forks could be based (such logic is be below the level of abstraction of UCMs).

As descriptions of system behavior, UCMs are analogous to board games, in which tokens are moved by human players along paths, following the rules of the game. The game board and the rules, together, enable many possible token-movement scenarios to be generated by players, but the scenarios themselves are not specified explicitly—they emerge during play. In exactly this way, a person may play scenarios along UCM paths—mentally or by moving actual tokens—to understand the operation of the system (next diagram, in which tokens are represented by pointing fingers). A UCM does not formally express the model a person forms in the mind's eye while doing this.

•Responsibilities affect system state
•Information flows along paths
•Preconditions become postconditions

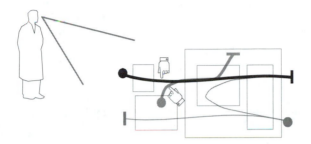

In general, even with the simplest maps, more than one scenario may be in progress at the same time (even along the same path). In such cases, we may refer to a set of concurrent scenarios as a single (compound) scenario. The path notation by itself (deliberately) does not indicate whether or not concurrent scenarios are possible (with one exception, AND-forks in paths, introduced in Section 5.3.4). The possibility of concurrent scenarios introduces the possibility of races: individual scenarios could, in principle, overtake and even pass each other. Races are an important design issue in concurrent systems that use case maps help us understand. A critical race—one that results in an error condition—can result from building into a component a wrong assumption about who will win.

Because UCMs are intended to provide insight by presenting relationships visually, the style of presentation should be as clean and uncluttered as possible. For example: Stimuli of related types that follow the same path, perhaps with minor variations, should have the same start point, not be OR-joined to the path from different start points; stimuli that come from the same source but carry information (e.g., data or commands) that requires them to follow different paths should have the same start point, with paths OR-forking after entering the system; paths should cross as little as possible; positions of the same components in different diagrams should not be arbitrarily switched around; names should be chosen to give clues to meaning; and so forth.

UCMs will mean nothing to anyone but their creators without proper documentation. Map documentation must include at least the following elements. Each scenario has a name, a short prose description, and an indication of which route is followed (or routes, for concurrent scenarios). Preconditions and postconditions of each scenario are defined in prose, including whether or not a new scenario may start while one is still in progress. Start and end points are named to give clues to the nature of triggering stimuli and observed results at the end. Stimuli and responses are named, described, and associated with start and end points (in general, this may be a many-to-one association). Any input quantities coming from the source of the stimulus, or output quantities at the end, are named and described. Legal and illegal routes through multipath UCMs are identified.

Responsibilities are named and explained by short, active prose statements that indicate their effect on the state of the component or the system (this must be informal, because these states are not defined by UCMs). Preconditions and postconditions may be defined for some responsibilities. Cross-reference lists are provided of short-form names on maps and associated long-form names and/or brief characterizing phrases. Where appropriate, identification of associated classes or types is provided (e.g., types of parameters, classes of components). A name dictionary provides descriptions and cross-references. If a UCM is part of set of related UCMS, then relationships among the members of the set are identified.

5.3.3 UCMs and Real Time

Real time (meaning wall clock time here) is implicitly assumed to be required to move

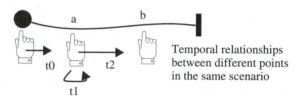

Temporal relationships between different points in the same scenario

along the segments of the paths between responsibility points (for example, t0, t2), and also to progress through each responsibility point (for example, t1). This is so even for unbound maps, because the assumption always is that resources will be required to perform each responsibility and to propagate the effects of a completed responsibility to the next responsibility along a path. For example, performing a responsibility may require executing some functions that belong to the component that has the responsibility, and propagating the effect along the path may require interactions between components that have different responsibilities. In all the examples of this book, times are additive along paths (the end-to-end time is the sum of the intervening responsibility and segment times).

   Unbound maps tell us nothing about the sizes of responsibility times or inter-responsibility times. They can only be resolved in bound maps in relation to components, and, in this book, only qualitatively (quantitative performance information can easily be associated with UCMs, but this idea is not developed in this book). For example, binding responsibility a to a process in one hardware box and responsibility b to a process in another would tell us that the ab path is realized by some interprocessor communication hardware and software. This can give us some qualitative feel for the nature of the delay along the path. If we know something about the speeds of the processors and the complexity of the responsibilities in relation to these speeds we would also get some qualitative feel for the total real time along the path in the absence of other activity. The maps themselves are not intended to do more than this for purposes of reasoning about design issues.

   UCMs may also contain explicit timers, but this subject will be left to examples in later chapters.

5.3.4 UCMs and CGs

Let us now return to the questions asked in Section 5.3.1 and see how they might be answered by UCMs. In doing so we shall develop UCMs without responsibilities, using the shapes alone to suggest meaning.

The following UCM gives a plausible requirements pattern that the final CG in Section 5.3.1 might be implementing. The paths indicate clearly that there are causal sequences joining ACE and BCD, independently, but not joining ACD and BCE. As well, there are independent causal sequences joining the top three processes and the bottom three processes, independently.

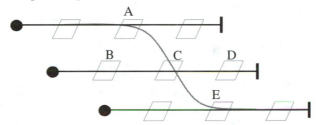

If the preconditions on the paths are such that scenarios can start down any of the paths at any time, then the paths identify a need for at least fourfold concurrency. The processes here provide ninefold concurrency, so there is excess concurrency relative to the path requirements as we understand them so far. Whether we need this much concurrency or not depends on more knowledge of the requirements than we have presented here, but in any case the UCM gives a clear view of the process architecture in relation to a particular set of requirements paths. IPC becomes a detail that can be deferred.

The minimum requirement for fourfold concurrency in the previous diagram suggests that a process architecture with four processes (next diagram) might be more appropriate if these paths express the full range of requirements. The idea is that each process controls one path, end to end. Objects not shown could be positioned along the paths at the points where the original processes were situated to perform responsibilities there under the control of this smaller set of processes. Observe how easy it is to manipulate process architectures in relation to use case paths.

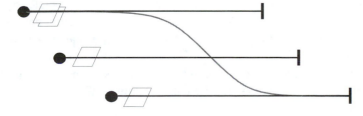

Returning to the original nine-process architecture, here follow two different path patterns (among many) that answer the questions in a different way. They use map notations called AND-forks and AND-joins to represent forking into parallel paths and synchronization of parallel paths, respectively. The next diagram shows a pattern in which a causal sequence runs through A and then splits into sequences through CD and CE that proceed in parallel (grey lines). The other paths continue to be independent. We now have fivefold path concurrency. We can imagine that further such developments might lead to a requirement for the ninefold concurrency provided by the nine processes.

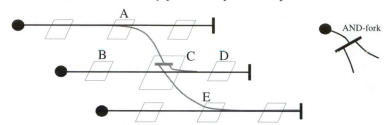

The next diagram shows a pattern in which paths from A and B are synchronized at C and then a single path progresses to D. The top and bottom paths remain independent. This is still fourfold path concurrency, but patterned in a different way from before.

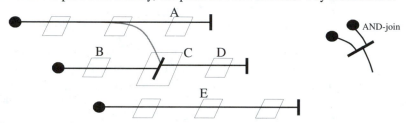

These are only a few among many possible requirements patterns that might be expressed with UCMs. CGs do not, by themselves, reveal the causal sequences in these patterns, and they swamp us in IPC detail even as they hide the causal sequences. This is why we need something like UCMs for high-level design.

Here is a quick overview of the nature of the relationship between the CGs that gave rise to this discussion and the resulting UCMs (later chapters explore the CG-UCM relationship in much more depth):

- *Intercomponent path segments:* A segment of a path that joins responsibilities of two different processes tells us that the processes must collaborate to realize the causal sequence, but not how they will do so. This collaboration must accomplish two purposes: first, hand over control of scenario continuation, and second, pass along any needed data. Among many other possibilities, these things could be accomplished by sending a message to the next process along the path. Choosing a suitable IPC arrangement may require consideration of all paths entering and leaving the process.

- *Intracomponent path segments:* A segment of a UCM path that traverses a process tells us that the process must perform the responsibilities thus bound to it, but not how it will do so. Among many other possibilities, responsibilities might be implemented as functions to be called by the body of the process after receiving a message from the previous process along the path. An internal AND-fork indicates that the process must somehow arrange for more than one other process to continue the path. Choosing a suitable solution may require consideration of all the paths traversing the process.

5.3.5 Do's and Don'ts for the UCM Notation

UCMs are useful for the following purposes:

- To reason from requirements to design solutions. UCMs help with this because their paths provide a context for addressing issues that affect the system as a whole.
- To explain the big picture to other people. UCMs can be used to explain how systems work (or are intended to work) to fellow team members, customers, managers, and new employees, to name but a few possibilities.
- To avoid the problems of big-bang integration (implementing complete components before integrating them into a system and then discovering the system has problems). Examples of such problems are end-to-end performance along paths through the system being unexpectedly unacceptable, or behavior along paths through the system being unexpectedly wrong. UCMs help by guiding us to the development of skeleton prototypes that support a few important paths end to end, to provide a sanity check of design ideas relative to these paths before committing to implementation of complete components.
- To guide design for testability. Test sequences for the implementation naturally follow from paths in the maps.

The main UCM don'ts are as follows:

- Don't intermix the UCM and CG notations in the same diagram. This will lead to confusion and misunderstanding. To show causal sequences running through a CG, remove everything from the CG except the components. Do not use AND-forks from UCMs in CGs to indicate broadcasting; this would just cause confusion, because Tempo does not support broadcasting and it would be unclear what was meant. Do not use the queue-like symbol called a *pool* from the extended UCM notation of Chapter 9 to indicate process queues associated with IPC connections in CGs; this would just cause confusion, because such queues are already implied by the connection notation (they are supported by the kernel and the kernel is assumed as an underlying layer that supports interactions over all IPC connections).
- Don't try to design detailed behavior with UCMs. Leave that to CGs and internal details of components.

- Don't try to capture control flow or data flow details with UCMs. For example, do not employ UCMs to show back-and-forth traversals in call-return interactions. Connections in CGs indicate this kind of thing better and more compactly. UCMs should abstract away from such details to show larger causal patterns.
- Don't vary the visual form of the component substrate in different diagrams. UCMs are intended to help humans understand systems in terms of understandable visual patterns, and this would defeat the purpose.

The unique feature that UCMs offer for designing real-time systems is an ability to relate solution decisions to stimulus-response scenario requirements in an explicit way. Here follows a brief description to give a sense of how this may be done (later chapters explore these suggestions in more depth).

An important rule is: *Let the paths tell you about the processes*. With this rule, UCMs can replace design magic with a rational and traceable progression from paths to processes. Once we have the processes, other components coalesce around them and detailed design with CGs follows systematically. The design technique is to experiment with different bindings between processes and maps, to understand how required concurrency, performance, and robustness can be achieved.

Typically, there will be processes at the "edges" of the software that interact with the environment. Such processes identify the need for ISRs. However, during high-level design, ISRs may be left as details.

Paths in UCMs provide a handy common denominator for mentally adding up the qualitative, end-to-end effects of IPC overheads, IPC queuing delays, time required to execute responsibilities, and so on, without requiring any commitment to actual IPC. Thus UCMs can be used to make rough, qualitative judgments during high-level design about performance tradeoffs between different candidate process architectures, such as pipelines, collaborating peers, client-servers, and so on, based on general real-time systems knowledge, without knowing specific details of how everything will be connected or programmed.

UCMs providing a starting point for designing to achieve robustness by telling us where paths may fail and what effects failures may have. Processes are positioned as arbiters of robustness of paths because they are the active components that control the paths and are generally associated with physical components that may fail (for example, they run on physical processors and manage interactions with physical I/O devices). For robustness of paths, the first and most obvious rule is that paths must never be caused to fail by the processes that control them. This may seem to be a small matter of programming. However, errors can easily creep in if programmers do not understand the end-to-end picture represented by paths, resulting in, say, incorrect handling of race conditions along and between paths.

If we can identify specific failure points along paths, then we can design for robustness by positioning processes on either side or on top of the failure points and giving the processes responsibility for discovering failures and keeping action along the paths going correctly (for example, using timeout-recovery techniques). If we cannot identify specific failure points along paths, then we can design for robustness by positioning watchdog processes off to one side and assigning them the responsibilities of monitoring system state variables for evidence of path breakage. Recovery might involve aborting broken paths (perhaps destroying the processes that control them, in case the processes are damaged) or restoring consistency to broken paths and then allowing them to continue (easy to say, but not do).

Teams are used in this exploration of design alternatives with UCMs to hide parts of the system that we do not want to design yet. Their lightweight nature at this level of abstraction (no interface design required) means that when we open them up for design, different internal configurations that might imply different interfaces can be easily explored without worrying about the interfaces.

Objects may enter the scene late because they tend to coalesce naturally around processes, teams, and responsibilities. Note that although we *define* the term *object* in Section 5.1 by saying it supports an abstraction through an interface, the actual *interfaces* of objects are below the level of abstraction of UCMs. The assumption is that the interface—when it is designed—will provide the means for other components to invoke it to perform its responsibilities.

5.4 SUMMARY

In this chapter we have described the basics of three design notations in an implementation-independent fashion, and indicated how they complement each other to bridge the gap from requirements to implementation:

- A component notation that is used throughout
- A collaboration graph (CG) notation for detailed design
- A use case map (UCM) notation for high-level understanding and design

This chapter lays the groundwork for the next one, which begins a case study to show how to reason from requirements to high level design with UCMs and how to proceed from high-level design to detailed design with CGs.

Design Case Study: Message Transfer Utility (MTU)

*T*his chapter stands well back from the details of code to make a first pass at applying UCMs and CGs to designing a simple computer communications system. In this chapter we keep the requirements very simple in order to illustrate the high ground of design techniques and issues for real-time systems (Chapter 7 continues this example in more depth).

A number of important topics are developed in this chapter: process discovery with UCMs; systematic development of CGs from UCMs; and ways of reasoning about detailed issues at a high level, for example, to make tradeoffs between high-level design alternatives based on rough estimates of performance differences. Thus the chapter aims to give insight into how to design.

6.1 THE PROBLEM

The UCM of Figure 6.1 gives the essence of the problem. Two computer systems called MTU1 and MTU2 send messages to each other (for simplicity, we shall assume that messages are short enough to be transferred whole). The paths start with the need to send a message and end with the message successfully received at the other end. The preconditions of the paths place no constraints on when scenarios may start down the paths, so, just like a highway, the map is simple, but paths in both directions may be crowded.

The main issue arising from paths being crowded is the possibility of overrunning available buffer space at the sending end if physical transmission is too slow, and at the receiving end if it is too fast. Generally, constraints on the speed of physical transmission are imposed by physical limitations and by communications protocols. However, let us imagine that there are no constraints, in order to see how the paths enable us to reason about such issues.

This application, although simple, embodies many of the issues that make designing real-time systems difficult, such as distribution, concurrency, and (as generalized in Chapter 7) continued operation in the presence of failures. The map of Figure 6.1, although incomplete because it does not include the possibility of failures, is enough to make a start; it expresses the full degree of problem concurrency, and the success scenarios in it will still be valid after we add failure scenarios (Chapter 7).

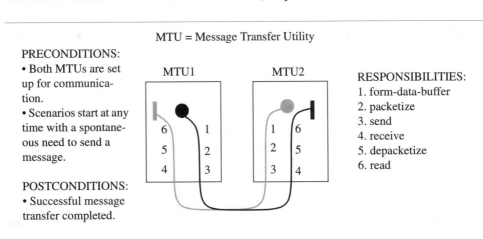

Figure 6.1 The initial problem: communication over a reliable link.

In this simple map, the short-form names of the responsibilities are small integers. It happens that the integers indicate the sequence in which the responsibilities are performed along the paths. However, that is only possible for simple maps like this; it is not possible in general, as later refinements will illustrate.

The responsibilities in Figure 6.1 are as follows:

form-data-buffer: For simplicity, each one-line message is assumed to be put in a fixed length data buffer that exactly fits into the space for data in a packet.

packetize: For generality, data is assumed to be sent as a data packet, which is a fixed-length, fixed-format byte string with space for data and a header containing identifying information.

send: Prepare a packet for sending via physical I/O (Section 6.1.1 explains why this responsibility is characterized this way).

receive: Accept a complete packet that has successfully been received through physical I/O (Section 6.1.1 explains why this responsibility is characterized this way).

depacketize: Remove the message.

read: Read the message contents.

6.1.1 Layering of Details

Layering means hiding supporting details by not showing them. Layering is often a useful trick to simplify high-level views. The preceding UCM implicitly layers physical I/O, meaning it assumes physical I/O will be performed in a manner that will make the responsibility sequences of the map happen, without indicating how. This layering is identified by the definitions of the *send* and *receive* responsibilities. As defined, the *send* responsibility is completed when a packet is ready for physical I/O and the *receive* responsibility starts after the packet has arrived via physical I/O. The implication is that physical I/O occurs along the path segment joining these two responsibilities. Because physical I/O is not explicitly shown along this segment (which indicates only causality), we say that it is layered under the segment.

In general, we may choose to layer any kind of detail under either path segments, as we have done here for physical I/O, or under responsibilities. However, we chose path segments for this example because this choice gives the simplest high-level view (simplicity is an important criterion in deciding how to present high-level views). It is simplest because it does not require explicitly distinguishing the different parts of physical I/O, namely local at one end, global through the network, and local at the other end; all are layered under one path segment in either direction. Local physical I/O could be layered under the *send* and *receive* responsibilities, by redefining them appropriately, but this would still leave network I/O layered under the path, resulting in a more complex view.

Of course, pushing details into layers does not get rid of them. We shall show in Section 6.3 how to use the assumptions we have made here about layering physical I/O as a starting point for bringing physical I/O explicitly into the design picture.

6.2 LET THE PATHS TELL YOU ABOUT THE PROCESSES

Discovering processes is an important aspect of high-level design for real-time systems, and is perhaps the most difficult part of designing real-time systems for novices, who may see it as design magic. This first example of high-level design focuses on employing UCMs to eliminate the design magic in discovering processes. The theme here is: *Let the paths tell you about the processes.* To start, all we need is a map that gives us an understanding of the full concurrency of the application. Figure 6.1 does that even though it is incomplete; we can start with it and then adjust the results to accommodate a more complex map later (Chapter 7).

However, the map as it stands is too large scale for process discovery. We need to zoom in on where the processes are, namely, the individual MTU systems. This requires factoring the map.

6.2.1 Factoring

Factoring was identified in Chapter 5 as a way of dealing with the following issue that arises with recursive decomposition of systems: treating a black box discovered during decomposition as a system in its own right. The present problem is a special case in which the initial decomposition has been given as a requirement (the MTU systems are given black boxes). Figure 6.2 does the required factoring (see the next page for an explanation).

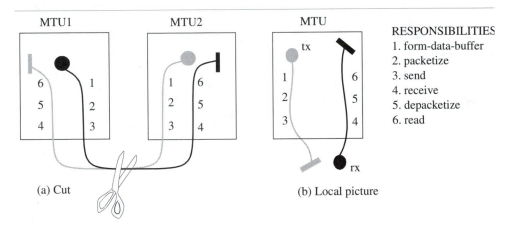

RESPONSIBILITIES
1. form-data-buffer
2. packetize
3. send
4. receive
5. depacketize
6. read

(a) Cut   (b) Local picture

NEW LOCAL PRECONDITIONS AND POSTCONDITIONS:
tx postcondition: physical transmission of a complete packet ends.
rx precondition: physical reception of a packet starts.

Figure 6.2   Factoring the MTU.

The map is factored as follows: First, cut the large map between the MTU teams, as shown by Figure 6.2(a) and then put start and end terminations on the dangling ends of the paths in an obvious way, as shown by Figure 6.2(b), to give a smaller local map. This gives a local picture of independent tx and rx paths, the first starting inside the team and ending in the environment, and the second vice versa. The preconditions and postconditions follow from our earlier assumptions about layering physical I/O. The other MTU has vanished from this picture (though it still forms an important part of the design context).

Observe that, taken together, the responsibility definitions, preconditions and postconditions imply that physical transmission is layered under the path segment between the *send* responsibility and the end of the *tx* path, and physical reception is layered under the path segment between the start of the *tx* path and the *receive* responsibility, as shown in the next diagram.

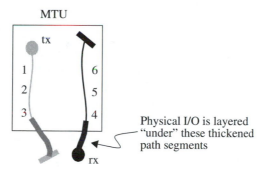

Physical I/O is layered "under" these thickened path segments

6.2.2 From Problem to Solution Concurrency

Having set the stage by factoring, we can now proceed with process discovery. We say that this is going from problem to solution concurrency because the paths express problem concurrency and the processes express solution concurrency.

However, the issue is more than just individual processes; it is also arrangements of multiple processes in relation to each other—in other words, process architectures. Examples of process architectures are collaborating peers controlling different paths and pipelines along paths. Architectures need connecting tissue for their components and here the connecting tissue is formed of the paths. *Architecture* is one of those terms that is so widely used in so many ways that it must be defined in context; in this book an architecture is expressed by bound UCMs. Diagrams in the style of CGs are sometimes called architecture diagrams elsewhere, but not in this book.

We know from Figure 6.2 that the 1-2-3 and 4-5-6 paths are, at a minimum, required to be concurrent relative to each other. We have left open the issue of how much concurrency there will be along each of them. There are many possible process architectures, with different degrees of process-level concurrency.

Figure 6.3 makes a first pass at identifying some possible process architectures. The issue here is not which is the "right" one, but the fact that diagrams like these display the alternatives in a way that helps us, with experience, to assess trade-offs between them by inspection. They are the high ground where requirements meet physical constraints. We want to give a sense here of how to use diagrams like this to reason about the issues.

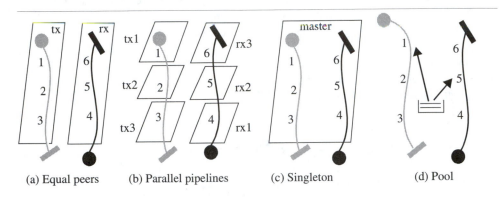

(a) Equal peers   (b) Parallel pipelines   (c) Singleton   (d) Pool

Figure 6.3 First candidate process architectures.

We can analyze the different architectures in a qualitative fashion as follows:

(a) Equal peers. All responsibilities along each path are allocated to one process. This mirrors in the solution domain exactly the minimum required concurrency in the problem domain. The tx process is responsible for the whole 1-2-3 path and the rx process for the whole 4-5-6 path. Thus the processes give the paths concurrency. The implication is that each path is run through from beginning to end by the process before it revisits the beginning. There are several variables to juggle, for example, the average rate of path completion, the average rate of path starting, and the ability for the ISR level to handle the rate of path completion. In this application, the rate of tx path completion could be too high for the ISR level unless the rate of tx path starting is constrained. The rate of rx path starting could also be too high for the rate of rx path completion if, for example, the path had to store messages in files. If neither of these issues arises, this would be a good solution. We shall return to these issues later.

(b) Parallel pipelines. Each responsibility along each path is allocated to a separate process in a pipeline of processes. This also satisfies the minimum problem-domain requirement that the 1-2-3 and 4-5-6 paths be concurrent, but it also allows progress along each path to be concurrent, for example, tx3 could be transmitting one packet, tx2 preparing a second one, and tx1 preparing a message to go into a third one, all concurrently. However, given the foregoing interpretation of the send and receive responsibilities, there is likely to be very little practical difference in concurrency between this architecture and the first one. This is because a single process can probably work through the path end to end faster than packets can be physically transmitted or received. The main effect of adding processes along the path to increase concurrency may be to add IPC overhead along the path. This conclusion would be invalidated if we decided to use a multiprocessor hardware configuration in which different physical processors handled the top and bottom ends, for example, one processor handled everything up to and including packet processing and another one handled everything above that. We have observed that novices tend to design organizations like this one under the erroneous impression that processes are a good way of achieving code modularity. They are not; they should be used to modularize behavior, not code.

(c) Singleton. This is a strawman architecture, meaning one set up to be knocked down. A single master process is effectively a mainline sequential program. Path concurrency could only be achieved by explicitly interleaving, in the process code, the execution of responsibilities along the different paths. The process would have to check periodically (poll) for stimuli at different start points in order not to lose stimuli. The process would also have to maintain the path context for all paths (when we use a process for each path, we effectively hand this administrative burden over to the kernel that supports the processes). All of this could be both complex to program and inefficient.

(d) Pool. Some successful solutions in industrial practice use an approach in which a pool of processes handles all responsibilities along different paths. The implementation solution is to have an interrupt-driven executive queue up the responsibilities for processes in the pool. The UCM states the requirement that this solution satisfies, namely that the pool processes perform the responsibilities in the appropriate path context (this is actually a structurally dynamic system that falls within the scope of Chapter 9, so the ideas are left incompletely explained here).

We will now set the stage for adding more structure to the architecture. Suppose that, for concurrency, we want processes positioned *along* paths, as in Figure 6.3(a), and that, for functional grouping, we want teams positioned cutting *across* paths, to group message, packet, and link responsibilities. Figure 6.4 suggests the idea, but a diagram that has component boundaries cutting across each other like this is meaningless. Are processes and teams intended to be part of each other? They can't be (at least not in the structurally static way suggested by this diagram), so we need to rethink our process bindings.

Warning: This is an illegal diagram, presented only to identify an issue.

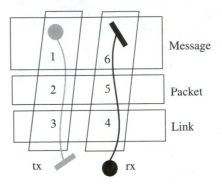

Figure 6.4 What does it mean to have processes cutting across other structures?

A different binding of processes lets us have our cake and eat it too. Figure 6.5 shows two different bindings with the same concurrency as Figure 6.3(a), but with more flexibility. In the binding of Figure 6.5(a), tx would directly *perform* 1 and would *control* 2 and 3, and rx would directly *perform* 4 and would *control* 5 and 6. In the binding of Figure 6.5(b), tx would *control* 1, 2, and 3, and rx would *control* 4, 5, and 6, but neither process would directly *perform* any of them. We would add teams or objects along the paths to perform the responsibilities that the processes do not directly perform. Process bindings like the ones of Figure 6.5 or Figure 6.3(b) are easily aligned with team structures like the one in Figure 6.4 simply by making the processes part of the teams.

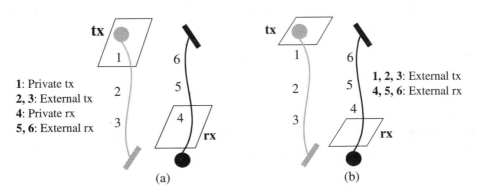

Figure 6.5 Process bindings with some organizational flexibility.

Figure 6.6 shows another slightly different process architecture; it is a pipeline, but it is motivated not by the pipeline concept itself but by the need to give different parts of the reception path different priorities in a uniprocessor. It adds one extra process to the rx path of Figure 6.5(a) to enable a higher priority to be given to the beginning path segment (by giving the rx1 process a higher priority). This will ensure that a new arrival could start along the rx path before the single process of Figure 6.5(a) had finished traversing it end to end. This is an example of low-level detail (process priorities in a uniprocessor) some-times needing to be taken into account in high-level design. We already pointed out in our discussion of Figure 6.3(a), which has the same level of concurrency as Figure 6.5(a), that one process along the reception path could not cover this situation adequately.

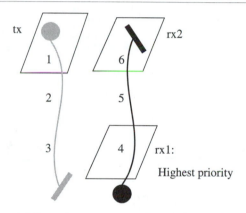

Figure 6.6 Positioning several processes along a path to give
its parts different priorities.

This is enough to give a sense of how to let the paths tell you about the processes (there is more in Chapter 7). Let us now move on to detailed design with CGs.

6.3 LET THE MAPS GUIDE YOU TO THE WIRING

In this section we are concerned with making the transition from high-level design with UCMs to detailed design with CGs (wiring). The design principle is *let the maps guide you to the wiring*. This in part requires human judgment and in part is relatively mechani-cal. This section gives helpful hints about the judgment part and guidelines about the mechanical part.

6.3.1 Teams in CGs

Although the principle we want to illustrate is *let the maps guide you to the wiring*, issues associated with interfaces and interconnections of teams may bring other principles into play that we need to understand first. Figure 6.7 sets the stage for discussing these issues for the MTU.

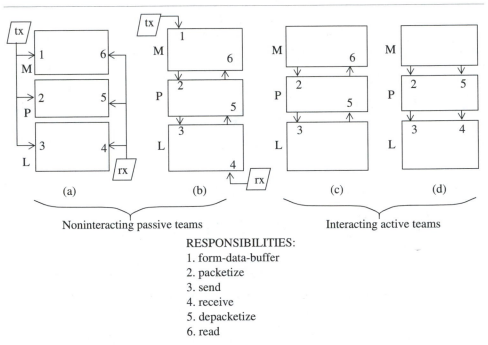

Noninteracting passive teams   Interacting active teams

RESPONSIBILITIES:
1. form-data-buffer
2. packetize
3. send
4. receive
5. depacketize
6. read

Figure 6.7 Different team interface and interconnection structures.

Before getting to the main point, we must first explain how to interpret the textual annotations in Figure 6.7. This figure deliberately does not commit to connection names, in order to illustrate a style of thinking that would precede such commitments. Obviously such commitments have to be made eventually, but explorations of alternatives must be made first. Figure 6.7 uses responsibility identifiers taken directly from the UCMs to *identify* (not name) connections that would implement the responsibilities. In general, there is not a one-to-one mapping from responsibilities to connections, as will become clearer when we open up the black boxes—some responsibilities will be implemented by several external and internal connections. Some responsibilities do not appear in some alternatives in this figure because they are associated with internal components and connections, for example, responsibility 4, `receive`, is an internal responsibility of L in Figure 6.7(c). Cross referencing the numbers to the responsibility list, we see that the phrases character-

izing the responsibilities are not necessarily indicative of names we would give to the
associated connections. For example, the connection from M to P at 5 in Figure 6.7(d)
would likely be called `get-data` rather than `depacketize` because M is only interested in data, not in all packets; the connection from tx to M at 1 in Figure 6.7(b) would
likely be called `send-data` rather than `form-data-buffer`; and so on.

There may be tension between, on one hand, choosing an alternative from
Figure 6.7 so that its control structure best reflects the underlying operational nature of the
application and, on the other hand, obeying software conventions that require control to be
hierarchical. A good principle for software design is to mirror the structure of the problem
in the structure of the solution, so such tension is worrying if it tends to force solution
structures that do not mirror the problem. Let us consider the different cases.

When we make teams passive servers and keep processes outside of them as controllers, as in Figure 6.7(a), we have a structure that mirrors very little of the operational
nature of the problem. Although the processes are in control, in the sense that they initiate
all calls to the teams, all the detailed knowledge of the application is in the teams (we shall
continue to use the term *team* for simplicity, because we can leave it to the CGs to tell us
which teams are modules—in this diagram, all of them are). Large-grained behavior patterns of the kind expressed by UCMs may be deeply buried in internal details of the teams.
However, the passive-server nature of the teams is a convenient one for software construc-
tion.

Figure 6.7(b) is just a stage on the way from Figure 6.7(a) to Figure 6.7(c) and (d).
The directions of the connections in Figure 6.7(b) mirror the nature of the communications problem, but the teams are still all passive, as in Figure 6.7(a), so some of the undesirable aspects of Figure 6.7(a) are retained (undesirable from the perspective of mirroring
the problem structure).

The structure of Figure 6.7(c) provides symmetrical peer-to-peer connections that
express the operational nature of the application, because the bidirectional call chains correspond to the bidirectional, concurrent paths in the corresponding UCM. It is also a flexible structure, relative to Figure 6.7(d), because it does not force unwanted processes on
us. The bottom team of Figure 6.7(c) needs a process that can make up-calls when input
arrives at the bottom via ISRs, but we would likely position a process there in any case to
handle reception. The connection structure does not require any additional processes
along the up-call chain from one team to another to act as controllers of the call chain. All
the calls in the chain can be controlled by the single reception process at the bottom. We
need a process in the bottom team to avoid requiring a reception ISR to make the up-calls.
We want to avoid this for the obvious reason that ISRs must do as little processing as possible, to say nothing of the fact that the up-calls might be to modules that are not designed
to handle calls from ISRs (for example, if interface functions access mutual-exclusion
semaphores).

In spite of its flexibility, the structure of Figure 6.7(c) is often avoided as a way of
organizing code, at least for largish teams. One reason is that the resulting modules must
have mutual visibility of each other, so that linking independently compiled code for the
teams becomes a problem. Another reason is that established programming conventions in

a development organization may require a one-way hierarchy of control among modules. Such conventions may be adopted to constrain software complexity, but as we shall see in the following discussion of Figure 6.7(d), they do not succeed in doing this for active teams with peer-to-peer operational relationships that are bidirectional.

The choice for CG structures in code is likely to be along the lines of Figure 6.7(d) because it presents no compilation-order problems and has a clear hierarchy of control. However, it expresses a one-way client-server relationship that masks the bidirectional operational nature of the application and makes implementing it awkward. In particular, it provides no direct means for the bottom spontaneously to send new receptions upwards. Getting new receptions requires down-calls from the top, requiring the presence of at least one process at the top to make the initial down-call. Because that process may get stuck at the bottom waiting for input, it may have to be a special process whose only purpose is to wait for and return input. Such processes are often called transporters (or listeners, or messengers). Transporters are extra processes, introduced to get around a constraining control structure. To deal with issues like this, we need to have clear in our minds at the level of UCMs what fundamental processes are required by the nature of the problem. Then we can evaluate whether extra processes required to get around constraints are harmful or not.

Advanced readers will know that a common trick to avoid the consequences of having only down-calls in a structure like Figure 6.7(d) is to implement dynamically bound up-calls that bypass the fixed, down-call structure. This is done at the code level by passing a process pointer downward, thus enabling the pointer to be used at the bottom for spontaneous delivery of new input directly to a process at the top. Because this is a structurally dynamic solution, we leave the details incomplete here (see Chapter 9). However, we note one consequence, which is that the result is complex. The simple look of the fixed, one-way connection structure of Figure 6.7(d) is misleading. Because Figure 6.7(d) does not mirror the operational symmetry of the application, this symmetry must appear in another form, in this case in the form of dynamically bound up-calls that bypass the fixed structure. On the other hand, a fixed structure that mirrors the operational symmetry may be too inflexible for many purposes simply because it is fixed, so the complexity may be tolerated as the price of flexibility. There is no free lunch.

6.3.2 Back to: *Let the Maps Guide You to the Wiring*

Figure 6.8 illustrates the principle: *Let the maps guide you to the wiring.* The general form of both the maps and the wirings in this figure will be familiar from what has gone before. However, we are now ready to see how one can lead to the other.

Example 1. Figure 6.8 how a map based on Figure 6.5(b) guides you to a wiring based on Figure 6.7(a). Before explaining the steps, some new elements in Figure 6.8(a) need explanation.

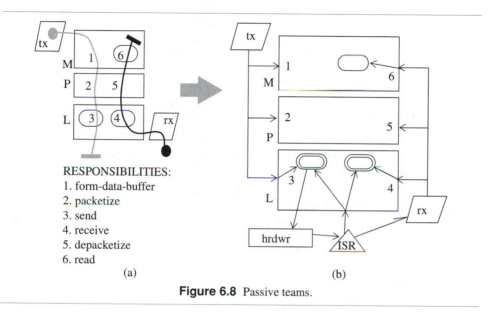

RESPONSIBILITIES:
1. form-data-buffer
2. packetize
3. send
4. receive
5. depacketize
6. read

(a)   (b)

Figure 6.8 Passive teams.

The map of Figure 6.8(a) shows a data buffering scheme that uses three fixed objects to store data. These objects are not individual data buffers themselves but are *data-manager* objects that may manage many data buffers, where the term *data buffer* indicates a storage place for a complete packet, either ready for transmission or received. The details of how data buffers are actually stored and passed around are thus deferred. This is good enough for our purposes here (Chapter 8 develops buffering details). The scheme of Figure 6.8(a) has one fixed buffer-manager object for transmission and one for reception in L and one fixed buffer-manager object for reception in M. There is no buffer-manager object in M for transmission and no buffer-manager objects of any kind in P. The responsibilities 3, 4, and 6 are bound to the buffer-manager objects. The absence of a transmission buffer-manager object in M and of any buffer-manager objects in P does not mean there is no manipulation of communications data in these places, it only means that data just passes through and any data manipulation is done "on the move" (meaning that in code, the data would be manipulated as parameters).

The objects in L in Figure 6.8(b) are shown as monitors because each is shared between an ISR and a process; the need for this sharing is not visible in Figure 6.8(a) because the ISR is layered below the map.

Now let us study the steps in going from Figure 6.8(a) to Figure 6.8(b). The transition is from a UCM in which physical I/O is layered under path segments to a CG that shows design details for handling physical I/O (next two diagrams).

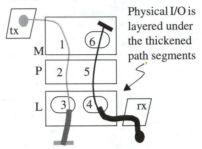

Such a transition requires delayering the map. The next diagram shows how the delayering of Figure 6.8 is accomplished: Each of the layered map segments is expanded into a CG pattern that is capable of supporting interrupt-driven, character-by-character I/O for that segment. The transmission CG implies the following sequence: After a complete transmission buffer is prepared, the first character is transmitted; thereafter, the ISR takes over and transmits each succeeding character when the previous one is done. The reception CG implies the following sequence: The ISR puts each received character into a buffer until the buffer is complete; the ISR then signals the rx process; finally, the rx process accesses the complete buffer.

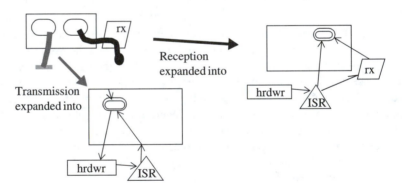

The following list steps through the paths of Figure 6.8(a) to explain how the CG of Figure 6.8(b) implements the paths. This list is not only helpful for understanding this particular figure, but is also helpful as a reference for remembering in general how CGs implement maps:

Transmission path starts: The tx process starts.

Transmission path passes through responsibility 1: The tx process calls the M team at 1; control returns to tx with the message data as a returned parameter.

Transmission path passes through responsibility 2: The tx process calls the P team at 2, passing the message data as a parameter; the call adds packet headers; control returns to tx with the modified data as a returned parameter.

Transmission path passes through responsibility 3: The tx process calls the L team at 3, passing the packet data as a parameter; the call is chained through to the buffer object to store the packet and on through to the hardware to start interrupt-driven transmission.

Transmission path ends: Control returns to the tx process and interrupt-driven transmission continues independently at a level of detail below the map. From the map perspective, the path ends when interrupt-driven transmission starts.

Reception path starts: Interrupt-driven reception fills the buffer and then the ISR sends a signal to the rx process. From the map perspective, the path starts when interrupt-driven reception ends.

Path passes through the rx process: The rx process returns from waiting for a signal from the ISR (presuming it has performed a call to wait previously, otherwise nothing happens until it does).

Path passes through responsibility 4: The rx process calls the L team to read the buffer. This call is chained through to the buffer object which returns the data as a parameter.

Path passes through responsibility 5: The rx process calls the P team at 5, passing the contents as a parameter; the call depacketizes it; control returns to rx with the message data as a returned parameter.

Path passes through responsibility 6: The rx process calls the M team at 6 with the message data as a parameter.

Path ends: Control returns from the call at 6 to the rx process.

Example 2. Figure 6.9 proceeds from a UCM in Figure 6.9(a) based on Figure 6.6 to a CG in Figure 6.9(b) based on Figure 6.7(c), except that buffer-manager objects have been added, as was done with the previous example. Fine points in the development from Figure 6.9(a) to Figure 6.9(b) are explained following the figure.

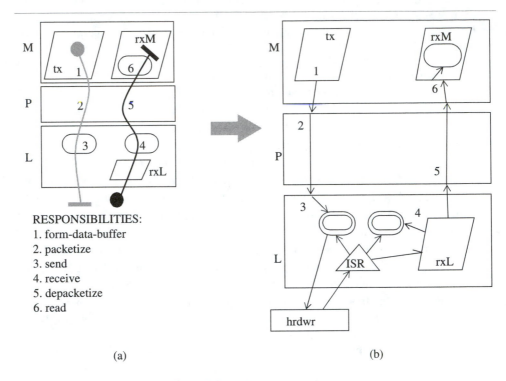

RESPONSIBILITIES:
1. form-data-buffer
2. packetize
3. send
4. receive
5. depacketize
6. read

(a)   (b)

Figure 6.9 Collaborating active teams.

As before, responsibilities are positioned near where they must be performed but local detail determines how they are performed. For example, responsibility 4 would be performed by waiting for a signal, returning from the wait when the signal arrives, and then retrieving the data from the reception buffer.

The connections are in the same direction as the paths, implying that all paths are achieved by chains of *call* and *sendwait* connections in the direction of the path. This is not necessary. The one-way structure of Figure 6.7(d) can be achieved with the same processes, except with the connections on the rx side reversed (using send-blocked *sendwait* connections for IPC), implying that the path is achieved through a chain of *returns* and *responses*. A general rule is: *Path direction in maps does not impose constraints on control direction in CGs.*

6.3.3 Physical I/O Revisited

Designing physical I/O frequently poses difficulties for novice real-time designers, because of the large conceptual gap between the picky details required at the programming level and the higher-level design concepts we have been discussing here. In this section we examine interrupt-driven reception and transmission in the MTU in some detail, to expose the issues. For concreteness, we identify the hardware device identified only by the label *hrdwr* in previous diagrams as a UART (see Appendix C for details of programming such devices). To expose the underlying issues, the UCMs that follow are separated into different diagrams for different scenarios instead of combining all scenarios into one diagram, as would be appropriate for design documentation. For simplicity, responsibilities are left implicit.

Figure 6.10 shows a use case path for moving a character from a UART into a packet buffer-manager object under interrupt control. The path could loop back to show that this is done repetitively to fill a packet buffer, but let's keep things simple here to expose more fundamental issues. Imagine this path as being followed every time a character arrives (deferring the case where the character fills the buffer, which is added later).

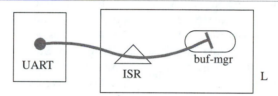

Figure 6.10 Basic character-arrival path.

Figure 6.11 shows suitable wiring to implement this path.

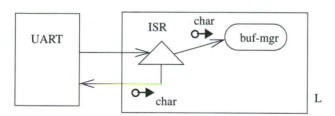

Figure 6.11 First cut at character reception wiring.

Figure 6.12 shows the path that would be followed when the character that has arrived fills the buffer. The path extends into P to pass on the complete packet.

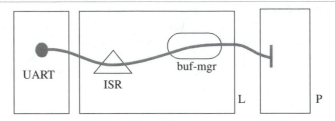

Figure 6.12 Arrival of a complete packet.

Figure 6.14 shows how an inexperienced designer might attempt to extend the wiring of Figure 6.11 to have the ISR deliver packets to P. Although the wiring is legal, it has several flaws. First, the entire arrival path from the start point to P would have to run with interrupts disabled. This has consequential performance implications. Second, the ISR's control penetrates a team other than the one where the ISR resides. This requires that P's functions be designed to preform correctly when called by an ISR (for example, they must not use mutex semaphores). This begs the following questions: Should all teams be designed so they can be called by ISRs? If not, how do we keep track of the ones that can and the ones that cannot? Thus, this innocent-appearing diagram raises large issues affecting the whole system. Third, because UARTs support character reception and transmission, not just character reception, disabling interrupts for a long period may slow down interrupt-driven transmissions in progress, not just receptions. Fourth, from a logical standpoint, the completion of a packet is a new event at the level of processes and should be reported to that level as soon as it occurs, on the spot.

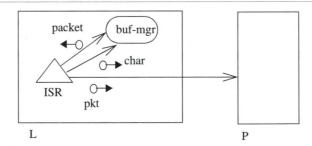

Figure 6.13 Bad reception wiring: extend the ISR's control?

Another solution is to use a semaphore in L, in a scheme like that in Figure 6.14. This is a reasonable programming solution, but it inverts the control relative to the path direction, so that P (or more correctly, a the process at the tail of the call chain from P, whether it is in P or elsewhere) must call to get a packet (and possibly wait).

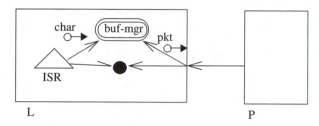

Figure 6.14 A solution with inverted control.

If a process is required to wait anyway, it is cleaner and more efficient to put it in L and keep the control direction from L to P. We need to go back to the UCM to add such a process (Figure 6.15). This is the design we showed earlier in this chapter and gives some additional insight into why it was chosen.

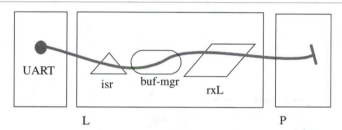

Figure 6.15 Add a reception process.

Figure 6.16 shows one possible IPC wiring for Figure 6.15, among many. The assumption of this figure is that the path from the ISR to the rxL process is a signal path that notifies rxL only that a packet has arrived but does not give it the actual packet (rxL is assumed to know where to look for it).

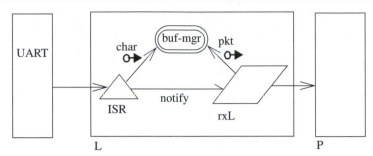

Figure 6.16 ISR-process communication.

Figure 6.17 shows some possible transmission paths through L. In Figure 6.17(a), the path brings in a packet to be transmitted and the first character is sent to the UART. In Figure 6.17(b), the ISR runs after the UART has transmitted the character, picks up the next character from the buffer, and outputs it to the buffer. This path is followed for each succeeding character in the buffer. The path ending at (c) represents the case where the ISR runs after the character has been transmitted, determines that a complete packet has been sent, and so has nothing more to do (notice that no character is sent to the UART).

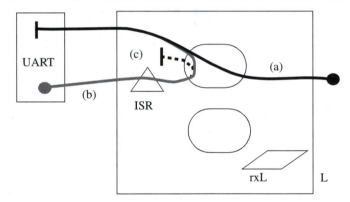

Figure 6.17 Transmission paths through the Link team.

There are no new wiring issues to be explored on the transmission side relative to what has gone before, so we leave the wiring as an exercise for the reader.

6.4 SUMMARY

In this chapter we have

- Shown how to use paths in UCMs to find processes.
- Shown how wiring diagram (CGs) flow systematically from UCMs without requiring design magic.
- Explained module interconnection issues that affect the flow from UCMs to CGs.
- Shown how maps can be used to bring the implications of low-level details such as IPC overheads and process priorities into high-level thinking about performance.
- Shown how to factor UCMs to treat components in them as systems in their own right.
- Used examples to illustrate general techniques that are reusable for other problems.

If all of this seems rather heavyweight for such a simple problem, remember that more complex problems often have at their core many of the same issues that we have discussed here. This will be illustrated in more depth later in the book, including in the next chapter. The point of this example is not that simple problems require heavy machinery, but that a systematic reasoning process can lead you (1) from requirements paths to UCMs embodying process architectures and (2) from UCMs to CGs defining module interconnection structures and IPC. Human judgment is required along the way, but mainly to decide clearly defined issues, not to perform design magic.

Design Case Study: Refining the MTU

*T*his chapter continues in more depth the study of the MTU example begun in Chapter 6. It deals with the following main issues: recovering from failures along paths (Section 7.1, in which a few additional features of the UCM notation are introduced as needed); maps as design patterns (Section 7.2), and performance and complexity issues (Section 7.3). The objective continues to be to illustrate general approaches with specific examples.

7.1 FAILURE AND RECOVERY

Let us begin as we did in Chapter 6 with a UCM to define the requirements, using the simple map of Figure 6.1 as a starting point. We will now build a failure recovery mechanism into that map, around identified failure points, using some new notation that we shall explain as we go along. The maps to come, like the ones that have gone before, are analogous to road maps on which possible end-to-end routes are traced with different colored marker pens (we use different line shadings, but the principle is the same). They have no deeper purpose than to enable you to trace possible scenarios through the map with your finger (although the concurrency of the scenarios described by these maps may require several independent fingers). The new notations that will be introduced along the way are no more than markings on the map to give you additional information that will help you trace scenarios with your fingers; they are not components with internal logic that makes the maps executable. Figure 7.1 begins the process.

- Figure 7.1(a) is a success scenario from the original map of Figure 6.1. Recall that there is one of these in each direction.
- Figure 7.1(b) adds a failure scenario. *Failure points* are identified by a ground symbol borrowed from electrical engineering; they indicate that a scenario *may* end abnormally at the point.
- Figure 7.1(c) uses AND-forks to express the following behavior: At the local end, the scenario simultaneously progresses toward the remote end and waits locally for an ack; at the remote end, the scenario simultaneously reads the message and sends an ack. Coupling at the local end between waiting for an ack and its arrival is provided by a *Coupler* component with two responsibilities, *notify* and *wait* (the coupling is assumed to take place through some internal mechanism of this component).
- Figure 7.1(d) adds the possibility of timing out the *wait* responsibility. An alternative path, to be followed after timeout, causes retransmission.

Although a component such as the *Coupler* in Figure 7.1 can be used to indicate interpath coupling, a more graphic notation is useful and is introduced in Figure 7.2. The elements of this notation will now be explained.

- Figure 7.2(a) shows a *waiting place* (a filled circle) along the local path; this notation expresses the idea of a *wait* responsibility and the coupling between it and a *notify* responsibility more graphically. *Wait* has disappeared as an explicitly identified responsibility, replaced by the waiting place. The *notify-wait* coupling is indicated by touching the end bar of the ack path tangentially to the waiting place (the ack path could also touch it tangentially in passing, if it had something else to do afterward, which it does not here).
- Figure 7.2(b) changes the waiting place into a *timed waiting place* to indicate the idea of waiting with timeout more graphically. The concept is that the path entering the timer symbol starts a timer and then waits. Two events enable the path to stop waiting: a *notify* event (which also clears the timer) or the timer running out.
- Figure 7.2(c) is a composite map that includes all paths in both directions. The documentation of this map would include labeling to identify the individual scenarios from which it was composed (following the recommendations of Chapter 5).

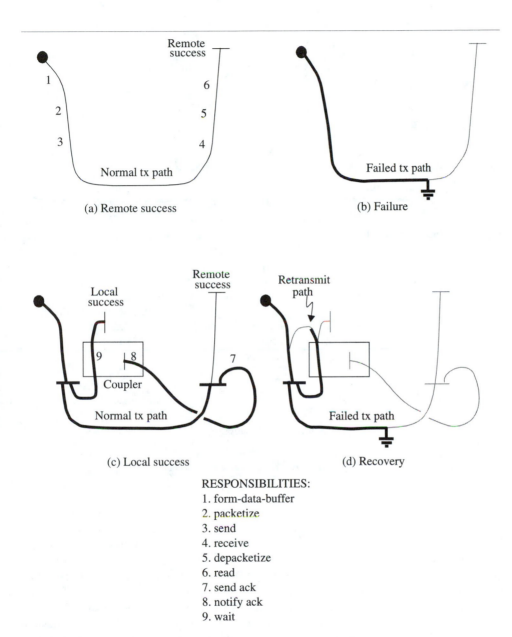

1
2
3
Normal tx path

Remote
success
6
5
4

(a) Remote success

Failed tx path

(b) Failure

Local
success
Remote
success
9   8
Coupler
7
Normal tx path

(c) Local success

Retransmit
path
Failed tx path

(d) Recovery

RESPONSIBILITIES:
1. form-data-buffer
2. packetize
3. send
4. receive
5. depacketize
6. read
7. send ack
8. notify ack
9. wait

Figure 7.1 Building a composite map.

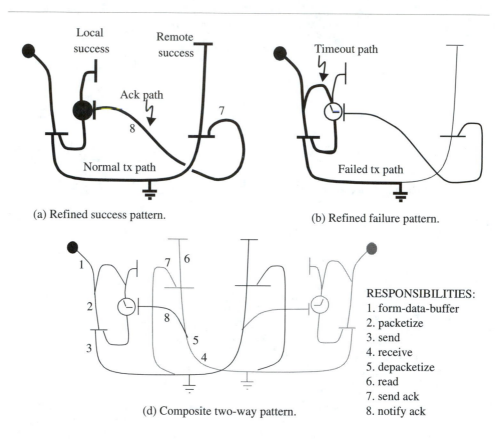

(a) Refined success pattern.

(b) Refined failure pattern.

(d) Composite two-way pattern.

RESPONSIBILITIES:
1. form-data-buffer
2. packetize
3. send
4. receive
5. depacketize
6. read
7. send ack
8. notify ack

Figure 7.2 Building up a composite map.

7.1.1 Unintended Scenarios

Because maps are formed as compositions of end-to-end paths with some shared path segments, there may be unintended sequences lurking in the composition (we may exclude
them by labeling but should not ignore them, because they may give insight into possible
new behaviors that could cause problems). For example, we may follow one end-to-end
path into a shared segment and then inadvertently switch to another path going out.
Exploring maps for unintended sequences is an important part of the high-level design
process; making sure unwanted sequences don't get into code is an important part of the
detailed design and implementation process.

Figure 7.3 identifies some unwanted sequences in the map of Figure 7.2:

- Cases (a) and (b) could occur if noise on the communications link alters transmitted bits sufficiently. However, usually this is prevented by mechanisms below the level of this map, such as checksums or cyclic redundancy codes.

- Case (c) could be a critical race if it is not handled properly. Retransmission after timeout when the other end has already received and acknowledged the original transmission could result in the other end seeing the retransmission as something new. Abandonment of transmission due to too many timeouts could result in a late ack being interpreted as an ack for a later transmission. There is also the issue of whether or not a nak (negative ack) should be included along this path to allow the other end to ask for retransmission if it receives a garbled transmission. The *possibility* of critical races is widespread in concurrent systems. Maps are helpful for spotting them. Critical races are hard to see at the level of the software components that implement segments of the paths.

Adding a negative acknowledgment will enable the other end to ask explicitly for retransmission and adding an alternating bit field in packets will enable acks to be identified uniquely with transmitted packets, to prevent the race described previously from becoming critical. Such features are typical of communication protocols and could have been specified up front from knowledge of the protocol field. The point in arriving at them via maps is not to re-derive standard features of communication protocols, but to show how to employ UCMs to reason about any kind of system in which failures may occur at points along paths.

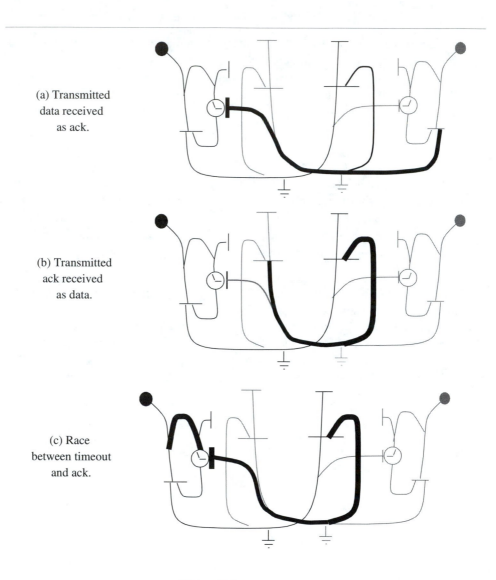

(a) Transmitted
data received
as ack.

(b) Transmitted
ack received
as data.

(c) Race
between timeout
and ack.

Figure 7.3 Unwanted sequences.

7.2 MAPS AS DESIGN PATTERNS

Figure 7.4 repeats the factoring process of Figure 5.2 for the refined map of Figure 7.2(e) to produce a local map that can be used as a starting point for detailed design.

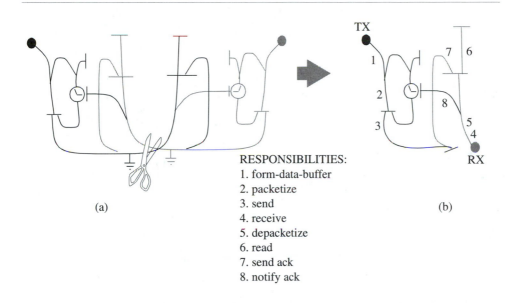

(a)

RESPONSIBILITIES:
1. form-data-buffer
2. packetize
3. send
4. receive
5. depacketize
6. read
7. send ack
8. notify ack

(b)

Figure 7.4 Factoring the refined map.

Because this unbound map has an invariant form relative to a wide class of process architectures to realize it, the map can be used as an invariant design pattern against which to evaluate architectures (Figure 7.5). In this case study (and we think in many practical problems) the designer has three independent variables to juggle: maps, teams, and processes. A general design approach is to hold one or more of these variables invariant while manipulating the others to evaluate issues. Here the teams and the maps are held invariant while the processes are varied. The particular set of process architectures in the figure was chosen to give a sense of the range of choices, not to be exhaustive. Observe that some teams may not have any processes in them (such teams are not empty because they may have interfaces and internal objects that are not shown because they have not been discovered yet).

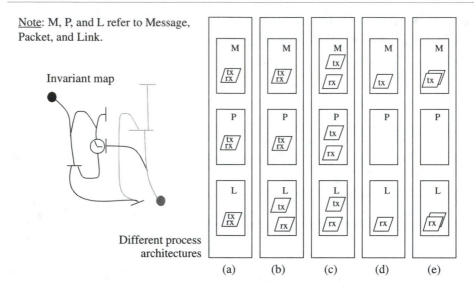

Note: M, P, and L refer to Message, Packet, and Link.

Invariant map

Different process architectures

(a)   (b)   (c)   (d)   (e)

Figure 7.5 Maps as invariant patterns to help evaluate design tradeoffs.

The different process architectures in Figure 7.5 all have pros and cons:

- Alternatives (a) through (c) provide flexibility in relation to the possible use of a multiprocessor. They do so by providing processes in teams that might be allocated to different processors. Alternatives (d) and (e) reduce uniprocessor overhead along paths by minimizing the number of process interactions along the paths.

- Alternative (d) follows directly from the fact that processes are needed for concurrency of reception and transmission. It is a natural one when the software will run on a single processor because it enables control of each path to be centralized in one process instead of decentralized among several, thereby minimizing overhead along paths. However, it is not a natural one when the software is split among several processors.

- Alternative (e) is a variation of (d) that would enable multiple transmissions and receptions to proceed concurrently along the same path, under the control of different processes. This alternative introduces interesting issues associated with process coordination. For example, processes may overtake other processes and even pass them along a path, unless detailed means, below the level of the map, are put in place to prevent it. The map warns of the possible problem and provides a context for thinking about it but does not solve the problem.

- The other alternatives come from anticipating that the teams might be allocated to different physical processors (for example, L might be in a front end processor, or perhaps both L and P). Alternative (a) has the minimum number of processes if each team is in a separate processor. The others are variations to provide full transmission and reception concurrency in each team.

Think of the map on the left of Figure 7.5 as superimposed on the architectures on the right, assuming the relative sizes and form factors are adjusted to make this possible. Figure 7.6 shows the result of such superposition for one of the alternatives.

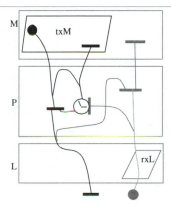

Figure 7.6 An example of superposition in relation to Figure 7.5(d).

Here are some points to note about Figure 7.6 that are also helpful as general reminders of how to develop detailed maps:

- Both the start and the end of the local transmission path are positioned inside the txM process to make clear that this process sees transmission as a path excursion that loops back to report end-to-end success.
- The join between the two transmission paths going from P to L is positioned in P to make clear that L does not see them as different paths.
- The retransmission path segment is confined to P to make clear that M and L are not aware of retransmission.
- The asynchronous coupling with timeout is positioned inside P to make clear that it is P's responsibility to do all the ack-timeout processing. Because there is no process in P, this places constraints on the CG to implement this map.
- The two AND-forks inside P do not mean concurrency of the forks is achieved there, because there are no processes there or elsewhere to achieve it.
- A design rule that clarifies maps is as follows: *Processes should be assumed to complete current responsibility sequences before going back to wait for new stimuli, unless otherwise specified*. The implications here are that txM completes the TX

path end to end before looking for something else to transmit and rxL completes the RX path end to end before looking for another reception.

7.2.1 Refined CGs from Refined Maps

Figure 7.7(a) repeats the map of Figure 7.6 with the crosscoupled parts highlighted with thick lines and the rest shown with thin lines. Figure 7.7(b) adds suitable crosscoupled connections (thick lines) to a basic CG (from Chapter 6). The slightly simpler look of the CG is misleading because all the end-to-end information that is in the UCMs is absent. To use the CGs alone to understand the end-to-end behavior, we would have to rely on the internal logic of components (which at this point in the design process has not yet been defined).

In general, the process of going from a UCM such as the one in Figure 7.7(a) to a CG such as the one in Figure 7.7(b) requires some careful thought; it is not just a linear process of substituting connections for path segments. The process requires separating the UCM into constituent paths representing individual scenarios, selecting appropriate connection structures for each constituent path from a mental library of possible structures (taking account of possible scenario concurrency), and then combining the connection structures in a coherent way. The latter step may require making adjustments to the selected individual connection structures to make them compatible in combination, and using the same connection structures for multiple purposes. The process for Figure 7.7 is outlined following the figure.

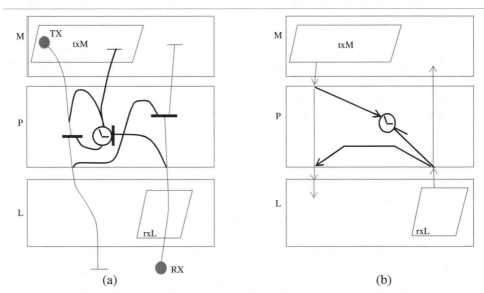

(a)   (b)

Figure 7.7 Refining the details (unchanged parts shown with lighter lines).

Before deciding CG connections, UCM concurrency must be understood. The next diagram shows where concurrency may be present in the highlighted area of Figure 7.7(a). The correspondence with Figure 7.7(a) is by visual shape not labeling. The concept of the following diagram is that each different line shading identifies a single path along which a concurrent scenario may progress. For example, path A starts at the top left and continues along the right hand branch of the AND-fork, and route B begins at the left hand branch of the AND-fork. A and B are concurrent, by definition. A property of the MTU system is that either C1 or C2 may be concurrent along with them.

A. Concurrency comes from txM in M
B. Concurrency comes from an ISR in L
C. Concurrency comes from rxL in L

In the next diagram (and the two following it), the correspondingly-shaded path segments in the UCM and arrows in the CG show possible connection structures that are capable of realizing the UCM. The purpose here is only to show plausible connection structures, not to prescribe how to select from among many possibilities (the intention is that the totality of examples in this book will give the reader a start on understanding how to do that). Numbered, small arrows indicate call-return sequencing in the CG. The first diagram focuses on the A-C1 combination of paths.

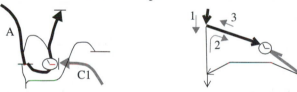

In the next diagram, we show that the B-C2 path-segment combination may use the same call-return connection from P to L for sending data and acks.

In the next diagram, we show that the timeout/retransmit path may be implemented with the already-defined connection structure. We could continue to explore the nuances of this example, but the foregoing is sufficient to give the main ideas.

To illustrate the mapping of CGs to code in Chapter 8, we use a slightly more general process configuration than the one in Figure 7.7. To pave the way for Chapter 8, Figure 7.8 shows a UCM and CG for this configuration. This figure is similar to Figure 7.7 except that it shows additional buffering and ISR details that were omitted from Figure 7.7 for simplicity. Figure 7.8 adds this information while continuing to defer many of the details of how data buffers are actually stored and passed around in programs (see Chapter 8 for that).

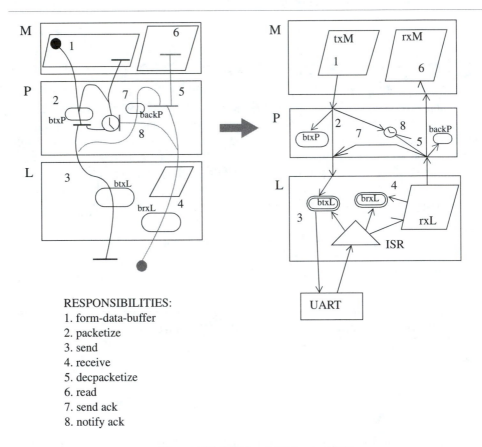

RESPONSIBILITIES:
1. form-data-buffer
2. packetize
3. send
4. receive
5. decpacketize
6. read
7. send ack
8. notify ack

Figure 7.8 UCM and CG for the MTU.

The objects in Figure 7.8 are buffer-manager objects, not actual buffer objects. The buffering concept is that buffer objects containing packet and message data (the assumption is there is room for both in a single object) are passed around from place to place, where they may be operated on or stored. The buffer-manager objects store the buffer objects. Buffer-manager objects are not needed everywhere because buffer objects are not stored everywhere (sometimes they simply pass though). For brevity we say "message" or "packet" when we mean, respectively, "a buffer object containing a message" or "a buffer object containing a packet."

Let us now step through the paths of this map to explain how the CG implements the paths. (This follows the style of a similar list presented in Chapter 6 but is presented here to consolidate the specific details of this design.)

Transmission:

> **Transmission path starts:** The txM process starts.

> **Transmission path passes through responsibility 1:** The txM process initializes a buffer object with a message. There is no buffer-manager object in M because the buffer object just passes through.

> **Transmission path passes through responsibility 2:** The txM process calls the P team, passing it the message, which is stored in the buffer-manager object btxP (packet header information is added here).

> **Transmission path splits at an AND-fork; left hand path passes through responsibility 3:** The txM process calls the L team, passing it the packet (which also stays in btxP); the call is chained through to the buffer-manager object btxL to store the packet for ISR-driven transmission, and on through to the hardware to start transmission.

> **Left-hand transmission path ends:** Control returns from the call to L and ISR-driven transmission continues independently at a level below the detail of the map. From the map perspective, the path ends when ISR-driven transmission starts.

> **Right-hand transmission path waits at a waiting place:** The txM process waits at the semaphore until it is signaled (indicating that an acknowledgment has been received from the remote system) or times out.

> **Right-hand transmission path splits at an OR-fork:** After an acknowledgment is received, control returns to the txM process. If the semaphore times out before an acknowledgment is received, the txM process calls the L team to retransmit the message, passing it the packet stored in btxP.

Reception:

> **Reception path starts:** Interrupt-driven reception fills a packet in brxL and then the ISR sends a signal to the rxL process. From the map perspective, the path starts when interrupt-driven reception ends.

> **Reception path passes through the rxL process:** The rxL process returns from waiting for a signal from the ISR (presuming that is has performed a call to wait previously, otherwise nothing happens until it does).

> **Reception path passes through responsibility 4:** The rxL process retrieves the packet from brxL.

Reception path passes into the P team and splits at an OR-fork: The rxL process calls the P team, passing it the received packet. Subsequent actions depend on whether the packet contains a message or an ack.

Reception path (message reception) splits at an AND-fork; right-hand path passes through responsibility 5: The packet is recognized as a message and the call is chained through to M to pass the message.

Reception path (message reception) passes through responsibility 6: The message is passed on to the rxL process, which handles it.

Reception path (message reception) passes through responsibility 7: An ack packet is obtained from the backP buffer manager and passed to the L team for transmission.

Reception path (ack reception) passes through responsibility 8: The packet contains an ack, so the call from rxL signals the semaphore where txM waits.

Reception path ends: Control returns from the call to P.

7.2.2 Exploring Alternative IPC Patterns

One can easily imagine other ack-timeout IPC patterns between rxL and txM than the one in Figure 7.7 or Figure 7.8. However, the UCMs of Figure 7.7(a) and Figure 7.8(a) impose constraints leading to this one as the only reasonable choice. Figure 7.9 gives two examples of technically acceptable ack-timeout IPC patterns that must be rejected because they do not fit the requirements of the maps. Both of these patterns could accomplish the purpose of txM waiting with timeout for an ack. Both are unsuitable because they violate the requirement of the maps that all responsibilities associated with acks and timeouts belong to P. This is a sensible requirement that should not be violated, because it centralizes all packet-level processing in one place, which is desirable for modularity.

- Figure 7.9(a) has txM waiting for an ack "at home." The notation indicates that txM sets a timer before waiting for any events (there is only one possible event here, an ack message from rxL) and then waits with timeout.
- Figure 7.9(b) has txM waiting for an ack at the source at rxL. We show the interface of rxL as supporting the means by which txM may wait, with timeout, for an ack; however, the same effect could be achieved by moving the shared semaphore implied by Figure 7.7(b) into L.

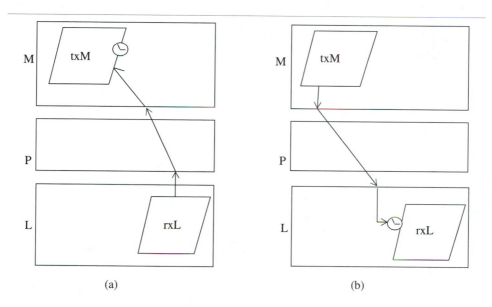

(a)   (b)

Figure 7.9 Legal but unsuitable ack-timeout CGs.

While rejecting the solution of Figure 7.9(a) for this specific problem, we note that it has one nice property that the other two do not, including the selected one of Figure 7.7(b). It offers the possibility that, for a slightly more general version of this problem, all waiting that txM might have to do for interactions with any other processes could be centralized in txM (including with processes not shown, for example, with a process bringing new messages to send from a source other than the console). In this specific problem, in which only one message may be outstanding (that is, awaiting an ack) at a time, there is no advantage because, when a message is outstanding, txM has nothing else to do but wait for an ack, so having it wait at a specific place outside itself (in P) causes no problems. In a slightly more general case, multiple messages could be outstanding, and the transmission process might be torn between waiting for new messages requiring sending and waiting in P (or elsewhere) for acks or timeouts for outstanding ones.

The following is a good design rule for processes: *Provide each process with only one place to wait*. This rule prevents the possibility of a process being stuck in one place while missing things at another. A companion rule is this: *Avoid having processes jump back and forth between different places where events may occur* (this is called *polling*, and it wastes processing resources).

Figure 7.10 shows one possibility for guaranteeing that txM has one place to wait. Put a process in P, txP, to do all transmission-oriented processing in P. This enables us to satisfy the one-place-to-wait rule for txM while also satisfying the requirement that all ack-timeout processing be the responsibility of P. The new process txP acts as a switchboard for all transmission-related action in P. The price we pay is more processes and more interactions. This is not an unusual price to pay for greater flexibility, but care must be taken not to carry it so far that the additional overhead causes performance problems and the additional complexity causes errors.

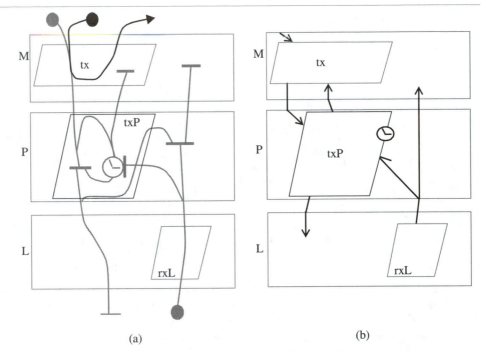

(a)   (b)

Figure 7.10 Satisfying the rule of one-place-to-wait.

7.3 PERFORMANCE AND COMPLEXITY ISSUES

7.3.1 Performance

Paths in UCMs can be used to integrate performance information from diverse sources to pinpoint possible performance problems (here we refer to some issues associated with object orientation, even though this book largely avoids that subject, and we refer to some concepts that are not explained until Chapter 9):

- The presence of multiple processes along paths alerts us to the possibility of IPC overhead that will degrade end-to-end performance.
- The presence of structural dynamics along paths (indicated by the presence of slots

for dynamic components—see Chapter 9) alerts us to the possibility of overhead that will degrade end-to-end performance due to the slowness of runtime mechanisms for dynamic creation.

- The presence of components along paths that may be derived from class hierarchies alerts us to the possibility of overhead due to object-oriented implementation techniques. For example, the buffer-manager objects of this chapter may be implemented through inheritance in an object-oriented programming language. In this case, inheritance paths may have to be traversed at runtime, causing overhead.

7.3.2 Complexity

Is the MTU example complex enough to be realistic? Have we somehow stacked the deck in favor of our methods by presenting only examples like the MTU to which it easily applies? We respond to these questions as follows:

- Complexity is not necessarily a function of size only. The tricky issues of race conditions, failure and recovery, performance, and structural dynamics are all representative of practical systems. Practical systems may have a lot of functional detail in them that makes them large (in terms of size of code). However, the impact of such detail on the big picture represented by UCMs can be kept small by modeling functionality in terms of point responsibilities along paths.
- The MTU system has the characteristic of displaying large-scale behavior patterns that are naturally represented by paths (we may call such systems path centric). For path-centric systems, the map model seems such a common-sense one that is hard to imagine it not being applicable to systems of any size or complexity. Most real-time and distributed systems we have encountered are path centric, so we think the techniques are widely applicable. However, there are systems that are not path centric; for example, signal processing systems in which data items ripple through a set of signal processing elements in a diffuse manner would not be characterized as path centric. However, we think that systems like this are likely to be subsystems of larger path centric systems and can be treated as layers in the larger context.

7.4 SUMMARY

In this chapter we have

- Shown how to refine maps to include recovery from path failure for the case in which failure points can be pinpointed along paths.
- Shown how to employ maps as design patterns to make tradeoffs between architectures.
- Shown how to make the transition from refined UCMs to refined CGs.
- Pointed the way to employing UCMs to pinpoint performance problems.
- Explained that the MTU problem is complex enough to be representative of many practical issues in real time systems, in spite of its relatively small size.
- Attempted to point the way to general approaches, rather than just develop solutions to one particular problem.

Implementation Case Study: Programming the MTU

This chapter completes the MTU example from the previous two chapters. In Section 8.1, we finish the high-level design of the MTU and begin the process of converting the CGs into code. Section 8.2 discusses detailed design issues that are below the level of CGs and contains the skinny C++ code for most of the components of the MTU. A staged approach for implementing the MTU as a series of prototypes is presented in Section 8.3.

8.1 FINISHING THE HIGH-LEVEL DESIGN FOR THE MTU

8.1.1 Adding a Simple User Interface

So far, we have intentionally ignored the question of how the MTU should interact with the user. This is because user interface issues are usually distinct from real-time issues. We have deferred discussing the MTU's user interface until now, because we did not want to cloud the important issues that were presented in the previous chapters.

Figure 8.1 steps back from the UCMs and CGs to present a uses diagram for a complete MTU that could be implemented as a project. The core of the MTU consists of the M, P, and L teams that were designed earlier. A control team (C) and a status team (S) have been added to provide a very simple user interface that allows limited user control of the MTU.

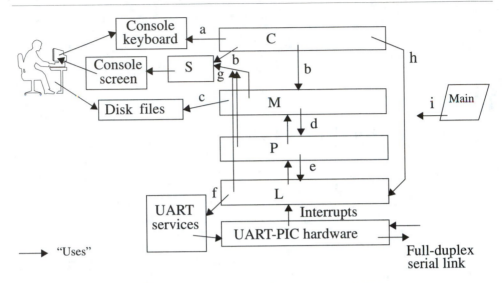

Figure 8.1 Uses diagram for the complete MTU.

The arrows in Figure 8.1 show uses relationships between the teams.

(a) C calls to get keyboard input occasionally.

(b) C calls M and S to send them commands.

(c) M calls standard C++ run-time library functions to open and close DOS files and to read and write the file contents (namely, messages).

(d), (e) M, P, and L interact with one another, as described in Chapters 6 and 7.

(f) L calls UART Services to perform UART operations.

(g) M, P, and L call S to display progress on the screen.

(h) C calls L to shut down the MTU (interrupt vectors must be restored and Tempo multitasking ended).

(i) Initialization is performed by the Main process (see Figure 8.5).

8.1.2 Requirements for the Control Team

This team gets everything started, then acts as a decoder of operator commands, and finally stops the program on operator request.

Console keyboard input is tested periodically (say, once a second). The team makes appropriate consequential calls to other teams. C provides no external functions to be called from anywhere else. It also stores no local state information, so it has no idea if the commands make sense in the context of sequences of previous commands and what the system is doing about them. It only knows what commands affect which teams.

Operator commands from the console keyboard are very simple. They are entered by typing a single character for each command:

1. **Send-Next** (character "S") requests a single message to be read from the file and sent. Every occurrence of this command causes a call to M.
2. **Send-All** (character "A") requests that all the messages in the file be sent, one after the other, starting from the first and ending with the last. Every occurrence of this call causes a call to M.
3. **Freeze-Status** (character "F") requests that the status display be frozen, so a fixed snapshot of the system's status is displayed. Unfreeze-Status (also character "F") reenables status display updates.
4. **Quit** (character "Q") requests that control be returned to DOS without waiting for message transmission and reception in progress to complete.

There are no operator commands for message reception, which is always enabled. Any other keystrokes than the ones listed here are ignored, there are no prompts, and no keystrokes are echoed on the screen.

Compared to most real-world programs this interface appears contrived, but that is because the MTU is a student project that deliberately puts issues of user interface design and programming to one side to focus on the real-time aspects.

8.1.3 Requirements for the Status Team

This team provides interface functions that are called by other parts of the system to log status information for display. The team writes this information to the screen periodically; for example, once every 5 seconds or so, to provide enough time for the user to read the screen. Another interface function accepts the Freeze-Status command from C.

8.1.4 Adding Control and Status Teams to the MTU Collaboration Graph

Extending the MTU CG from Chapter 7 to include the control and status teams from Figure 8.1 is straightforward. We present this in Figure 8.2 and Figure 8.4. The C and S teams introduce a requirement for additional concurrency: Periodic checking for commands and updating of the status display is independent of the transmission and reception paths in the M, P, and L teams. This concurrency is provided by a process in each of the C and S teams.

Figure 8.2 shows how the ctrl process in C is wired to M to deliver Send-Next and Send-All commands to txM. To prevent the figure from becoming cluttered, the S team is not shown here (see Figure 8.4).

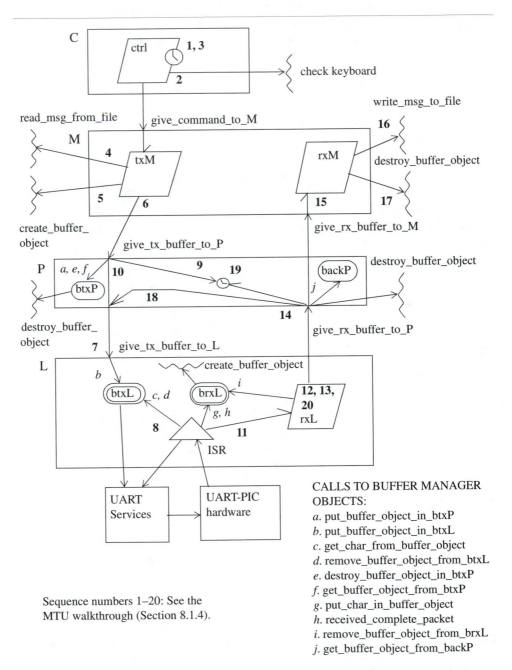

Figure 8.2 Collaboration graph for the MTU (message transmission and reception).

We begin the process of converting the CG to code by adding to Figure 8.2 names for the interface functions provided by the teams and the buffer-manager objects.

The following list steps through the CG in Figure 8.2, listing the functions calls made by the program during message reception and transmission (status logging and system initialization and shutdown are not considered here). Although a UCM is not shown in this figure, this sequence traces through the MTU UCM that was presented in Chapter 7. Readers are urged to compare this walkthrough to the similar one in Chapter 7, which explains how the CG implements the paths in the UCM.

1. **The ctrl process wakes up:** The ctrl process returns from a call to Tempo's `process_sleep()` kernel function.

2. **The ctrl process handles a single user command:** The ctrl process checks for a single-character command entered at the keyboard. Send-Next and Send-All commands are delivered to M by calling M's `give_command_to_M()`, passing it the character code for command. This function calls Tempo's `send()` function to deliver the command to the txM process.

3. **The ctrl process sleeps:** The ctrl process returns from `give_command_to_M()` and puts itself to sleep for one second by calling `process_sleep()`.

Transmission Path

4. **The txM process starts:** The txM process returns from a call to Tempo's `receive()` function, saves the command sent by the ctrl process, then gets the text for a single message by calling `read_msg_from_file()`.

5. **The txM process forms a tx buffer:** The txM process allocates and initializes a new buffer object by calling `create_buffer_object()` and passing it the message text, which is copied into the buffer.

6. **The txM process packetizes the tx buffer:** The txM process passes the buffer object to P by calling `give_tx_buffer_to_P()`. This function initializes the packet header in the buffer object, then saves the buffer in P's buffer-manager object, btxP, by calling `put_buffer_object_in_btxP()` (function *a* in Figure 8.2) in case the packet must be retransmitted.

7. **The txM process causes the packet to be sent:** The txM process, executing function `give_tx_buffer_to_P()`, passes the buffer object to L by calling `give_tx_buffer_to_L()`. The call is chained through to buffer-manager object btxL—`put_buffer_object_in_btxL()` (function *b*) is called to store the buffer object—then on through to the UART Services team to start interrupt-driven transmission, if it is not already in progress.

8. **The txM process returns from L while the packet is transmitted:** txM returns from `give_tx_buffer_to_L()` to `give_tx_buffer_to_P()`. Interrupt-driven transmission continues independently at a level below the detail of the CG.

The ISR repeatedly calls btxL's `get_char_from_buffer_object()` (function *c*) to extract characters from the packet and delivers them to the UART Services team. The ISR calls btxL's `remove_buffer_object_from_btxL()` (function *d*) after the packet has been transmitted. (See Section 8.2.11 for the code for interrupt-driven transmission.)

9. **The txM process waits at a timed waiting place:** The txM process, executing function `give_tx_buffer_to_P()`, calls `wait_semaphore()`, specifying a time-out value. The process waits until the semaphore is signaled (indicating that an acknowledgment or negative acknowledgment has been received from the remote system) or times out.

10. **The txM process finishes waiting**: If an acknowledgment is received, the txM process (executing `give_tx_buffer_to_P()`) deallocates the buffer object that was just transmitted by calling `destroy_buffer_object_in_btxP()` (function *e*). The txM process then returns from `give_tx_buffer_to_P()`. Depending on whether the last command was Send-Next or Send-All, the txM process calls Tempo's `receive()` (to wait for another command) or allocates and initializes another buffer object for transmission. However, if a negative acknowledgment is received or the semaphore times out before an acknowledgment is received, `give_tx_buffer_to_P()` calls `get_buffer_object_from_btxP()` (function *f*) to get the buffer object that was saved earlier. It then calls `give_tx_buffer_to_L()` to retransmit the packet.

Reception Path

11. **A packet arrives:** Interrupt-driven reception fills a buffer object with a packet. The ISR stores characters received from the UART by repeatedly calling buffer-manager object brxL's `put_char_in_buffer_object()` (function *g*). When a complete packet has arrived, the ISR calls brxL's `received_complete_packet()` (function *h*), then calls Tempo's `signal()` to inform the rxL process. (See Section 8.2.11 for the code for interrupt-driven reception.)

12. **The rxL process executes:** The rxL process returns from Tempo's `wait()` after it has been signaled by the ISR (presuming that the process called `wait()` before the ISR signaled; otherwise the signal is remembered until `wait()` is called).

13. **The rxL process gets an rx buffer:** The rxL process calls brxL's `remove_buffer_object_from_brxL()` (function *i*), which returns the buffer object containing the newly received packet.

14. **The rxL process passes the rx buffer to P:** The rxL process passes the buffer object to P by calling `give_rx_buffer_to_P()`. Subsequent actions depend on whether the packet in the buffer object contains a message, an ack, or a nak.

15. **The rxL process handles message reception:** If the packet contains a message, the rxL process, executing `give_rx_buffer_to_P()`, passes the buffer object to M by calling `give_rx_buffer_to_M()`. This function calls Tempo's `send()` function to send the buffer object to the rxM process.

16. **The rxM process stores the message:** The rxM process waits for an rx buffer by calling Tempo's `receive()`. After receiving the buffer object, the rxM process asks the buffer object to return the text of the message contained in it. It then calls `write_msg_to_file()` to save the message.

17. **The rxM process deallocates the rx buffer:** The rxM process calls `destroy_buffer_object()` and then calls `receive()` to wait for another rx buffer.

18. **The rxL process acknowledges reception of the message:** The rxL process, executing `give_rx_buffer_to_P()`, obtains a buffer object containing an ack packet by calling backP's `get_buffer_object_from_backP()` (function *j*). Next, rxL calls `give_tx_buffer_to_L()`, passing it the buffer object for transmission to the other computer.

19. **The rxL process handles ack/nak reception:** If the packet is an ack or nak packet, `give_rx_buffer_to_P()` (executed by rxL) calls `signal_semaphore()`, where txM waits. A shared data object (not shown) is updated to indicate which type of packet was received. The buffer object containing the ack/nak packet is then deallocated by calling `destroy_buffer_object()`.

20. **The rxL process returns from P (reception path finished):** rxL returns from `give_rx_buffer_to_P()` and calls `wait()` to wait for the arrival of another packet.

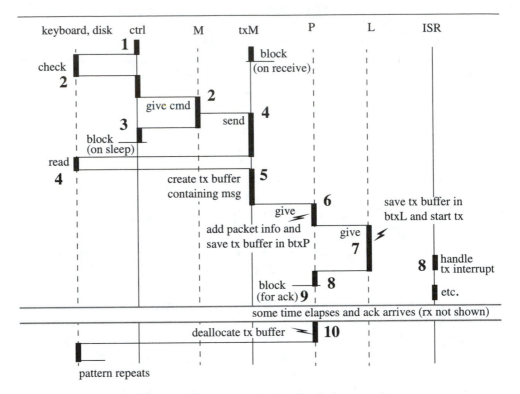

Figure 8.3 Simplest send-all transmission scenario.

Figure 8.3 shows a timing diagram for the simplest transmission scenario that corresponds to the Send-All command. Labels 1 through 10 correspond to steps in the CG walkthrough. To help us think about the concurrency issues, the timelines for the processes and the ISR are drawn as if they were physically concurrent. (Attempting to show how their execution would be interleaved on a single processor would complicate the diagram unnecessarily.) Drawing a timing diagram for the reception scenario is left as an exercise for the reader.

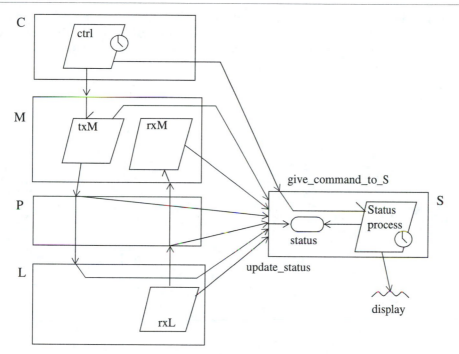

Figure 8.4 Collaboration graph for the MTU (status recording).

Figure 8.4 redraws the CG from Figure 8.2, hiding most of the connections within the M, P, and L teams and adding the wiring to the S team. M, P, and L call S (`update_status()`) to deposit status information in a buffer for pickup by the status process. The status object is not a monitor for efficiency reasons, so transient errors may occur in the status display due to process interference. The ctrl process in C calls S (`give_command_to_S()`) to deliver the Freeze-Status and Unfreeze-Status commands.

8.1.5 System Initialization and Shutdown

Figure 8.5 shows MTU initialization. The Main process created by Tempo at startup initializes the C team by calling its *init* interface function. This call is chained through to the *init* functions of the S, M, P, and L teams. As indicated by the dashed create arrows, these functions create processes and semaphores. The L team's *init* function also calls `init_uart_services()` to initialize the UART and install the UART ISR.

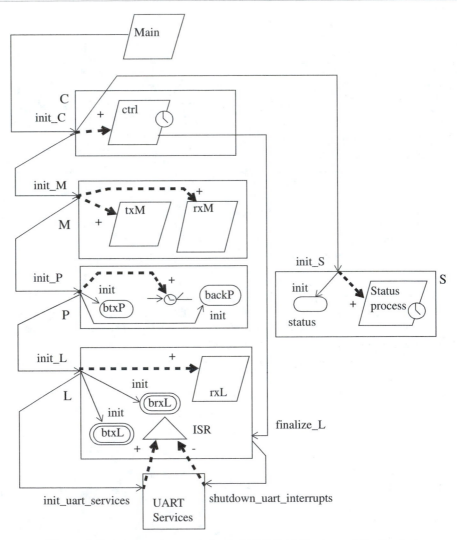

Figure 8.5 Collaboration graph for the MTU (initialization and finalization).

P and L's *init* functions also call the *init* functions of their buffer-manager objects. Similarly, the S team's *init* function calls a second *init* function to initialize the object that records status information.

Figure 8.5 also shows how the MTU is shut down. The ctrl process calls the L team's *finalize* interface function, which disables UART interrupts and restores the UART interrupt vector by calling `shutdown_uart_interrupts()`.

8.1.6 Packets, Buffer Objects, and Buffer-Manager Objects

As we developed the MTU in the previous two chapters, our efforts were focused on designing process architectures and IPC structures for the system, and the question of how to manage data within the system received relatively little attention. Before describing how the MTU CG is mapped to code, a few words are needed to clarify how data are managed.

Conceptually, messages and packets flow through the MTU as shown in Figure 8.6. On the transmission side, M is responsible for preparing messages and passing them to P. Upon receiving a message, P is responsible for building a data packet that consists of a *packet header* followed by the complete message. P then hands the data packet to L for transmission over the serial link. L adds a framing byte to either end of the packet (for reasons explained in Section 8.2.9) and transmits the frame across the serial link.

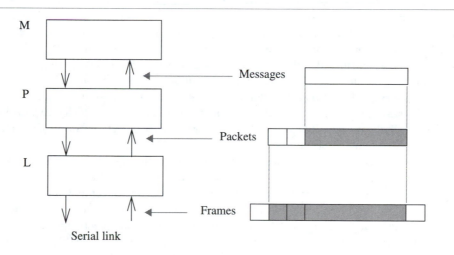

Figure 8.6 Relationship among messages, packets, and frames.

The reception side reverses this process. L receives a frame from the remote computer, extracts the packet by stripping the framing bytes, and passes the packet to P. If it is a data packet, P extracts the message from the packet and passes it to M. P is also responsible for acknowledging that a data packet has been received by preparing and sending an ack packet. If P receives a packet that contains an unrecognizable header, it transmits a negative acknowledgment (nak) packet back. No ack packet is sent when an ack or nak packet is received; in other words, acks are sent only in response to the arrival of a data packet.

Thinking about how to transfer messages and packets between teams reveals some interesting performance issues. Looking at Figure 8.6, you might expect complete messages to be copied between M and P and complete packets to be copied between P and L; furthermore, the figure suggests that within P, messages must be copied into and out of packets. If messages are large, copying messages and the packets containing them would be a time-consuming operation.

Here is how the MTU buffers data efficiently. The contents of data packets (that is, packets containing messages), ack packets, and nak packets are stored in *buffer objects* (often simply referred to as *buffers*). Even though the design concept is that buffer objects are passed around the MTU, for efficiency reasons these objects are passed around by passing *pointers* to them.

For each message that is transmitted, M allocates a new buffer object that is large enough to hold a complete data packet (that is, the packet header and the message). M stores the message data in the buffer and then passes P a pointer to the object. M does not alter the packet header; that is the responsibility of P. P packetizes the buffer object by initializing its packet type and alternating-bit fields and then passes the pointer to the buffer to L. The pointer to the buffer object is stored in L until the packet it contains has been transmitted. On the reception side, each incoming packet is stored by L in a buffer and, when a complete packet has been received, a pointer to the buffer is passed to P. When P determines that a buffer object contains a data packet, it passes the pointer to the buffer to M, and M is responsible for extracting the message from the buffer and storing it.

In the CGs, the btxP object in P represents a *buffer-manager object* that conceptually stores a single buffer object containing the most recently transmitted data packet for retransmission. In practice, the buffer-manager object stores the pointer to the buffer object. Similarly, the backP object in P is a buffer-manager object that stores a (pointer to a) buffer object containing ack/nak packet.

The transmission side of L needs storage for two buffer objects to handle the case in which a message and an ack need to be sent so close together in time that the corresponding buffer objects could overrun each other arriving at L. The reception side of L needs storage for two buffer objects to prevent overruns if the other computer sends a message and an ack close together in time. The btxL and brxL objects in L each represent a buffer-manager object that holds two buffer objects (actually, pointers to two buffer objects).

8.1.7 Buffer-Manager Teams

Objects in design diagrams are primitive components, meaning that pictorially they cannot contain other components. All this means is that at the scale of the diagrams we ignore internal details; it does not mean that there cannot be internal details. In the case of the buffer-manager objects, there are internal details that might usefully be shown pictorially.

This is done by converting the objects to teams.

Figure 8.7 shows that the btxL buffer-manager object from the transmission side of L can be represented as a buffer-manager team that holds two buffer objects. Inside the team, the shapes drawn with dashed outlines are *slots* for the objects. This notation is new here and is explained fully in Chapter 9. For now, recall that buffer objects are allocated in M and then wind their way through P and L. Imagine that, when a buffer object is passed to L, it is moved into an empty slot in the buffer-manager team, shown by the dashed move-arrow connecting the team's interface function and the slots. The parameter indicates the object that is moved into the slot.

The btxL buffer-manager object is represented as a buffer-manager team that stores a pair of buffer objects. The brxL buffer-manager can be decomposed the same way.

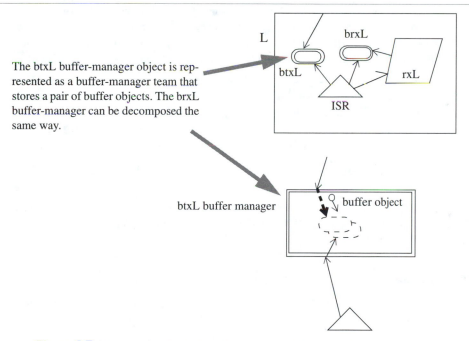

Figure 8.7   Representing the btxL buffer-manager object as a buffer-manager team.

Drawing the buffer objects with solid outlines would imply that the buffer manager contains two fixed buffer objects that exist for the lifetime of the program. By using the slot notation we indicate that, as the program runs, buffer objects will be moved into and out of the buffer manager. Although not shown here, the other buffer-manager objects are decomposed in a similar way.

8.2 MAPPING THE MTU COLLABORATION GRAPH TO CODE

The process of converting the MTU CGs to a program running under Tempo is a straight-forward application of the techniques presented in Chapters 2, 3, and 4. Here is a summary of the important ideas:

- Each team is implemented as a skinny C++ source (.cpp) file containing the team's functions, along with an associated header (.h) file.
- Every process in a CG requires a root function, and the source file for each team contains the root functions for the processes inside it. These root functions call object interface functions, team interface functions, and Tempo's IPC functions.
- Processes within teams must be created by calls to Tempo's create_process() kernel function, and this is handled by the team's initialization function, which is called when the program starts. This function also creates the team's semaphores and calls the initialization functions of the objects and teams nested within the team.
- Callwait connections to teams and objects correspond to skinny C++ function calls.
- IPC structures often map directly to Tempo's IPC functions; for example, semaphore connections are implemented by calling signal_semaphore() and wait_semaphore(), and send connections correspond to calls to Tempo's event queue functions. Sendwait connections are not directly supported by Tempo but can be realized easily by combinations of kernel functions.

The following sections present the skinny C++ code for selected MTU components. (The code for the complete MTU is available over the World Wide Web from the site listed in the Preface.)

8.2.1 The Main Process: MTU Initialization

The root function for the MTU's Main process is shown in Figure 8.8. Main starts the system initialization shown in Figure 8.5 by calling C's init_C() interface function, and then exits.

```
// The root function for the MTU's main process.
void Main()
{
    init_C(); // init the control team
}
```

Figure 8.8 Root function for the MTU's Main process.

8.2.2 The C Team

The code for the C team is shown in Figures 8.9 and 8.10. Figure 8.9 contains interface function `init_C()`. Initialization continues by chaining the call to `init_C()` through to `init_S()` and `init_M()`. After these calls return, `init_C()` creates the ctrl process (see Figure 8.5).

```
// Control (C) team for the MTU

void ctrl_root();

// init_C - initialize this team
void init_C()
{
    Process ctrl;

    init_S(); // init the Status team
    init_M(); // init the Message team
    ctrl = create_process(ctrl_root, 0);
}
```

Figure 8.9 The C team (part 1 of 2).

The root function for the ctrl process is shown in Figure 8.10.

```
// ctrl_root - root function for the ctrl process
//
// This process periodically checks for commands from
// the user. Send-Next and Send-All commands are sent to
// the M team, Freeze/Unfreeze-Status commands are sent
// to the S team, and the Quit command causes the
// system to shutdown in an orderly fashion.

// # of ticks to sleep (about 1 second)
const unsigned int SLEEP_TIME = 19;

void ctrl_root()
{
    char command;

    for(;;) {
        do {
            // sleep for a while before checking for
            // a command
            process_sleep(SLEEP_TIME);
        } while (!command_available());
        command = get_command();
        if ((command == SEND_NEXT) ||
            (command == SEND_ALL))
            give_command_to_M(command);
        else if (command == FREEZE_STATUS)
            give_command_to_S(command);
        else if (command == QUIT) {
            // When a quit command is received, we shut
            // down immediately; i.e., we don't wait for
            // any packets that are moving along the
            // tx paths to be processed.
            // Before returning to DOS, we MUST restore
            // UART interrupt handling to the way it
            // was before the MTU started; otherwise
            // the next UART interrupt that occurs
            // will likely cause the system to crash.
            finalize_L();
            terminate_multitasking();
        } else // unknown command
            CS(cout << command <<
                    " is not a valid command" << endl);
    }
}
```

Figure 8.10 The C team (part 2 of 2).

8.2.3 The M Team

The code for the M team is shown in Figures 8.11 through 8.14. Figure 8.11 contains init_M(), which creates the txM and rxM processes after calling P's *init* function (see Figure 8.5). Figure 8.11 also contains give_command_to_M() (see Figure 8.2). This function copies its argument, a single-character command, and sends it to txM.

```
// Message (M) team for the MTU

Process txM, rxM;
void txM_root(), rxM_root();

// initialize the M team - create the txM and rxM
// processes
void init_M()
{
    init_P();
    txM = create_process(txM_root);
    rxM = create_process(rxM_root);
}

const int COMMAND_QUEUE = 0;

// send a comamnd to the txM process
void give_command_to_M(char command)
{
    char *cmd_buf = NULL;

    CS(cmd_buf = new char);
    if (cmd_buf == NULL)
        panic("give_command_to_M: new failed");
    *cmd_buf = command;
    send(txM, COMMAND_QUEUE, (message)cmd_buf, NO_ACK);
}
```

Figure 8.11 The M team (part 1 of 4).

Notice that give_command_to_M() calls panic() if new is unable to allocate memory for a Tempo message. Function panic(), which is presented in Section 8.2.6, does not return to its caller. Instead, it displays the error message that is passed to it, then shuts down the MTU in an orderly manner.

The root function for the txM process is shown in Figure 8.12. This process loops forever, waiting for Tempo messages that contain commands and processing them. After verifying that it has received a Send-Next or Send-All command, txM calls handle_send_command() to read a message from disk, initialize a new buffer object with the message, and pass the buffer object to the P team.

```
void handle_send_command(char);

// root function for the txM process
void txM_root()
{
    message msg = NULL;
    Process correspondent;
    int queue, ack_queue;
    char cmd;

    for (;;) {
        // Wait for a new command to arrive
        queue = receive(msg, correspondent, ack_queue);
        cmd = *(char *)msg;
        CS(delete msg);
        msg = NULL;

        if ((cmd != SEND_NEXT) || (cmd != SEND_ALL)) {
            CS(cout << "txM: " << cmd
                    << " is not a valid command");
        } else
            handle_send_command(cmd);
    }
}

void handle_send_command(char cmd)
{
    int no_more_msgs;
    char s[80];

    Buffer_object *tx_buf = NULL;

    for (;;) {
        // Get the text for one message
        no_more_msgs = read_msg_from_file(s);
        if (no_more_msgs)
            return;
        // Init a new buffer object with the message
        tx_buf = create_buffer_object(s);
        // Pass the buffer to P
        give_tx_buffer_to_P(tx_buf);
        tx_buf = NULL;
        if (cmd == SEND_NEXT)
            return;
    }
}
```

Figure 8.12 The M team (part 2 of 4).

Figure 8.13 contains the root function for the rxM process. This process loops forever, waiting for buffer objects that contain data packets and processing them. After receiving a buffer object, rxM calls `get_message_data()`, `message_text()`, and `message_length()` to extract the message. It then writes the message to disk and deallocates the buffer object.

```
// root function for the rx process
void rxM_root()
{
    message msg;
    Process correspondent;
    int queue, ack_queue;

    Buffer_object *rx_buf = NULL;
    Message_data *md;
    char *text;
    unsigned int length;

    for(;;) {

        // wait for a new rx buffer object to arrive
        queue = receive(msg, correspondent, ack_queue);
        rx_buf = (Buffer_object *)msg;

        // extract a pointer to the message data from
        // the buffer object
        md = get_message_data(rx_buf);

        // now get the length and the text of the message
        // stored in the message data
        text = message_text(md);
        length = message_length(md);
        write_msg_to_file(text, length);

        // deallocate the buffer object
        destroy_buffer_object(rx_buf);
        rx_buf = NULL;
    }
}
```

Figure 8.13 The M team (part 3 of 4).

Figure 8.14 shows the code for the `give_rx_buffer_to_M()` interface function. This function is passed a buffer object containing a data packet received from the serial link, and sends it to the rxM process.

```
const int GIVE_RX_BUF = 0;   // send rx buffer objects to
                             // this queue

void give_rx_buffer_to_M(Buffer_object *rx_buf)
{
   if (rx_buf == NULL)
      panic("give_rx_buffer_to_M: NULL rx_buf");
   send(rxM, GIVE_RX_BUF, (message)rx_buf, NO_ACK);
}
```

Figure 8.14 The M team (part 4 of 4).

8.2.4 The P Team

The code for the P team is shown in Figures 8.15 through 8.17. Figure 8.15 contains the interface function init_P(), which creates the team's semaphore, requests the btxP and backP buffer-manager objects to initialize themselves, and calls L's *init* function.

```
// Packet (P) team for the MTU

Semaphore ack_sem;   // wait for acks/naks here
int ack_or_nak;      // tells if an ack or nak packet
                     // was received

// initialize the P team
void init_P()
{

   ack_sem = create_semaphore();

   init_btxP();  // init the tx buffer-manager object
   init_backP(); // init the ack buffer-manager object
   init_L();
}
```

Figure 8.15 The P team (part 1 of 3).

Figure 8.16 contains the interface function give_tx_buffer_to_P(). This function is passed a buffer object by M, and is responsible for packetizing the buffer, passing the buffer to L for transmission, and handling the acknowledgement-timeout-retransmit protocol that is described in Chapter 7 and Section 8.1.4.

```
void give_tx_buffer_to_P(Buffer_object *tx_buf)
{
    int status;

    if (tx_buf == NULL)
        panic("give_tx_buffer_to_P: NULL tx_buf");

    // packetize the buffer object
    set_packet_type(tx_buf, DATA);
    set_altbit(tx_buf, flip_altbit());

    // save the tx buffer object in the
    // tx buffer-manager object
    put_buffer_object_in_btxP(tx_buf);

    give_tx_buffer_to_L(tx_buf);
    for (;;) {
        // wait for an ack or nak
        status = wait_semaphore(ack_sem, 100);
        if (status == TIMED_OUT) {
            // timeout, so retransmit
            tx_buf = get_buffer_object_from_btxP();
            give_tx_buffer_to_L(tx_buf);
        } else if (ack_or_nak == NAK) {
            // got a nak, so retransmit
            tx_buf = get_buffer_object_from_btxP();
            give_tx_buffer_to_L(tx_buf);
        } else {
            // got an ack, so deallocate the buffer
            // object & we're done
            destroy_buffer_object_in_btxP;
            return;
        }
    }
}
```

Figure 8.16 The P team (part 2 of 3).

Figure 8.17 contains the interface function `give_rx_buffer_to_P()`, which is passed a buffer object containing a packet that was received over the serial link. This function is responsible for routing buffer objects containing data packets to M, acknowledging message reception, and handling ack/nak packet reception (see steps 15, 18, and 19 in the walkthrough presented in Section 8.1.4).

```
void give_rx_buffer_to_P(Buffer_object *rx_buf)
{
    if (rx_buf == NULL)
        panic(give_rx_buffer_to_P: NULL rx_buf);

    char ptype = packet_type(rx_buf);
    if ((ptype != ACK) || (ptype != NAK) ||
        (ptype !=DATA) || bad_altbit(rx_buf)) {
        // packet header is garbled - send a nak
        Buffer_object *nak_buf =
                        get_buffer_object_from_backP();
        set_packet_type(nak_buf, NAK);
        copy_altbit(rx_buf, nak_buf);
        give_tx_buffer_to_L(nak_buf);
        destroy_buffer_object(rx_buf);
        return;
    }
    if ((ptype == ACK) || (ptype == NAK)) {
        // We received an ack or nak packet.
        // Notify txM only if it is the ack/nak
        // for the last data packet sent.
        if (altbit_matches(rx_buf)) {
            ack_or_nak = ptype;
            signal_semaphore(ack_sem);
        }
        destroy_buffer_object(rx_buf);
        return;
    }
    if (ptype == DATA) {
        // We received a data packet.
        // Send an ack packet in response.
        Buffer_object *ack_buf =
                        get_buffer_object_from_backP();
        set_packet_type(ack_buf, ACK);
        copy_altbit(rx_buf, ack_buf);
        give_tx_buffer_to_L(ack_buf);
        // Now pass the rx buffer object to M
        give_rx_buffer_to_M(rx_buf);
    }
}
```

Figure 8.17 The P team (part 3 of 3).

8.2.5 The L team

The code for the L team is shown in Figures 8.18 and 8.19.

```
// Link (L) team for the MTU

Process rxL;
void rxL_root();

// initialize the L team
void init_L()
{
    // initialize the buffer-manager objects
    init_btxL();
    init_brxL();

    rxL = create_process(rxL_root);

    init_uart_services();
}

// Store buffer object txbuf in the buffer-manager object
void give_tx_buffer_to_L(Buffer_object *txbuf)
{
    if (txbuf == NULL)
        panic("give_tx_buffer_to_L: NULL txbuf");
    put_buffer_object_in_btxL(txbuf);
}

void finalize_L()
{
    shutdown_uart_interrupts();
}
```

Figure 8.18 The L team (part 1 of 2).

Figure 8.18 contains the interface function `init_L()`, which asks the btxL and brxL buffer-manager objects and the UART Services team to initialize themselves and creates the rxL process. Figure 8.18 also contains interface function, `give_tx_buffer_to_L()`, which passes its argument (a pointer to a buffer object that has been passed to L for transmission) to the btxL buffer-manager object.

The root function for the rxL process is shown in Figure 8.19. The process loops forever, waiting for new packets to arrive in brxL and passing them to the P team.

```
// The UART ISR (which is defined in another file) and the
// rxL process have a producer/consumer relationship,
// with the brxL buffer manager serving as the bounded
// buffer between them.  The ISR produces packets from the
// frames received by the UART (see the rx FSM).  Each
// packet is placed in a dynamically allocated buffer
// object, and buffer objects are stored in brxL.
// The rxL process consumes buffer objects by removing
// them from the buffer manager and passing them to
// the P team.

// root function for the rxL process
void rxL_root()
{
    Buffer_object *rx_buf = NULL;
    int queue;

    for (;;) {
        // wait for a new packet to arrive
        queue = wait();
        rx_buf = remove_buffer_object_from_brxL();
        give_rx_buffer_to_P(rx_buf);
        rx_buf = NULL;
    }
}
```

Figure 8.19 The L team (part 2 of 2).

8.2.6 The panic() Function

The M, P and L teams create buffer objects dynamically. What should a team do if it is unable to allocate a buffer object at run-time? Several MTU functions expect to be passed pointers to buffer objects. What should a function do if it passed a null pointer?

The simplest approach is to consider these to be unrecoverable errors; that is, if one of these errors occurs, the MTU should not attempt to continue operating. Instead, the MTU provides a function called panic() (see Figure 8.20), which is called by processes when they detect an unrecoverable error. This functions displays its argument (a character string that typically identifies the nature of the error), then shuts down the MTU in an orderly manner.

```
// Print error message err, then shut down the MTU.
void panic(char *err)
{
    CS(cout << err << endl);
    finalize_L();
    terminate_multitasking();
}
```

Figure 8.20 The panic() function.

8.2.7 Data Structures for Messages and Packets

How should messages and packets be coded? Readers with object-oriented programming experience will realize that they could be implemented as C++ classes. We haven't done this because we feel that C++ class design is a sufficiently complex topic that it would draw attention away from the real-time issues that are the focus of this book, so we will stick with the programming conventions introduced in Chapters 2, 3, and 4. Messages and packets can be programmed as C/C++ data structures and a set of functions that manipulate them (these functions are described in Section 8.2.8).

P must be able to distinguish three different types of packets: data packets (which contain messages) and ack and nak packets (which contain no message data). To do this, each packet needs a packet header that identifies the packet type.

The alternating-bit protocol is used to avoid the possibility of a late-arriving ack packet being misinterpreted as an ack for a new message. Every packet has an alternating-bit field in its header that takes one of two possible values, 0 or 1. This field in an ack or nak packet has the same value as the alternating-bit field in the data packet it acknowledges. The value is switched on alternate, new data packets (*not* counting retransmissions). When an ack or nak packet is received, its alternating-bit field is compared to the field in the outstanding data packet and if there is no match, the ack or nak is ignored. The name of the protocol suggests that the field should be a bit, but for our purposes it is easier to use a character and alternate the values stored in the byte between characters '0' and '1'.

This suggests the following data structure for a packet header:

```
struct Packet_header {
    char type; // packet type: data, ack, or nak
    char altbit; // for alternating-bit protocol
};
// packet types
const char ACK = 'A';
const char NAK = 'N';
const char DATA = 'D';
```

Data packets store messages in a `Message_data` structure:

```
const int MAX_MSG_LEN = 80;

struct Message_data {
    unsigned int size;      // # of chars in message
    char text[MAX_MSG_LEN]; // message text
};
```

The message can consist of up to MAX_MSG_LEN characters and is stored in array text; the size field records the length of the message.

Recall from Section 8.1.6 that data packets are stored in buffer objects. There is no need to declare separate data structures for data packets and buffer objects—instead, we declare the buffer object structure to have the format of a data packet:

```
struct Buffer_object { // holds a data packet
    Packet_header ph;   // header
    Message_data msg;   // message
};
```

Ack and nak packets have the same header format as a data packet, but they are smaller —they do not contain a Message_data structure:

```
struct Ack_nak_packet {
    Packet_header ph;
};
```

8.2.8 Implementing Buffer Objects

The code for the functions that manipulate buffer objects is shown in Figures 8.21 through 8.25. Figure 8.21 shows create_buffer_object(), which allocates a buffer object large enough to hold a data packet and initializes the Message_data part of the object with character string msg.

```
// Creates a new buffer object by allocating space for a
// complete data packet. The message data field inside the
// buffer is initialized by copying up to the first
// MAX_MSG_LEN characters from character string msg.
// The terminating null in msg is not copied into the
// packet. Returns a pointer to the buffer object.

Buffer_object *create_buffer_object(char msg[])
{
    CS(Buffer_object *p = new Buffer_object);
    if (p == NULL)
        panic("create_buffer_object: new failed");
    CS(unsigned len = strlen(msg));
    if (len > MAX_MSG_LEN) // use only the first
                           // MAX_MSG_LEN chars
        len = MAX_MSG_LEN;
    p->msg.size = len;
    CS(strncpy(p->msg.text, msg, len));
    return p;
}
```

Figure 8.21 Buffer object functions (part 1 of 5).

Function `get_message_data()` (see Figure 8.22) performs the depacketize operation. It simply returns a pointer to the `Message_data` structure contained inside a data packet. Function `message_text()` returns a pointer to the characters stored in a `Message_data` structure. Function `message_length()` returns the length of the message stored in a `Message_data` structure.

```
// Returns a pointer to the message data structure
// in the buffer object pointed to by p.

Message_data *get_message_data(Buffer_object *p)
{
    if (p == NULL)
        panic("get_message_data: NULL pointer");
    return &(p->msg);
}

// Returns a pointer to the message text in the
// message data structure pointed to by md.
// This character string is NOT null-terminated.
char *message_text(Message_data *md)
{
    if (md == NULL)
        panic("message_text: NULL pointer");
    return md->text;
}

// Returns the length of the message stored in the
// message data structure pointed to by md.
unsigned int message_length(Message_data *md)
{
    if (md == NULL)
        panic("message_length: NULL pointer");
    return md->size;
}
```

Figure 8.22 Buffer object functions (part 2 of 5).

Figure 8.23 contains functions to read and write the packet type and alternating-bit fields in a packet's header.

Function packet_size(), shown in Figure 8.24, returns the size, in bytes, of the packet that is stored in the specified buffer object. For data packets, this value includes the length of the message stored in the packet.

Function read_byte_from_packet() (Figure 8.24) allows buffer objects to be accessed as a contiguous block of bytes. It returns the value of the specified byte in the packet.

```
// Sets the packet type member of the buffer object
// pointed to by p to "type".
void set_packet_type(Buffer_object *p, char type)
{
    if (p == NULL)
        panic("set_packet_type: NULL pointer");
    if ((type == DATA) || (type == ACK) || (type == NAK)) {
        p->ph.type = type;
    } else {
        CS(cout << "set_packet_type: bad packet type"
                << type << endl);
        panic("");
    }
}

// Returns the type of packet in the buffer object
// pointed to by p.
char packet_type(Buffer_object *p)
{
    if (p == NULL)
        panic("packet_type: NULL pointer");
    return p->ph.type;
}

// Sets the alternating-bit member of the packet in
// the buffer object pointed to by p to "altbit".
void set_altbit(Buffer_object *p, char altbit)
{
    if (p == NULL)
        panic("set_altbit: NULL pointer");
    if ((altbit == '0') || (altbit == '1')) {
        p->ph.altbit = altbit;
    } else {
        CS(cout << "set_altbit: bad altbit value "
                << altbit << endl);
        panic("");
    }
}

// Returns the alternating-bit value of the packet
// in the buffer object pointed to by p.
char altbit(Buffer_object *p)
{
    if (p == NULL)
        panic("altbit: NULL pointer");
    return ((Buffer_object *)p)->ph.altbit;
}
```

Figure 8.23 Buffer object functions (part 3 of 5).

```
// Returns the size, in bytes, of the packet in the
// buffer object pointed to by p. If p points to a data
// packet, the size includes the length of the message
// stored in the packet.
unsigned int packet_size(Buffer_object *p)
{
    if (p == NULL)
        panic("packet_size: NULL pointer");
    if (p->ph.type == ACK)
        return (sizeof(Ack_nak_packet));
    if (p->ph.type == NAK)
        return (sizeof(Ack_nak_packet));
    if (p->ph.type == DATA)
        return (sizeof(Packet_header) +
                sizeof(p->msg.size) +
                p->msg.size);
    CS(cout << "packet_size: bad packet type: "
            << p->ph.type << endl);
    panic("");
}

// Returns byte "n" from the packet in the buffer
// object pointed to by p. Byte 0 is the first byte
// in the packet, byte 1 is the second byte, etc.
char read_byte_from_buffer(Buffer_object *p,
                           unsigned int n)
{
    if (p == NULL)
        panic("read_byte_from_buffer: NULL pointer");
    if (n >= packet_size(p)) {
        CS(cout << "read_byte_from_buffer: "
                << "can''t read byte " << n);
        panic("")
    }
    if ((packet_type(p) == ACK) || (packet_type(p) == NAK)
        || (packet_type(p) == DATA)) {
        char ch = ((char *)p)[n];
        return ch;
    } else {
        CS(cout << "read_byte_from_buffer: "
                << "bad packet type" << endl);
        panic("")
    }
}
```

Figure 8.24 Buffer object functions (part 4 of 5).

Function `destroy_buffer_object()` (Figure 8.25) deallocates buffer objects by using the C++ `delete` operator to return the buffer's memory to the system.

```
// Deallocate the buffer object pointed to by p,
// returning its memory to the system.
void destroy_buffer_object(Buffer_object *p)
{
    if (p == NULL)
        panic("destroy_buffer_object: NULL pointer");
    CS(delete p);
}
```

Figure 8.25 Buffer object functions (part 5 of 5).

8.2.9 Frames

The smallest unit of transmission and reception seen by the software is the character (the line actually sees bits, but these are handled by UARTs). Characters are received and transmitted through UARTs in an interrupt-driven fashion. L only transmits characters when it has a complete packet to transmit, and a transmission interrupt is generated by the UART after it transmits each character. L is always ready to receive characters (except for short periods when interrupts are disabled while an ISR runs, or during the update of some data object shared between an ISR and a process). Interrupts signaling the arrival of characters may occur at any time. Packet transmission and reception occur on a character-by-character basis, and packet lengths vary, so how does L determine when it has finished receiving one packet and started receiving the next?

Figure 8.26 shows how. L wraps each packet in a *frame* by adding framing characters to either end of the packet. STX (start-transmission) denotes that beginning of a new frame and ETX (end-transmission) indicates when the frame has finished. On the reception end, L detects the start and end of a new frame by checking the incoming character stream for these framing characters.

Figure 8.26 also shows what happens if the STX and ETX characters are contained within the packet. In order that they not be treated incorrectly by the reception side as false start-transmission or end-transmission characters, the transmission side inserts an *escape sequence* into the frame when it detects either of these characters in the packet. STX is converted into the two-character sequence DLE/STX (DLE is the data-link-escape character); ETX is converted into DLE/ETX. To handle the case where DLE is in the packet (and so should be treated as packet data, not the escape character), the transmission side replaces DLE with the two-character sequence DLE/DLE. It is the responsibility of the reception side to recognize these escape sequences and convert them into their single-character equivalents.

There is no need to build a complete frame data structure (containing a packet) in memory prior to transmitting a frame. Instead, frames can be built as transmission proceeds. On the transmission side, STX is output to the UART before the first character in the packet is sent, and ETX is transmitted after the last character in the packet. While the packet is transmitted, escape sequences are inserted into the outgoing stream of characters as required. Similarly, on the reception side, entire frames are not stored in memory. As a new frame is received the framing characters are discarded; only the contents of the packet are saved.

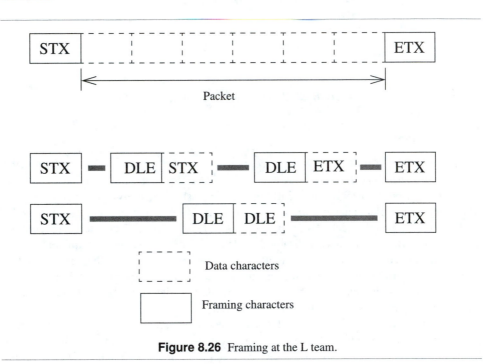

Figure 8.26 Framing at the L team.

8.2.10 Handling Framing Errors

Because the MTU must support reliable communication of messages over an unreliable serial link, it includes an acknowledgment-timeout-retransmission protocol to provide detection and recovery from communication failures. Figure 8.27 shows the different kinds of framing errors that can occur. L does not check the contents of received packets in detail to see if they have been garbled by the link during transmission. It only checks framing characters (and discards them). An error at this level results in the discarding of the entire received frame without any other action or warning (recovery relies on timeout and retransmission by P on the other computer). Specifically, *no naks* are sent by this team.

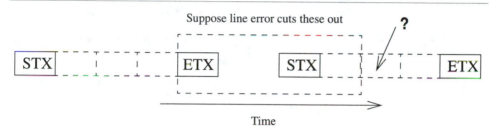

Time

If the character located at ? in the second frame is:

- ETX, then the 1st packet will be received correctly but the 2nd one discarded
- STX, then the 1st packet will be discarded and the 2nd one received incorrectly
- any other char (except the second DLE of a DLE-DLE sequence), then the 1st and 2nd packets will be received as one packet incorrectly
- the second DLE of a DLE-DLE sequence, then both packets will be discarded

Figure 8.27 Framing errors.

Figure 8.28 shows the finite state machine for receiving frames and detecting framing errors. Because incoming frames are converted into packets as they are received, instead of being stored in memory for processing by the rxL process, this state machine must be implemented in the UART ISR. Each time a character reception interrupt happens, the ISR checks the current state and the newly received character. It performs the appropriate action and updates the current state as required.

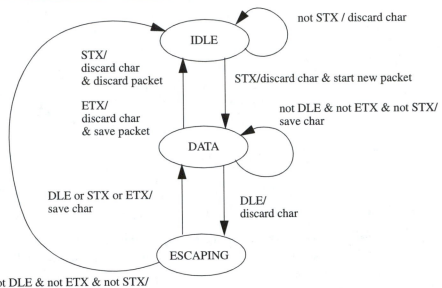

Note: TX state machine is similar, except instead of stripping STX, DLE, and ETX characters, it inserts them into the data stream

Figure 8.28 Framing state machine (reception).

For two of the cases listed in Figure 8.27, an incorrect packet will be received by L and passed to P. Furthermore, L cannot detect if a line error has garbled the packet's header or message data. Certain errors (an illegal packet type or alternating-bit value) will be discovered in P and result in the transmission of a nak packet, but it is still possible for incorrect messages to be received and passed to M.

How can we increase the level of error detection? We could add support for checksums or cyclic redundancy check codes (CRC codes) to L. This would find many of the errors that garble packets, but not all. Anything beyond this would require L to have too much detailed knowledge of what is supposed to be in packets; so further error checking would have to be added to the P and M teams, requiring additional information to be stored in the packet header.

8.2.11 The UART ISR

Because frames are received and transmitted by the UART on a character-by-character basis, and because character I/O is interrupt-driven, it is the ISR's responsibility to handle the frame reception and transmission protocols. Figure 8.29 shows how the UART ISR is organized. Logically, the framing state machines described in Section 8.2.10 are contained in objects inside the ISR. Each time it runs, the ISR determines whether it was triggered by a reception or a transmission interrupt and then calls the corresponding state machine object. This object updates its current state and performs the actions associated with the state transition by calling the appropriate buffer-manager object.

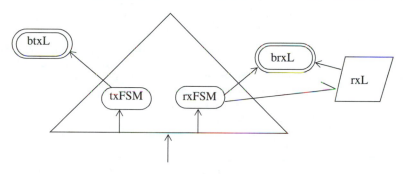

Figure 8.29 Inside the UART ISR.

The UART ISR, which is shown in Figure 8.30, handles two of the four types of interrupts generated by the 8250 family of UARTs (the 8250, 8250A, and 8250-B):

- Received Data Available (the UART has received a new character from the serial link)
- Transmitter Holding Register Empty (the UART can accept a new character for transmission)

Received line status interrupts and modem status interrupts are not supported.

Notice that the ISR does not exit immediately after servicing the interrupt. Instead, the body of the ISR consists of a loop, and one pending interrupt is handled each time through the loop. Why do things this way? Remember that, internally, the 8250 has four independent, prioritized interrupt sources. While one interrupt (such as received data available) is being serviced, the state of the UART may change (for example, the transmitter holding register becomes empty) so now a second interrupt is pending. In theory, this should cause the processor to be interrupted a second time (after interrupts have been reenabled at the processor and EOI sent to the PIC). However, because of the way the PIC is programmed in a PC-compatible machine, and because different members of the 8250 family assert their interrupt output signal in different ways, the PIC may not recognize the second interrupt request, the processor will not be interrupted, and the pending interrupt will not be serviced. So the ISR contains a loop. After an interrupt is serviced the ISR checks if a further interrupt is pending, and if so, services that interrupt. This ensures that no interrupt requests are lost, regardless of which version of the 8250 is installed in the computer.

```
void interrupt uartisr(...)
{
    unsigned char temp;
    char ch;

    outportb(PIC_CMD, EOI);
    temp = int_source();
    do {
        // rxFSM() handles the finite state machine for
        // receiving packets, while txFSM() handles the
        // state machine for transmitting packets.
        // Determine the interrupt source and call the
        // appropriate FSM function.
        if (temp == RDAI) {
            // received data available
            ch = inportb(RBR) & 0x7f;
            if (rxFSM(ch))
                // tell the rxL process that a new packet
                // is available for pickup
                signal(rxL, NEW_PACKET);
        } else if (temp == THREI) {
            // transmitter holding register empty
            txFSM();
        }
        temp = int_source();
    } while ((temp & 0x01) == INT_PENDING);
}
```

Figure 8.30 The UART ISR.

Figure 8.31 shows the code for the framing state machine of Figure 8.28. Notice the calls to buffer-manager object brxL to start a new packet, add received characters to the packet, finish reception of the packet, and discard the packet when an error occurs.

```
// rx FSM - state machine for frame reception

static States state = IDLE_STATE;

// rxFSM - update reception framing state machine.
//          ch contains a copy of the char that has
//          just been received by the UART.
//          Returns 1 when the last character of a
//          complete packet has been received;
//          otherwise, returns 0.

int rxFSM(char ch)
{
    if (state == IDLE_STATE) {
        if (ch == STX){  // receiving a new packet
            state = DATA_STATE;
            start_new_buffer_object();
        }
    } else if (state == DATA_STATE) {
        if (ch == STX) {
            state = IDLE_STATE;
            discard_packet();
        } else if (ch == ETX) {
            state = IDLE_STATE;
            received_complete_packet();
            return 1;
        }else if (ch == DLE) {
            state = ESCAPING_STATE;
        } else {  // not DLE && not ETX && not STX
            put_char_in_buffer_object(ch);
        }
    } else if (state == ESCAPING_STATE) {
        if ((ch == DLE) || (ch == STX)
                        || (ch == ETX)) {
            state = DATA_STATE;
            put_char_in_buffer_object(ch);
        } else { // not DLE && not ETX && not STX
            state = IDLE_STATE;
            discard_packet();
        }
    }
    return 0;
}
```

Figure 8.31 The reception framing state machine.

Figure 8.32 contains the code for the transmission framing state machine.

```
// tx FSM - state machine for frame transmission

static States state = IDLE_STATE;

// txFSM - update transmission framing state machine.

void txFSM()
{
   static char ch;
   int done;

   if (state == IDLE_STATE) {
      txchar(STX);
      state = DATA_STATE;
    } else if (state == DATA_STATE) {
       done = get_char_from_buffer_object(ch);
       if (!done) {
          if ((ch == DLE) || (ch == ETX) || (ch == STX)) {
             // save char (ch is static) and send DLE
             txchar(DLE);
             state = ESCAPING_STATE;
          } else {  // not DLE && not ETX && not STX
             txchar(ch);
          }
       } else { // packet has been sent
          txchar(ETX);
          state = IDLE_STATE;
          if (!remove_buffer_object_from_btxL()) {
             // There are no unsent packets in btxL,
             // so there will be no further tx
             // interrupts from the UART until a new
             // tx buffer object is placed in the
             // tx buffer-manager object.
             tx_is_now_idle();
          }
       }
    } else if (state == ESCAPING_STATE) {
       // send saved char
       txchar(ch);
       state = DATA_STATE;
    }
}
```

Figure 8.32 The transmission framing state machine.

8.2.12 Buffer-Manager Teams

Figure 8.33 contains the code for the btxP buffer-manager object.

```
// btxP - buffer-manager object for tx buffer objects

Buffer_object *btx;

void init_btxP()
{
   btx = NULL;
}

void put_buffer_object_in_btxP(Buffer_object *tx_buf)
{
   if (tx_buf == NULL)
      panic("put_buffer_object_in_btxP: NULL tx_buf");
   btx = tx_buf;
}

Buffer_object *get_buffer_object_from_btxP()
{
    return btx;
}

void destroy_buffer_object_in_btxP()
{
    destroy_buffer_object(btx);
    btx = NULL;
}
```

Figure 8.33 Buffer-manager object btxP.

Figure 8.34 contains the code for the backP buffer-manager object.

```
// backP - buffer-manager object for ack buffer objects

Buffer_object *back;

void init_backP()
{
    // Allocate a new packet for acks and naks.
    // Cast the pointer returned by new so that the
    // packet can be treated as a buffer object.
    CS(ap = (Buffer_object *) new Ack_nak_packet);
    if (ap == NULL)
        panic("init_backP: new failed");
    back = ap;
}

Buffer_object *get_buffer_object_from_backP()
{
    return back;
}
```

Figure 8.34 Buffer-manager object backP.

The code for the brxL buffer-manager object is shown in Figures 8.35 and 8.36.

```
// brxL - buffer-manager object for rx buffer objects

// The buffer-manager object holds up to two rx buffer
// objects
Buffer_object* buf[2];

// When curbuf == 0 or 1, received characters are stored
// in buf[curbuf].
int curbuf;

// buf[pickup] is the next buffer object that should be
// given to the rxL process.
int pickup;

// rx buffer objects are filled one character at a time,
// so we need to keep track of how many characters have
// been received.
int pos;

void init_brxL()
{
    // initialize buf with two empty rx buffer objects
    if ((buf[0] = create_buffer_object("\0")) == NULL)
        panic("init_brxL: can''t create rx buffer");
    if ((buf[1] = create_buffer_object("\0")) == NULL)
        panic("init_brxL: can''t create rx buffer");
    curbuf = 0;
}


// After this function returns, the next received
// character will be stored at the start of the rx buffer
// object in buf[curbuf].
void start_new_buffer_object()
{
    short saved_flags = disable_ints();
    pos = 0;
    restore_flags(saved_flags);
}
```

Figure 8.35 Buffer-manager object brxL (part 1 of 2).

```
// This function is called when the UART ISR determines
// that the rx buffer object in buf[curbuf] is invalid.
// As long as this function is always followed by a call
// to start_new_buffer_object(), this function doesn't
// have to do anything.
void discard_packet()
{
}


// Store ch in the rx buffer object in buf[curbuf].
void put_char_in_buffer_object(char ch)
{
    short saved_flags = disable_ints();
    write_byte_to_buffer(buf[curbuf], pos, ch);
    pos++;  // position of next char to fetch
    restore_flags(saved_flags);
}


// Called when a complete packet has been stored in
// buf[curbuf].
// Flips curbuf to point to an empty buffer object.
void received_complete_packet()
{
    short saved_flags = disable_ints();
    pickup = curbuf;
    // see remove_buffer_object_from_brxL()
    curbuf = 1 - curbuf;
    restore_flags(saved_flags);
}


// Removes a full rx buffer object from the buffer
// manager, and replaces it with an empty buffer object
Buffer_object* remove_buffer_object_from_brxL()
{
    short saved_flags = disable_ints();
    Buffer_object* rx = buf[pickup];
    if ((buf[pickup] =
                create_buffer_object("\0")) == NULL) {
        restore_flags(saved_flags);
        panic("remove_buffer_object_from_brxL:
                can''t create rx buffer");
    }
    restore_flags(saved_flags);
    return rx;
}
```

Figure 8.36 Buffer-manager object brxL (part 2 of 2).

The code for the btxL buffer-manager object is shown in Figures 8.37 and 8.38.

```
// btxL - buffer-manager object for tx buffer objects

// The buffer-manager object holds up to two tx buffer
// objects
Buffer_object* buf[2];

// The next tx buffer object will be stored in
// buf[nextbuf]
int nextbuf;

// When curbuf == 0 or 1, buf[curbuf] is the tx buffer
// that is currently being transmitted.  When no tx buffer
// is being transmitted, curbuf == -1.
int curbuf;

// tx buffer objects are transmitted one character at a
// time,so we need to keep track of how many characters
// have been transmitted.
int pos;

void init_btxL()
{
   buf[0] = NULL;
   buf[1] = NULL;
   nextbuf = 0;
   curbuf = -1;
}
// If the tx buffer object in buf[curbuf] contains unsent
// characters, returns 0, with the next character to send
// in ch.
// If all characters in buf[curbuf] have been sent,
// returns 1, and ch is undefined.
int get_char_from_buffer_object(char&  ch)
{
   int done;

   short saved_flags = disable_ints();
   done = (pos == packet_size(buf[curbuf]));
   if (!done) {
      ch = read_byte_from_buffer(buf[curbuf], pos);
      pos++;  // position of next char to fetch
   }
   restore_flags(saved_flags);
   return done;
}
```

Figure 8.37 Buffer-manager object btxL (part 1 of 2).

```
// After the tx buffer object in buf[curbuf] has been
// transmitted, call this function to remove the buffer
// object from the buffer manager.
// Returns 1 if the buffer manager contains another tx
// buffer object that has not yet been transmitted;
// otherwise, returns 0.
int remove_buffer_object_from_btxL()
{
    short saved_flags = disable_ints();
    buf[curbuf] = NULL;
    curbuf = 1 - curbuf;
    if (buf[curbuf] == NULL) {
        // there are no other tx buffer objects stored
        // in the buffer manager.
        curbuf = -1;
        restore_flags(saved_flags);
        return 0;
    } else {
        // buf[curbuf] contains an unsent tx buffer object.
        pos = 0;
        restore_flags(saved_flags);
        return 1;
    }
}


void put_buffer_object_in_btxL(Buffer_object* tx_buf)
{
    if (tx_buf == NULL)
        panic("put_buffer_object_in_btxL: NULL tx_buf");
    short saved_flags = disable_ints();
    if (buf[nextbuf] != NULL)
        panic("put_buffer_object_in_btxL: no room");
    buf[nextbuf] = tx_buf;
    // Now check to see if the UART transmitter is idle.
    // If it is, force a tx interrupt, to start
    // transmission of the packet in the buffer.
    if (tx_is_idle()) {
        // need to remember which buffer is being
        // transmitted
        curbuf = nextbuf;
        pos = 0;
        tx_is_now_busy();
        enable_tx_interrupt();
    }
    nextbuf = 1 - nextbuf;
    restore_flags(saved_flags);
}
```

Figure 8.38 Buffer-manager object btxL (part 2 of 2).

8.3 BUILDING THE MTU IN STAGES

Novice real-time system developers often find that testing and debugging a real-time program is a tedious and time-consuming process, even when considerable effort has been
spent designing the system prior to coding. Most software engineers and computer scien-
tists realize the importance of coding and testing a system's modules separately (that is,
performing so-called unit testing of modules), followed by integration testing of completed modules as they are linked together. Our students, while working on MTU-scale
projects, are often surprised when they first link their collection of individually tested
teams into a complete program, only to find that suddenly nothing works. The reason for
this goes back to the fundamental nature of real-time systems: They must respond to
unpredictable stimuli. The programmer cannot predict when events will arrive from the
environment (or when expected events will fail to arrive) relative to the state of the program's execution. Interrupts occur, ISRs run and signal processes (making them ready to
run), and processes are scheduled according to their priorities. The reality is that a real-
time system never runs exactly the same way twice. Bugs mysteriously disappear and then
reappear, much to the frustration of programmer (especially as the deadline for shipping
the system looms).

Despite this, constructing a correct real-time program need not be a trial-and-error
exercise. The UCMs that were developed earlier can assist us at this stage. In Chapter 6,
we followed these two design principles: *Let the paths tell you about the processes* and *let
the maps guide you to the wiring*. To this we add a programming principle: *Let the maps
guide the development*. Traditional top-down and bottom-up approaches to program
development focus on developing each module independently and defer working on the
system as a whole until the end. For real-time systems, we instead recommend using a
staged approach based on UCMs, in which we implement complete paths through a set of
incomplete components. First, we code and test a prototype to exercise only the critical
paths that span the entire system. (We often refer to this testing as *confidence testing*,
because it reminds us that the goal of the tests is to obtain confidence that the paths are
correct.) Next, we refine the prototypes to implement the minor paths and perform more
confidence testing. The idea is that we should concentrate first on getting things working
along critical paths and not on making components complete. To make the behavior of the
prototypes predictable and repeatable, sources of external stimuli (interrupts, timeouts)
are not coupled into the prototypes until late in the process.

We will now sketch how to use this approach to build the MTU. Figure 8.39 shows
two map-based MTU prototypes. Notice that the UART/PIC hardware and software, the
UART ISR, and the timed semaphore are not included in the stage 1 and stage 2 MTU prototypes. Without these, the behavior of the program is completely predictable: Knowing
the process priorities, we can determine when each process will run. Even though it consists of multiple processes, the program as a whole (with the kernel) is simply a sequential
piece of code that will run the same way each time it is executed.

The prototypes do not use the serial link; instead, one copy of the MTU running on
a single computer serves as both the local and remote computer. To do this, the L team

provides loopback; packets passed to L for transmission are "received" by the rxL process in the same team.

Before building the first prototype, we code and test the buffer objects and buffer-manager objects. These objects are not autonomous; that is, they are executed sequentially under the control of a process or an ISR, so they can be tested using traditional unit testing techniques for sequential code. The completed objects can now be used during the development of the MTU prototypes.

In Figure 8.39(a) we show the stage 1 prototype that sends a single message to exercise the main transmission and reception path that spans the M, P, and L teams. The tx path is coupled to the rx path in L, so in a correctly operating prototype, rxL will deliver to P a buffer object that is identical to the one that is passed by txM to L. It is the responsibility of the P team to verify that the received buffer is the same as the one that was passed to L. Notice that a UART-proxy team substitutes for the UART Services team and UART ISR from Figure 8.2. This team simply copies a buffer object from btxL to brxL and then signals the rxL process.

Figure 8.39(b) shows the stage 2 prototype to exercise the paths for sending and receiving acknowledgments. The M team is complete and the P team is complete except for timeouts. UART support and the ISR are still missing from the L team, so packets sent for transmission are looped back to the P team through the UART-proxy team. To test nak processing, we can modify rxL so that it garbles the header of the received data packet. After rxL passes the garbled packet to P, P should respond by sending a nak packet to L.

After these prototypes have been tested, we complete P by adding timeouts (the interface function called by txM will now perform a timed wait on the semaphore). Timeouts can be exercised by decoupling the tx and rx paths in L, so that packets sent to L for transmission are simply discarded.

We are now ready to complete the MTU, adding the additional components shown in Figure 8.2. The ISR is added to the L team and the UART device driver is connected to the system. Final confidence testing now requires two computers connected by the serial link, each running a copy of the MTU.

(a) Stage 1

(b) Stage 2

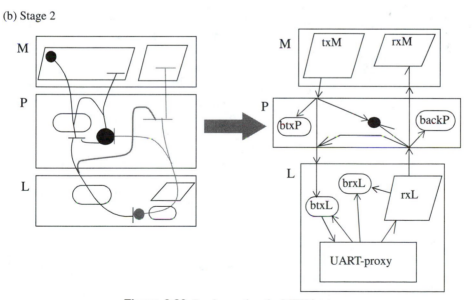

Figure 8.39 Implementing the MTU in stages.

8.4 SUMMARY

In this chapter we have

- Presented CGs for the complete MTU.
- Described the detailed design of messages, packets, buffer objects, and buffer-manager teams.
- Explained how packets are transmitted and received using frames and described how reception errors are handled.
- Described the code for selected components in the MTU and provided a framework for understanding the code for the complete MTU.
- Described how to build the MTU by using UCMs to guide the incremental coding and testing of a set of prototypes.

CHAPTER 9

Structurally Dynamic Systems

*T*his chapter shows how to use the same design notations as in Chapter 5, with some extensions, for systems that are structurally dynamic in a large-scale, coarse-grained fashion. The extensions are not major, but the issues are sufficiently deep that introducing the extensions earlier would likely have confused rather than enlightened the reader, by giving the misleading impression that the extensions are needed in all situations where the programming technology does things dynamically.

The notations of this chapter are both uniquely expressive about structurally dynamic systems and nonstandard, compared to other software design notations, including emerging standards such as UML. However, the nonstandardness adds something that is missing rather than conflicting with something already there, so the concepts are complementary and portable.

9.1 THE APPROACH IN A NUTSHELL

Chapter 1 said that structurally dynamic systems continually rewire themselves as they run and so may be viewed in terms of wiring diagrams that change over time (morph) on the same time scale as ordinary operation. It also said that, although this view is valid and provides a good starting point for thinking about the issues, it is not very practically useful because it does not scale up; too many diagrams are required, and important information is missing. This chapter develops a different view. As a starting point, Figure 9.1 identifies two distinct types of structural dynamics: (a) full structural dynamics, in which both components and wires change, and (b) partial structural dynamics, in which only wires change. Both may be treated with the general techniques to be presented in this chapter, but the partial case may sometimes benefit from more specialized treatment. We shall develop the general techniques first, as if they were the only ones, and then show where specialized treatment may be useful.

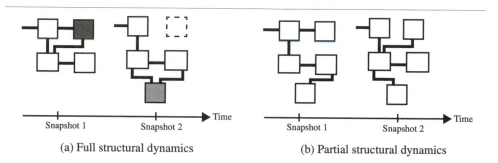

(a) Full structural dynamics   (b) Partial structural dynamics

Figure 9.1 Morphing wiring diagrams.

The key to finding a different way than morphing wiring diagrams of representing fully structurally dynamic systems is realizing that components in them that produce the morphing effect by appearing and disappearing have two possible forms, one as operational units and the other as data. We shall call such components *dynamic components (DCs)*. In the data form, DCs may be stored and passed around, just like any other type of data (whether this is done literally, as with Java byte code, or figuratively, as with Tempo process identifiers, is irrelevant to the principle). Wiring diagrams show only one of the forms of DCs explicitly—the operational form—and leave out the data form. Morphing is *caused* by DCs being created/destroyed and passed around *in data form*. This may be called *assembly*, suggesting finding the pieces of a puzzle and putting them together (not assembly language programming). Leaving the data form of DCs out of the picture leaves us with no means of describing assembly explicitly.

The solution of this chapter for full structural dynamics has the following parts:

- Extend the component notation to express the existence of DCs in two forms, as operational units and as data.
- Avoid explicit representation of the DCs themselves, to avoid the need for diagrams that morph. Instead, provide notations for organizational *slots*, where DCs may become operational units, and storage *pools*, where DCs may be held as data.
- Extend the CG and UCM notations with notations to indicate creating, destroying, saving, retrieving, and moving the data form of DCs and to show transforming this form into the operational form and vice versa.
- Use fixed CGs, with slots and pools wired in as fixed components, and fixed UCMs, with slots and pools associated with paths in the same way as fixed components, to

imply structural dynamics by indicating the creation and movement of DCs as data (no morphing).

The notational extensions for this purpose are both simple and expressive, as will now be explained.

9.2 FULL STRUCTURAL DYNAMICS

9.2.1 Additional Component Notations

Figure 9.2 summarizes the additional component notations needed for both CGs and UCMs. The places where DCs may exist in their two different forms are indicated by notation elements called *slots* and *pools*.

Slots are places in which DCs may be operational. Slots are treated as ordinary components of design diagrams, having connections in CGs and responsibilities in UCMs. In this way, they define *roles* for DCs. Any DC capable of filling the role may occupy a slot. Slots are of the same types as fixed components and are shown with the same notation, except for dashed outlines to symbolize the idea that they are not necessarily always occupied. When occupied, slots are, in effect, fixed components (the DC *becomes* the slot); otherwise they are nonoperational empty holes in the system structure.

Pools are places in which DCs may be stored as data. The notation does not by itself imply any particular storage/retrieval mechanism (for example, first-in-first-out), nor does it imply that all DCs in a pool must be of the same type. Such details must be indicated by other means in a particular context.

DCs themselves are not shown but left implicit.

Fixed components, having no data form (at least not outside initialization/finalization phases), cannot normally appear in either pools or slots (with one exception, aliasing—see Section 9.2.6).

These notations do not, by themselves, indicate if or when slots or pools are occupied or empty. This is left to CGs or UCMs.

Slots indicate places where DCs may appear   Pools indicate places where DCs may
as operational units.   be held as data.

Figure 9.2 Component notations for structural dynamics.

Caveats

Do not assume that the existence of these notations requires them to be used for everything that is done dynamically in programs. Nothing could be farther from the truth. They should be used only when structural dynamics is so large scale and coarse grained that the system picture cannot be understood without expressing it. As we have seen many times in this book, small-scale, fine-grained structural dynamics is often best left as programming detail.

Distinguish this usage of the term *pool* from another usage that is relatively common in the computer field, one that expresses the idea of a *service pool* containing many active components, ready to perform service (for example, a service pool of printer-driver processes). A service pool can be interacted with immediately, whereas a pool of the type indicated in Figure 9.2 cannot. Furthermore, a service pool is not necessarily structurally dynamic, although it may be. In the notation of this book, a service pool would be represented by either a stack of fixed processes or a stack of process slots with an associated pool of the type indicated in Figure 9.2.

Do not use the pool notation to represent queues associated with IPC connections in CGs. Remember that such queues are implied by the connection notations and do not require specific representation. This misuse is easy to slip into because pools can be legitimately used to represent process queues, as in the service-pool example of the previous paragraph. However, such process queues are in the application program, not in Tempo.

9.2.2 Extensions to the CG Notation

Pools are just fixed components that hold DCs as data, so interactions with them are shown with ordinary connections, with DCs as data parameters.

The movement of DCs as data into or out of slots is indicated with special dashed arrows pointing at them that are not literally *connections*. The arrows *do not indicate interaction with the slot occupant,* but rather make *assertions* about occupancy. Interactions with empty slots are not possible because empty slots are just holes in the system organization, so the arrows cannot be interpreted as a means of asking empty slots to fill themselves. The dashed arrows are as follows:

create/destroy a component in the slot pointed to by the arrow. As described in earlier chapters, this notation may also be used to indicate creation/destruction of a fixed component during initialization/finalization (fixed components now include pools). Remember that the term *fixed* means *unchanging during normal operation,* which is compatible with a component being dynamically created/destroyed during initialization/finalization.

move a component into or out of the slot pointed to by the arrow (the component is identified by the parameter). This has meaning only for slots but *not* fixed components (including pools).

Slots eliminate the need for notations to show dynamically changing connections in CGs. Connections between slots and other components (including other slots) are fixed but *imply* dynamic connections with slot occupants. Thus all *connections* in CGs remain fixed.

Additional notation is needed for the case in which a component is created in a location in the system separate from the location where it will move into a slot or pool.

This case is shown as it would be programmed, by showing an actual call connection to a factory layer that supplies new components, using the following notation (which was introduced in Chapter 5). The new call gets a new component that can then be moved

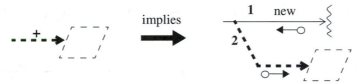

into a pool or slot elsewhere; the old call disposes of the component. The wiggly line represents the existence of the factory layer without showing it. The relationship among the *create*, *move*, and *new* notations is illustrated by the following diagram. The numbers indicate the required call sequence. For Tempo processes, new is the kernel function create_process; however, the convention applies to all types of slots, not just process slots. Here, one notation implies the use of the other two, but the three notations can also be used independently.

To keep in mind the difference between the dashed and solid arrows, imagine the slot is an empty manager position in a human organization. The dashed arrows indicate that the position is to be filled, but would *not* be interpreted as indicating the empty position is invoked to fill itself (there is nothing to invoke in an empty position). Accordingly these are *not* connections in the sense of paths for interaction. To fill the position we must invoke a supplier of managers (the factory layer). The solid *new* arrow that indicates this *is* a connection in the sense of a path for interaction.

Figure 9.3 provides an example following the pattern of Figure 9.1(a). The notation avoids the need for morphing wiring diagrams by replacing them with fixed diagrams that indicate how assembly operations are to be performed. The example arbitrarily assumes a pool of processes that is replenished by emptying process slots and depleted by populating them, but many other arrangements are possible (see the examples toward the end of this chapter). Although this diagram shows assembly *operations*, it does not show *sequences* of them. These may be shown by numbering the arrows. However, interaction sequences for assembly are perhaps better *implied* using associated UCMs that express assembly sequences more simply (Section 9.2.5).

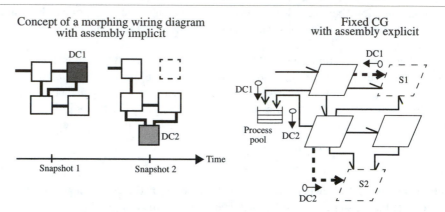

Figure 9.3 Replacing a morphing wiring diagram with a fixed CG.

The beauty of this notation is the ease with which it expresses relatively advanced features of systems, such as dynamically provisioning device handlers from a central site in a network (Figure 9.4). This CG provides enough information to give a very clear picture of the idea. A nondistributed version of this could easily be implemented as a Tempo program.

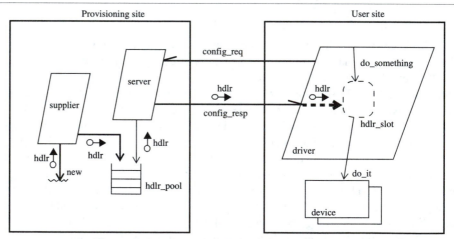

Figure 9.4 A device-handler provisioning example.

9.2.3 Interfaces of DCs

The fact that DCs are left implicit in system CGs means that there is no place for the total interface of a DC to be explicitly shown in a system context. The interface of a DC is the union of the interfaces of all slots in which the DC may appear in the system, but this is too indirect a description for documentation of DCs. For purposes of documenting DCs, the simplest solution is to draw a separate CG for each DC, showing it in isolation, with dangling interface connectors representing its total interface. It may also be useful to show slots with dangling connectors that indicate unused interface elements of DCs in the particular slot.

9.2.4 Implementing Assembly in Code

In the programming technology of this book, manipulations on the data forms of DCs translate into pointer manipulations (full implementation of the idea in Figure 9.4 would require something a little more general).

Movement of DCs as data translates into changing the visibility of DCs by passing their pointers around.

A slot may have an explicit, associated pointer variable in the place in the code where the slot is shown. This is a good solution if the component in the slot is required to perform responsibilities for different purposes over a period of time. In such cases, an empty slot is indicated by a null value of the pointer variable.

Local pointer variables for slots may not always be necessary. For example, a function that returns a pointer to DC may be the argument of another function that uses the pointer to access the DC, without going through a local pointer variable at the slot location. In such cases, an empty slot means not making the call.

In general, the meaning of a slot becoming occupied is that all code elements that need to have access to a DC are given that access, however this is achieved.

Pools are just implemented as data objects where pointer variables for DCs are kept in readiness for use. The storage structure of pools is unspecified (for example, it could be an array, a linked list, or a tree, to name but a few possibilities).

Be careful not to be confused by process parameters in assembly diagrams. As we shall see in Chapter 10, Tempo maintains process descriptor (PD) objects for each process. The identifiers returned from `create_process` calls are actually pointers to PD objects, not to processes. The PD objects are not themselves processes, only containers of information about processes. Outside the kernel, we don't care about this, because we never use the identifiers directly as pointers, only as data to be stored and passed around. Thinking about them as process identifiers (or actual processes) is a convenient fiction. However, when we cross the kernel interface boundary, we must remember that processes and PD objects are different things. For example, when we pass a receiver process identifier to Tempo as a parameter of a `send` call, we should not imagine that Tempo then uses this to pass the message to the PD object so identified, somehow, to "call" the process associated with the PD object. This is not at all what happens. What does happen is that the message is stored inside the kernel until the process *corresponding to* this PD object starts running and makes a `receive` call.

9.2.5 Extensions to the UCM Notation

Slots and pools carry directly over into UCMs. With the notations of Figure 9.2, UCMs are more expressive about sequences of assembly operations than CGs. The arrow notation implying DC movement is summarized next (the tail of a move arrow identifies the source of a move operation and the head of the arrow identifies the destination):

> **move:** A DC moves from a path to a pool or slot (or vice versa). The DC leaves the source and *remains at the destination after the move operation is completed*. Note that this is *not* movement along a path.
>
> **move-stay:** A DC both moves to the destination and remains there (same as move) and also stays at the source (different from move). Move-stay permits DCs to be aliased (see Section 9.2.6).
>
> **create** and **destroy:** A new DC is created *before* the move (and initialized), or an existing DC is destroyed *after* the move. These notations imply the existence of a factory layer, without specifying how it is used.
>
> **copy:** This is like move-stay, except that instead of moving the same DC, a copy of it moves (so there is no aliasing). Note that this does *not* mean the same thing as create followed by move-stay (the notation looks like it might mean that); create followed by move-stay requires use of both symbols, one after the other.

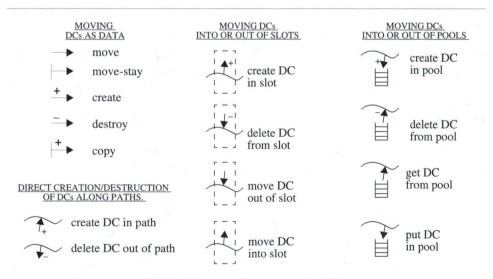

Figure 9.5 Assembly notations for UCMs.

Our convention is to show pools to one side of paths because this makes for clearer diagrams, but the meaning is that the pool is actually a fixed component with responsibilities to get a DC (as data) from storage or put it (as data) into storage. If we represented a pool as an ordinary fixed component named `componentPool` with responsibilities `get` and `put`, we would draw the path crossing the component in the usual way, but we do not represent a pool this way because we want all aspects of structural dynamics to be visually identified as an aid to understanding.

Figure 9.6 shows how to replace a morphing wiring diagram with a fixed UCM (compare with Figure 9.3). The slot occupancy changes imply new visibility relationships at the code level, without showing them explicitly. The corresponding CG (Figure 9.3) gives details from which these may be inferred.

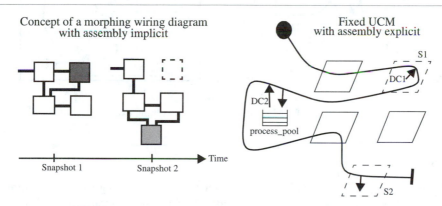

Figure 9.6 Replacing a morphing wiring diagram with a fixed UCM.

Figure 9.7 shows the earlier handler provisioning example (Figure 9.4) in UCM terms. The sweep of events is clearly seen, uncluttered by CG details. The paths starting from A and B illustrate typical behavior. Many variations may be imagined and easily shown.

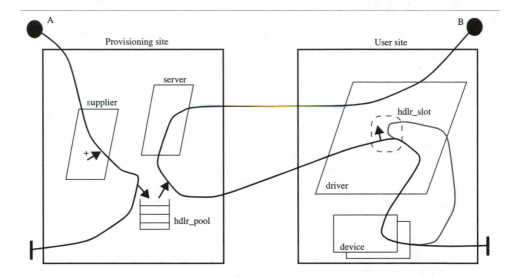

Figure 9.7 A UCM for the handler provisioning example.

9.2.6 Aliasing

In code terms, aliasing means having an identifier for the same thing stored in different program variables in different places in the code. Because the variables in the different places will have different names, they are "aliases" in the ordinary English meaning of the term.

In design terms, a DC is aliased when it occupies more than one slot at the same time. This may be visualized in terms of a dynamically established "wormhole" that bypasses intervening structure to make the same DC visible from two different places (next diagram). The wormhole is not part of the notation, only a way of visualizing things.

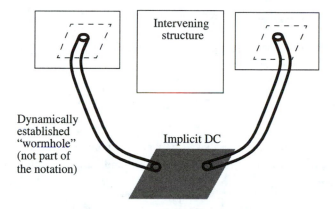

Aliasing in CGs

The difference between aliased and unaliased moves of DCs into slots is difficult to show explicitly in CGs. The usual default in code is aliasing (failure to null pointer variables will leave DCs aliased). To make moves unaliased, explicit program action is required to null pointer variables, and such details are below the level of CGs. For example (next diagram), does the process p end up in both S1 and S2, or is S1 left empty? The CG does not say. The intent must be established by documentation, or naming or programming conventions. The CG notation could also be extended to indicate the difference, at the cost of extra notational complexity.

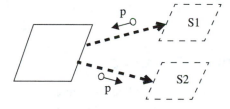

Aliasing in UCMs

UCMs express aliasing in a very direct and simple fashion:

- A dynamic component may be aliased among slots by *move-staying* it from one slot and *moving* it into another.

- A fixed component may be aliased between its home place and one or more other slots by *move-staying* it from its home place and *moving* it into one or more slots elsewhere.

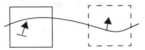

- No other move notations may be applied to fixed components. By definition, a fixed component can never be moved out of its place in such as way as to leave the place empty and can never be replaced by moving a different component into its place. Therefore the following constructions would either be incorrect or intended to mean there is an internal pool not shown.

9.3 PARTIAL STRUCTURAL DYNAMICS

Partial structural dynamics of the kind identified in Figure 9.1(b), in which only wires among fixed components change, may require special treatment.

The concept may be represented in two ways (apart from morphing diagrams). One of them treats the fixed components as aliased in slots. The other one pushes the details down to an underlying layer. Both approaches have their uses, as will now be explained. We shall continue to use the wormhole model introduced in Section 9.2.6 to describe the ideas, because this allows us to explain them independently of whether CGs or UCMs are used to express the design solutions. However, the wormhole model is slightly different with fixed components (next diagram), because there is no implicit DC.

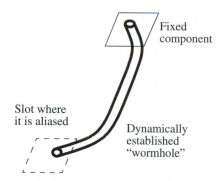

As an example of fixed components being aliased in slots, consider a process that fills two roles in a system, as controller and as an inspector (next diagram). In the controller role, it collaborates with one set of components to handle application events. In the inspector role, it collaborates with a different set of components to get periodic reports of system status from many places so that it will have a good enough picture to handle errors sensibly if they occur, and it handles recovery from errors when errors occur. The two roles of the process in the system are quite distinct, and keeping them distinct in design diagrams may be deemed desirable. A person could just draw separate diagrams and *say* they represent different roles, but the slot notation provides a means of showing the roles explicitly and of allowing roles to change dynamically (next diagram). One of the roles is designated as a main one, represented by a fixed component, and the other as a subsidiary one, represented by a slot. The fixed component is then aliased in the slot. We leave it as an exercise for the reader to draw CGs and UCMs for this example and approach.

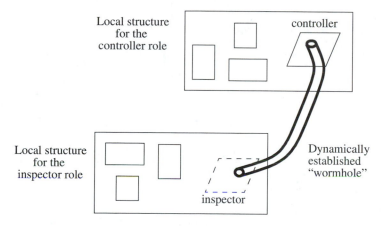

As an another example, imagine a client-server system in which slots for clients at the server location indicate that the server is required to provide responses directly to continually changing clients (next diagram). The slot approach seems too heavyweight for this example. It is not wrong, because the example is clearly structurally dynamic in the sense of Figure 9.1(b); the client-server relationship must be continually rewired as clients come and go. It just seems too cluttered for such a simple requirement.

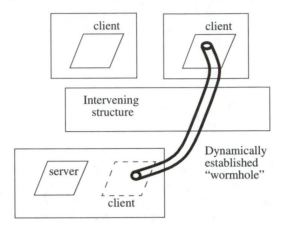

Now consider the approach of pushing the details down to an underlying layer. This solution is suggested by the following wormhole diagram for the same client-server problem. There are no slots in this diagram. Instead, the wormhole goes directly between client and server. The concept is that the client makes requests through normal channels as a peer of the server, providing an identifier indicating where responses are to be sent, but the server bypasses bypass normal channels to send responses directly, by going through a layer that knows how to interpret the identifier to send responses. This concept is very simple to represent in either CGs or UCMs.

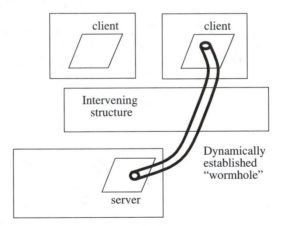

Here follows a CG representing the layer approach for the client-server example. In this CG, the request and response parameters are assumed obviously needed and so are left out, for simplicity.

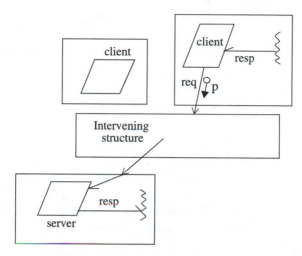

Here follows a UCM representing the same approach for the same example. Path A requires a client to make a request at rq. This request is satisfied by the server at rs. Some other path B gets the response at rp (B may be just a continuation of A, but it could be a separate path triggered by a new event). No path excursion back to the client from rs is shown for responses, because the response path from rs to rp is assumed to go through an underlying layer.

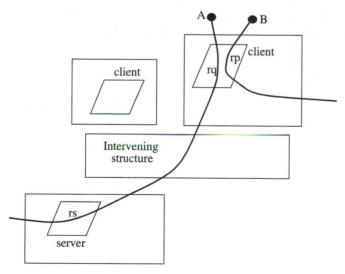

9.4 SUMMARY

In this chapter we have

- Explained that practical programs are routinely structurally dynamic, but that we do not always want to show this.
- Introduced the concepts of *operation* and *assembly* as distinct aspects of the behavior of structurally dynamic software systems and explained that assembly needs new notations.
- Explained that the problem of describing assembly is eased by identifying two distinct forms of dynamic components (DCs), an operational form and a data form, and two new types of system components, slots for the operation form and pools for the data form.
- Explained simple CG and UCM notations for showing how the data form of DCs is manipulated and moved around to achieve assembly.
- Cautioned against going too far in the direction of developing assembly details with CGs, because the diagrams can very quickly become cluttered and difficult to understand. Basic CGs that provide operational scaffolding without becoming obsessive about expressing assembly details, supplemented by UCMs, may often be a better approach.
- Explained that modeling structural dynamics explicitly is useful when the behavior of the system cannot be properly understood without taking it into account, but pointed out that structural dynamics that is localized in the software or in time, or below a certain scale, can often be pushed down as detail.
- Provided several examples.

A Look Inside the
Tempo Kernel

*I*n Chapter 4 we introduced special notations for representing IPC connections in CGs, to provide insight into the relationships between processes. When we draw connections like this

we are using a visual shorthand for the following diagram, which more closely represents IPC the way it actually occurs in our programs, through calls to Tempo kernel functions.

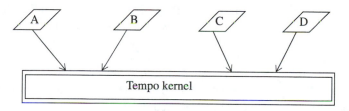

This convention enables designers to work with processes and IPC as first-class design abstractions, without having to bring the kernel explicitly into every design diagram. However, this is only a convention to reduce clutter (both pictorial and mental). In fact the kernel is implemented in a straightforward manner that can be depicted with the same design notations we have used until now, as this chapter will show.

The purpose of this chapter is to explain the essence of how Tempo works. Tempo and this chapter use full C++, but even readers who don't know C++ should gain an understanding of how Tempo works, because familiar notations are used to describe the kernel's organization and behavior before any of its code is presented.

This chapter uses only CGs to explain the kernel. Although the other important notation of this book, use case maps, can be used to provide a compact, high-level description of how the kernel works, and doing so can provide useful insight, for brevity we do not do so here (we leave it as an exercise for interested readers). We do not use any other notations in this chapter to explain the kernel, because we do not need to. Readers with object-oriented experience may be surprised at the absence of class diagrams, such as inheritance trees. They are not needed here because the C++ classes that provide the objects to populate our CGs are all stand-alone classes, not related by inheritance.

10.1 TEMPO VIEWED IN TERMS OF COMPONENTS

Chapter 4 explained how Tempo can be viewed as a large-scale monitor team, with its interface functions (the kernel functions) providing mutual exclusion protection on its internal data structures. This a convenient fiction from the skinny C++ perspective of the previous chapters of this book, but it is not quite how the kernel is actually organized. Figure 10.1 shows that Tempo consists of several components: a kernel interface object, process descriptor objects, semaphore objects, a scheduler object, pools of process descriptors, and an ISR that handles interrupts generated by the system timer.

To write multitasking programs in skinny C++ we need a kernel like Tempo that supports concurrent processes, because processes are not provided by C++. Although we consider Tempo processes to exist outside the kernel, because their root functions are programmable, Tempo needs to keep track of the state information of each process. To do this, for every process created by create_process(), a corresponding process descriptor object is created by the kernel.

Every semaphore created by create_semaphore() corresponds to a semaphore object. Semaphores are considered to exist inside Tempo because, although semaphore functions are called by processes, the semaphores themselves are not programmable.

Tempo also contains a scheduler object, which performs the responsibilities associated with sharing the processor between processes.

The kernel interface object provides the interface between processes and the other components inside Tempo. (The partial double outline indicates that this object is partly a monitor and partly just a collection of unprotected functions.)

The pools represent queues of process descriptor objects, and from now on they will be referred to as queues, not pools, because this is what they are called in the kernel's code. When we imagine a process being placed in a queue (for example, while waiting on a semaphore), what really happens is that the process descriptor for the process is placed in the queue.

The queue labeled sleepQ and the timer ISR support process_sleep() and the versions of `wait()`, `receive()`, and `wait_semaphore()` that permit processes to time out.

The objects inside Tempo are now described in more detail.

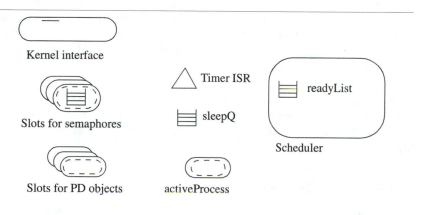

Figure 10.1 Components inside the Tempo kernel.

10.1.1 Kernel Interface

Process descriptors, semaphores, and the scheduler are implemented as C++ objects; that is, they are instances of C++ classes. To write Tempo programs in skinny C++, it is necessary to hide these C++ objects so that process root functions do not have to deal with them directly. To do this, Tempo's kernel functions are part of a kernel interface object, and the process descriptor, semaphore, and scheduler objects hide behind this interface. Processes see only the functions provided by the kernel interface but do not see the objects behind the interface.

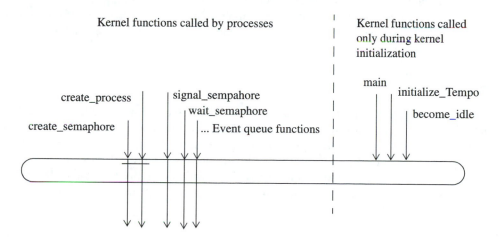

The short horizontal line in the kernel interface object indicates that the object has a monitor part and a nonmonitor part, so only part of the object is drawn with a double outline. Two functions provided by the kernel interface, `create_semaphore()` and `create_process()`, call the C++ run-time library to create new objects, so they enforce mutual exclusion through interrupt lockout. For these two functions, the kernel interface acts like a monitor. The kernel interface functions for semaphore and event queue operations are part of the nonmonitor part of the object. Calls to these functions are chained through to the appropriate semaphore or process descriptor object, which enforces mutual exclusion.

Kernel functions `main()`, `initialize_Tempo()`, and `become_idle()` are called when a Tempo program starts and are responsible for initializing the kernel. These functions are never called by processes. (Kernel initialization is described in Section 10.2.7.)

10.1.2 Process Descriptors

As a Tempo program runs, only one process is scheduled for execution at any time. All other processes in the system will be in a nonrunning state, either eligible to run, blocked while waiting for a semaphore to be signaled, or blocked while waiting for a signal or message to arrive at an event queue. Tempo must keep track of the state of each process so that it can block running processes (to wait for events), make blocked processes eligible to run (when events occur) and reschedule the processor among ready-to-run processes. When Tempo context switches between processes, it must save enough information about the currently running process to be able to cause the process to resume execution exactly where it left off.

Tempo stores this information about processes in *process descriptor objects (PD objects)*. Each process has its own PD object, which is allocated when the process is created and stored in one of the PD slots shown in Figure 10.1. The `activeProcess` slot shown in Figure 10.1 contains the PD object for the currently executing process.

PDs are actually small-scale monitors supplied by the kernel. These monitors provide mutual exclusion on their data structures (the semaphore count and queue) and provide delayed services.

10.1.3 Scheduler

The responsibility for sharing the processor between processes belongs to Tempo's *scheduler*. This object maintains Tempo's queues of ready-to-run processes. `readyList` is actually an array of queues (one queue for each process priority level); each element in a queue is a PD object for a process that is eligible to run. When a process becomes eligible to run, its PD object is added to the queue associated with its priority level, and when the process is scheduled for execution, its PD object is moved into the `activeProcess` slot.

The scheduler also contains the PD object for Tempo's idle process, which is executed when no other process is eligible to run.

10.1.4 Semaphores

Recall from Chapter 4 that semaphores are actually small-scale monitors supplied by the kernel. These monitors provide mutual exclusion on their data structures (the semaphore count and queue) and provide delayed services. When `create_semaphore()` is called, a slot inside the kernel is filled with a semaphore. In Figure 10.1, the queue inside a semaphore represents the queue of PD objects for processes that are waiting on the semaphore). Calls to `wait_semaphore()` and `signal_semaphore()` pass a semaphore id to the kernel that is used to select the corresponding semaphore.

10.2 VISUALIZING TEMPO'S BEHAVIOR

In this section we use CGs to illustrate what happens when a process calls Tempo kernel functions to create a process, create a semaphore, and wait on and signal a semaphore.

When reading these examples it is important to remember that Tempo is not a process, so user processes do not context switch to it when they call Tempo functions. Instead, Tempo functions are always executed in the context of the calling process.

An important consequence of the mutual exclusion protection provided by Tempo is that while a process executes a Tempo function, modifying the kernel's internal state, it cannot be preempted by a higher-priority process. That doesn't mean that the process executes the function to completion, without delay. Executing the function may cause the calling process to become ineligible to run (while it waits for an event that has not yet arrived) or it may cause a blocked, higher-priority process to become eligible to run. This results in a context switch to another process, causing the first process to be delayed inside Tempo until a subsequent context switch causes that process to resume.

The important thing to remember is that each process executes sequentially, just like an ordinary C++ program, even when the process is executing a kernel function. If the kernel function causes a context switch, the processor simply switches from executing one sequential chunk of code (one process) to another sequential chunk of code (another process).

We're now ready to look at a few examples.

10.2.1 Creating a New Process

Figure 10.2 shows what happens when `create_process()` is called. The `new()` function in the C++ run-time library called to create a new PD object for the process, which in turn asks the PD to initialize itself. (For readers who know about C++ classes, the initialization code is in the object's constructor.) Space is allocated for the process's stack, the PD is initialized so that the process will begin in its root function, and the process priority level is set to the specified value. The constructor then calls the scheduler's `addNewProcess()` function, which changes the process state to ready-to-run by calling the PD object's `makeProcessReady()` function (in the diagram, the required visibility of PD by the scheduler is indicated by showing the scheduler populating and accessing a PD slot). This call is chained through to the scheduler's `addready()` function to place the PD in the appropriate ready-to-run queue (in `readyList`). The new process is now eligible to run. Finally, `create_process()` returns the identifier for the new process (a value of type `Process`) to its caller.

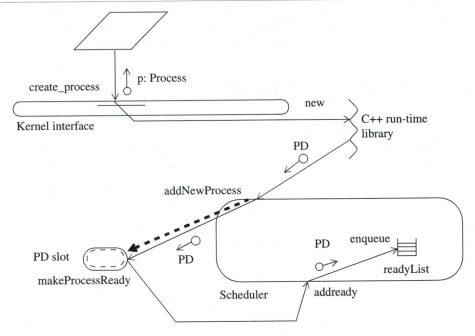

Figure 10.2 Creating a Tempo process (part 1 of 2).

The new process (outside Tempo) and the new PD object (inside Tempo) are related but are not the same thing. Although the PD for the new process exists after the operations shown in Figure 10.2 are completed, the process has not yet started to execute its root function. Figure 10.3 completes the picture. Eventually, the PD for the new process will be at the head of its queue in `readyList`, and there will be no PDs with higher priority in the `readyList`. The process that is currently running will call `process_sleep()` (or any other kernel function that causes rescheduling), which in turn calls `resched()` to request the scheduler to reschedule the processor. The scheduler moves the PD for the new process into `activeProcess` and then performs a context switch to that process by loading the processor's registers from the PD. The new process then begins execution, as implied by the dashed arrow between the scheduler and the process. (A new notation is used here for the first time. The dashed arrow labeled *Start* asserts that the process is started, implying that the processor registers have been loaded with their initial values.)

What happens to the PD of the switched-out process depends on the kernel function caused the context switch. Some examples will be given in Sections 10.2.3 and 10.2.4.

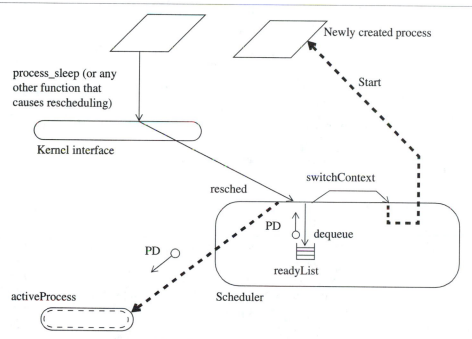

Figure 10.3 Creating a Tempo process (part 2 of 2).

10.2.2 Creating a New Semaphore

Figure 10.4 is a CG showing how `create_semaphore()` creates a new semaphore inside Tempo. The semaphore is instantiated by the C++ `new()` function, which in turn asks the semaphore to initialize its count and its internal queue. The diagram shows the new semaphore (Sem) moving into a slot inside Tempo. Finally, `create_process()` returns the identifier for the new semaphore (a value of type Semaphore) to its caller.

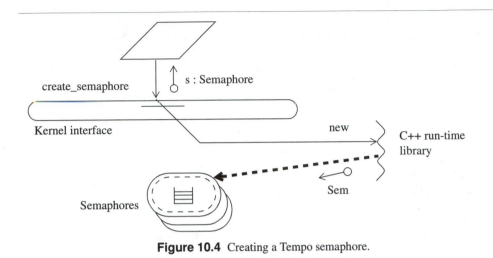

Figure 10.4 Creating a Tempo semaphore.

10.2.3 Waiting on a Semaphore

Figure 10.5 is a CG showing what happens when a process calls Tempo's `wait_semaphore()` function. This function uses the semaphore id passed by the caller to select a semaphore and then calls its `wait()` interface function. If the semaphore count is positive when this function is called, the count is decremented and the function exits. If the count is zero, the calling process must block, but how does a process block itself? The answer is surprisingly straightforward. `activeProcess` contains the process object for the process that is running; that is, the process that called `wait_semaphore()`. First, the semaphore calls the PD's `makeProcess-Blocked()` function to change the process's state to blocked. It then moves the PD out of `activeProcess` and adds it to the semaphore's queue, which contains the PDs for all processes that are waiting on the semaphore. Finally, the semaphore calls the scheduler's `resched()` function. Although not shown in this diagram, scheduling another process for execution happens exactly as depicted in Figure 10.3.

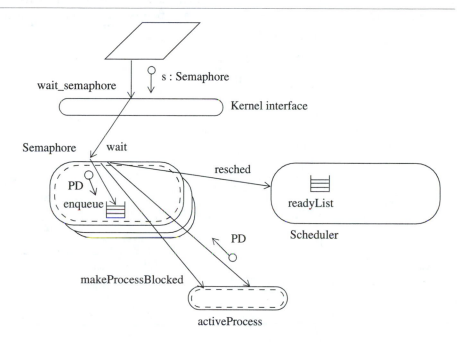

Figure 10.5 Waiting on a Tempo semaphore.

10.2.4 signaling a Semaphore

Figure 10.6 is a CG showing what happens when a process calls Tempo's `signal_semaphore()` function. This function is passed a semaphore id, which it uses to select the appropriate semaphore and call its `signal()` interface function. If no processes are blocked on the semaphore when the function is called, `signal()` simply increments the semaphore count and returns. If, however, processes are waiting on the semaphore, `signal()` must unblock a waiting process. It does this by removing a PD from the head of the semaphore queue, placing it in `p`, calling its `makeProcess-Ready()` function to change the state of the process from blocked to ready-to-run. This call is chained through to the scheduler's `addready()` function to move the PD to its ready-to-run queue in `readyList`.

At this point, a context switch is required if the priority of the unblocked process is greater than that of the active process (the process that called `signal_semaphore()`). To arrange this, the semaphore calls the scheduler's `relinquish()` function. This function asks the PD in `activeProcess` to change its state from running to ready-to-run, by calling `makeProcessReady()`. The PD then calls `addready()` to move that PD to `readyList`. Finally, `resched()` is called to schedule the processor. Either the

unblocked process is scheduled (and a context switch occurs) or the active process continues (no context switch is needed), depending on which process has the higher priority.

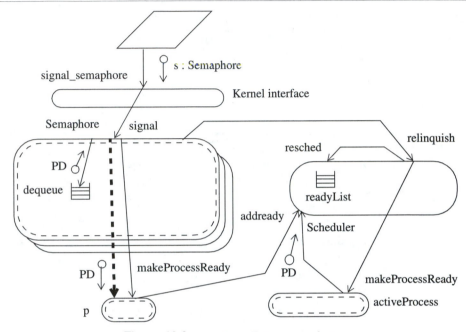

Figure 10.6 Signaling a Tempo semaphore.

10.2.5 Event Queue Kernel Functions

Calls to Tempo's event queue functions are chained by the kernel interface to the appropriate PD. The behaviors of `wait()` and `signal()` are similar to `wait_semaphore()`
and `signal_semaphore()` (each event queue acts like a semaphore that belongs to a
single process), so CGs for these functions are not provided in this chapter. The functions
that support message passing—`send()`, `receive()`, and `reply()`—are more complicated, because messages are stored in and removed from the event queues; however,
these functions can be represented with CGs that are only slightly more complex than the
diagrams in this chapter. As an exercise in using the notations, we suggest that readers
reverse engineer the source code for the event queue functions into CGs.

10.2.6 Sleeping and Timeouts

When a process calls `process_sleep()`, as shown in Figure 10.7, the call is chained
to `activeProcess`, which contains the PD for the calling process. This object's
`process_sleep()` function first calls `makeProcessSleepBlocked()` to change

the process's state from running to sleep-blocked. The PD is then moved to `sleepQ`, which stores the PDs of all processes while they sleep. Finally, `resched()` is called to schedule another process for execution.

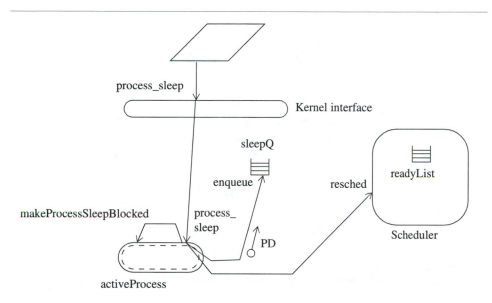

Figure 10.7 Putting a process to sleep.

Sleeping process are wakened by Tempo's timer ISR, as depicted by Figure 10.8.Each time the ISR runs, it begins by checking `sleepQ` for processes that are to wake up when that timer tick occurs. The PDs in `sleepQ` are ordered according to the length of time the processes are to sleep; the PD for the process that is to be wakened first is always at the head of the queue. If it is time for this process to wake up, the timer ISR moves the PD from `sleepQ` to `wakeUp`. Next, the PD is asked to change its state to ready-to-run (`makeProcessReady()` is called), and `addready()` is called to add the PD to `readyList`. These steps are repeated until every process that is ready to be wakened has been moved from `sleepQ` to its ready-to-run queue in the scheduler.

At this point, a context switch is required if the priority of one the processes that was removed from `sleepQ` is greater than that of the active process (the process that the timer ISR interrupted). To arrange this, the semaphore first asks the PD in `activePro-cess` to change its state from running to ready-to-run, by calling `makeProcess-Ready()`. The PD calls `addready()` to move that PD to `readyList`. Finally, `resched()` is called to schedule the processor. Either a newly awakened process is scheduled (and a context switch occurs) or the active process continues (no context switch is needed), depending on which process has the higher priority.

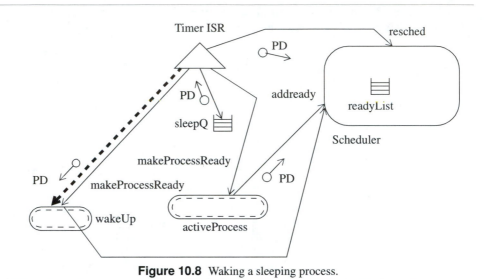

Figure 10.8 Waking a sleeping process.

Processes that time out after calling `wait()`, `receive()`, or `wait_semaphore()` are handled in a similar fashion:

- If a process calls `wait()` or `receive()` with a timeout value and has to wait, its PD is placed in `sleepQ`. A timeout while waiting for a signal or message to arrive at an event queue is handled exactly as shown in Figure 10.8.
- If a process calls `wait_semaphore()` with a timeout value and has to wait, aliases are used to store its PD in both the semaphore queue and `sleepQ`. A timeout while waiting for the semaphore to be signaled is handled as shown in Figure 10.8; in addition, the timer ISR removes the PD from the semaphore queue (not shown).

10.2.7 Kernel Initialization

In Chapter 2, we noted that a Tempo program starts executing as an ordinary, sequential C++ program. During kernel initialization it becomes a multitasking program with an idle process and a Main process. Figure 10.9 shows how this happens.

A sequential C++ program begins by executing a function in the C++ run-time library that initializes the run-time environment and then calls `main()`. In a Tempo program, `main()` is part of the kernel and is responsible for initializing Tempo. It calls the `new()` function in the C++ run-time library to create the scheduler object, which in turn calls the scheduler's constructor to initialize `readyList`. The constructor then creates a PD object for Tempo's idle process, which is placed in `readyList` by the PD object's constructor. After the scheduler's constructor returns control to `main()`, `create_process()` is called to create the Main process, as shown in Section 10.2.1.

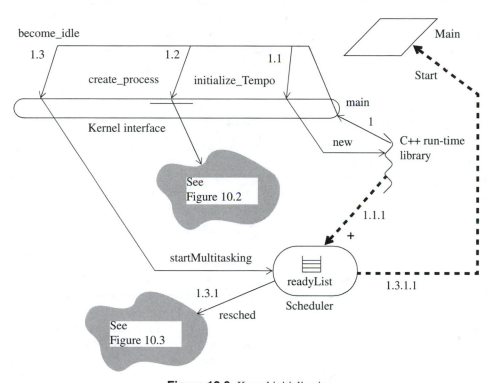

Figure 10.9 Kernel initialization.

.When `create_process()` returns, there are two PD objects in `readyList`—one for the idle process and one for the Main process—but the computer is still executing a sequential C++ program. The transformation to a multitasking program happens when `main()` calls `become_idle()`, which in turn calls the scheduler's `startMultitasking()` function. This function makes the idle process the active process, not by performing a context switch but in such a way that it appears as though the `startMultitasking()` was called by the root function of the idle process. In effect, through some software sleight of hand, `main()` has become the root function of the idle process. The idle process then relinquishes the processor, and because the Main process is ready to run, Tempo performs a context switch to this process. The Tempo program is now a multitasking system.

10.3 MAPPING TEMPO COMPONENTS TO C++

PD objects, semaphores, and the scheduler are C++ objects; that is, they are instances of C++ classes. Most of the kernel functions provided by the kernel interface are ordinary C/C++ functions (for efficiency reasons, a few of them are implemented as inline functions; however, this is transparent to processes that call them). These functions simply call the member function of the appropriate C++ object. Several examples of this will be shown in the remainder of this section.

10.3.1 Process Descriptors and the PD Class

Each PD object is an instance of class PD, and in the CGs in Section 10.2, each parameter labeled PD corresponds to one of these objects. For efficiency reasons, moving a PD into a queue or a slot is accomplished by moving a pointer to the object, and not the entire object.

Several kernel functions expect or return process identifiers (values of type Process). These values are simply pointers to PD objects:

```
typedef PD *Process;
```

Figure 10.10 contains the declaration for Tempo's PD class. A PD object's private member data includes variables for storing the process state, process priority, and processor registers. Tempo saves a copy of these registers in the PD before it switches context to another process; when it later switches back to this process, the registers are reloaded from these saved values. link is an object of class QueueLink. Tempo uses this object to place PD objects in ready-to-run queues and semaphore queues. The PD also contains the data structures that implement the process's event queues.

```
// PD (process descriptor) class
//
class PD
{
private:
   friend void interrupt timertick(...);
   friend class Sem;
   friend class Scheduler;

// Processes are kept in queues.
   QueueLink link;

   int priority;       // Process priority
   int state;          // Process state

// During a context switch, processor registers
// are saved here.
   ProcessorRegs registers;

// Each process has its own array of event queues.
   EventQueue eventQueue[MAX_QUEUES];

// When a signal or a message is received, the following
// records which event queue was signaled.
   int signaledOn;

// The following is set if a waiting process times out
// while waiting.
   int timedOut;

// This function is executed when a process returns by
// executing a return statement or "falling of the
// end" of its root function.
   static void processDone();
```

Figure 10.10 Tempo's PD (process descriptor) class (part 1 of 2).

```
public:

// These 7 functions change the process state.
   void makeProcessReady()
       {state = PROCESS_READY;}
   void makeProcessActive()
       {state = PROCESS_CURRENT;}
   void makeProcessBlocked()
       {state = PROCESS_BLOCKED;}
   void makeProcessQueueBlocked()
       {state = QUEUE_BLOCKED;}
   void makeProcessSleepBlocked()
       {state = SLEEP_BLOCKED;}
   void makeProcessSemaphoreTimedBlocked()
       {state = SEM_TIMED_BLOCKED;}
   void makeProcessQueueTimedBlocked()
       {state = QUEUE_TIMED_BLOCKED;}

   int myState() {return state;}

// The next function is called by the
// process_sleep() wrapper function.
   void process_sleep(unsigned int time);

// These functions are called by the event queue
// wrapper functions.
   void signal(int queue_number);
   int wait();
   int wait(unsigned int timeout);
   void send(int queue, message msg, int ack_queue);
   int receive(message &msg, Process& correspondent,
               int &ack_queue);
   int receive(message &msg, Process &correspondent,
               int &ack_queue, unsigned int timeout);
   void maskqueue(int queue_number);
   void unmaskqueue(int queue_number);

// The object's constructor creates a new process with
// the specified root function, priority, and stack size.
   PD(void (*rootFnPtr)(),
      int priority = LOWEST_PRIORITY,
      unsigned stackSize = DEFAULT_STACK);
   ~PD() {}
};

typedef PD *Process;
```

Figure 10.11 Tempo's PD (process descriptor) class (part 2 of 2).

Class `PD` provides the public member functions shown in Figure 10.11. The functions that change and report the process state (`makeProcessReady()`, `makeProcessActive()` and so on) are used by the objects within Tempo but are not directly called by processes. The `process_sleep()` member function implements the `process_sleep()` kernel function. Function names like `send()` and `receive()` are familiar; these are the functions that implement Tempo's event queue functions.

10.3.2 The create_process() Function

Figure 10.12 contains the code for Tempo's `create_process()` function. After ensuring mutual exclusion by disabling interrupts, this function dynamically allocates a PD object (an instance of class `PD`) by calling `new()`:

```
p = new PD(rootFnPtr, priority);
```

When the object is created, its constructor is automatically called by the C++ run-time environment, with the address of the process's root function and its priority passed as arguments. When the constructor has finished, `new()` returns a pointer to the new PD object. After interrupts are reenabled, this value is returned by `create_process()` as the identifier for the new process.

```
// create_process() - create a new Tempo process
Process create_process(void (*rootFnPtr)(),
                       int priority)
{
    Process p;
    short savedFlags;

    savedFlags = disable_ints();
    p = new PD(rootFnPtr, priority);
    restore_flags(savedFlags);
    return p;
}
```

Figure 10.12 The `create_process()` function.

The real work associated with creating a new PD object is handled by the class constructor. The code is shown in Figure 10.13.

This constructor begins by invoking the constructor for the QueueLink object contained in the PD object. Then the process's stack is allocated and the saved-register area in the PD object are then initialized so that when Tempo first schedules this process for execution, it starts in its root function. After saving the process's priority level and initializing the event queues, the scheduler's `addNewProcess()` function is called to install the PD in the scheduler's ready-to-run queues.

```
//   Constructor for class PD
//
PD::PD(void (*rootFnPtr)(),
        int processPriority,
        unsigned stackSize)
      : QueueLink()
{
    short *stackPointer;

// Initialize the stack so that the root function
// for this process returns to processDone().
    stackPointer = (short*)Scheduler::InstancePtr->
                    allocStackSpace(stackSize);
    *stackPointer = (short)PD::processDone;

    initProcessorRegs(&this->registers,
                    (short)stackPointer,
                    (short)rootFnPtr);

    priority = processPriority;

// Init the process' event queues
    for (int i = 0; i < MAX_QUEUES; ++i) {
        eventQueue[i].count= 0;
        eventQueue[i].mask = UNMASKED;
    }
    signaledOn = -1;

// Ask the scheduler to add this process to its
// list of ready-to-run processes.
    Scheduler::InstancePtr->addNewProcess(this);
}
```

Figure 10.13 The constructor for the PD class.

10.3.3 The Scheduler Class

Tempo's scheduler is implemented by class `Scheduler`. The declaration of the private part of this class is shown in Figure 10.14.

```
class Scheduler
{
private:

// For each process priority level, the scheduler
// maintains a queue of process descriptors for
// processes that are ready to run.
    QueueLink readyList[PRIORITY_LEVELS];

// The total number of user processes, including the
// Main process.
    int numprocesses;

// A pointer to the process descriptor for Tempo's
// idle process.
    PD *idleProcess;

// The context switcher.
    void switchContext(ProcessorRegs *from,
                       ProcessorRegs *to);
```

Figure 10.14 Tempo's `Scheduler` class (part 1 of 2).

`idleProcess` holds the pointer to the PD object for the idle process. `readyList` is the array of ready-to-run queues (one for each process priority level).

The public part of class `Scheduler`, shown in Figure 10.15, declares two functions for moving PD objects on to the ready-to-run queues (`addready()` and `addNew-Process()`) and two functions (`relinquish()` and `resched()`) that cause processor rescheduling. `activeProcess` corresponds to the slot of the same name in the CGs in Section 10.2. It holds the pointer to the PD object for the currently running process.

```
public:
// Tempo creates a single Scheduler object during
// initialization. InstancePtr points to it.
   static Scheduler *InstancePtr;

// The following points to the active process.
   PD *activeProcess;

void startMultitasking();

// The next function is called when a process is
// created, to allocate its stack.
   char *allocStackSpace(unsigned size);

// These functions add processes to the ready
// queues.
   void addready(PD *p) ;
   void addNewProcess(PD *p);

// relinquish() is called by the active process
// when it is willing to give up the processor.
// resched() reschedules the processor among all
// ready-to-run processes.
   void relinquish();
   void resched();

   Scheduler();
   ~Scheduler() {}
};
```

Figure 10.15 Tempo's `Scheduler` class (part 2 of 2).

10.3.4 Semaphores and the Sem Class

Each semaphore is an instance of class `Sem`, and in the CGs in Section 10.2, a parameter labeled Sem corresponds to one of these objects.

Several kernel functions expect or return semaphore identifiers (values of type `Semaphore`). These values are simply pointers to Sem objects:

```
typedef Sem *Semaphore;
```

Figure 10.16 contains the declaration for this class.

```
//
//   Sem (semaphore) class
//
class Sem : QueueLink
{
private:
    int count;

public:
    void wait();
    int wait(unsigned int timeout);
    void signal();

// The constructor allocates a new semaphore object
// with a default initial count of 0.
    Sem(int initialCount = 0);
    ~Sem() {}
};

typedef Sem *Semaphore;
```

Figure 10.16 Tempo's Sem (semaphore) class.

A semaphore maintains a queue of waiting processes, so class Sem is considered to be a specialized form of queue and is implemented as a subclass of class QueueLink. The private part of a Sem object holds the signal count.The public member functions support the wait, wait-with-timeout, and signal operations.

10.3.5 The create_semaphore() Function

Figure 10.17 shows how the create_semaphore() function allocates a new Sem object and returns a pointer to the object. Because class Sem is a subclass of class QueueLink, the constructor for QueueLink runs before the constructor for Sem, which simply initializes the semaphore count.

```
Semaphore create_semaphore(int initial_count)
{
    Semaphore s;
    short savedFlags;

    savedFlags = disable_ints();
    s = new Sem(initial_count);
    restore_flags(savedFlags);
    return s;
}

//   Sem::Sem
//   Constructor for objects of class Sem
//
Sem::Sem(int initialCount)
{
    count = initialCount;
}
```

Figure 10.17 The create_semaphore() function.

10.3.6 The wait_semaphore() Function

The code for Tempo's wait_semaphore() function is shown in Figure 10.18. The calling process passes the function an argument of type Semaphore, which is a pointer to a semaphore object. Using this pointer, wait_semaphore() calls the semaphore object's wait() function.

```
void wait_semaphore(Semaphore semaphore)
{
    semaphore->wait();
}

void Sem::wait()
{
    short savedFlags;

    savedFlags = disable_ints();
    if (count > 0)
    {
        --count;
    } else {
        // block the caller
        PD *active = Scheduler::InstancePtr->
                    activeProcess;
        active->makeProcessBlocked();
        // move the active process to the
        // semaphore queue
        enqueue(&active->link);
        Scheduler::InstancePtr->resched();
    }
    restore_flags(savedFlags);
}
```

Figure 10.18 Tempo code for wait_semaphore().

10.3.7 The signal_semaphore() Function

The code for `signal_semaphore()` function is shown in Figure 10.19. The calling process passes the function an argument of type `Semaphore`, which is a pointer to a semaphore object. Using this pointer, `signal_semaphore()` calls the semaphore object's `signal()` function.

```
void signal_semaphore(Semaphore semaphore)
{
      semaphore->signal();
}

void Sem::signal()
{
    short savedFlags;
    PD *p;

    savedFlags = disable_ints();
    if (empty())
    {
        // No processes blocked on the semaphore
        ++count;
    } else {
        // Get the process at the front of the
        // semaphore queue.
        p = (PD*)dequeue();

        // If the process specified a timeout
        // when it called wait_semaphore(),
        // remove the process from the sleep
        // queue.
        if (p->myState() == SEM_TIMED_BLOCKED)
            (void)sleepQ.deltaRemoveElement(p);

        p->makeProcessReady();
        Scheduler::InstancePtr->relinquish(p);
    }
    restore_flags(savedFlags);
}
```

Figure 10.19 Tempo code for `signal_semaphore()`.

10.3.8 The QueueLink Class

Class `QueueLink` is the building block for the queues maintained by Tempo (see Figure 10.20). Any object containing a `QueueLink` object (for example, a PD object) can be stored as a node in a queue of objects. The queue is implemented as doubly linked lists, so that the nodes may be removed efficiently from the middle of queues. Each QueueLink object maintains a forward link to the next QueueLink object in the queue and a backward link to the previous QueueLink object in the queue. The public member functions provide the fundamental queue operations (adding the QueueLink object to the rear of the queue, removing and returning the QueueLink object from the head of the queue, and so on).

```
class QueueLink
{
private:
// forward link to the next node in the queue
    QueueLink *next;
// backward link to the previous node in the queue
    QueueLink *prev;

public:
// Return 1 of the queue is empty, 0 if not.
    int empty();

// Add the object pointed to by link to the read
// of the queue.
    void enqueue(QueueLink *link);

// Remove the object from the front of the queue,
// and return a pointer to it.
    QueueLink *dequeue();

// Remove this object from whatever queue
// it is currently in.
    void remove();

// The constructor points the forward and backward
// links to this QueueLink object.
    QueueLink() {next = prev = this;}
    ~QueueLink() {}
};
```

Figure 10.20 Tempo's QueueLink class.

10.3.9 Tempo's process_sleep() Function and the Timer ISR

The code for process_sleep(), which corresponds to Figure 10.7, is shown in Figure 10.21. When a process calls this function, the call is chained through to the process_sleep() function provided by the process's PD object.

```
inline void process_sleep(unsigned int time)
{
    Scheduler::InstancePtr->activeProcess->
                         process_sleep(time);
}

// process_sleep() - the calling process is put
// to sleep for "time" ticks of the system timer

void PD::process_sleep(unsigned int time)
{
    short savedFlags;

    savedFlags = disable_ints();

    if (time > 0) {
       makeProcessSleepBlocked();
       sleepQ.deltaEnqueue(this, time);
       Scheduler::InstancePtr->resched();
    }
    enable_ints(savedFlags);
}
```

Figure 10.21 Tempo code for `process_sleep()`.

The code for the timer ISR, which corresponds to Figure 10.8, is provided in Figure 10.22.

```
void interrupt timerISR(...)
{
    PD *wakeUp;
    short savedFlags;
    int contextSwitchNeeded;

    // daisy chain to the old timer ISR
    oldhandler();

    // When we return from the old ISR, interrupts
    // have been enabled and EOI has been sent to the
    // PIC. Now check for blocked processes that have
    // timed out and sleeping processes that must be
    // awakened.
    savedFlags = disable_ints();
    contextSwitchNeeded = FALSE;
    PD *active
        = Scheduler->InstancePtr->activeProcess;
    sleepQ.deltaDecrement();

    // remove a process from the sleep queue
    wakeUp = sleepQ.deltaDequeue();
    while (wakeUp != NULL) {
        if (wakeUp->myState() == SEM_TIMED_BLOCKED) {
            // A process that is blocked on a
            // semaphore has timed out. Remove it
            // from the semaphore queue.
            wakeUp->link.remove();
            wakeUp->timedOut = TRUE;
        }
        wakeUp->makeProcessReady();
        if (wakeUp->priority > active->priority)
            contextSwitchNeeded = TRUE;

        wakeUp = sleepQ.deltaDequeue();
    }

    if (contextSwitchNeeded) {
        active->makeProcessReady();
        Scheduler::InstancePtr->resched();
    }
    enable_ints(savedFlags);
}
```

Figure 10.22 Tempo's timer ISR.

10.4 USING FULL C++ WITH TEMPO

This section is intended for readers with experience in developing object-oriented programs in C++, and it answers two questions that our students often ask about programming object-oriented, real-time systems:

- Are there any problems with Tempo programs using C++ classes; in other words,
  with Tempo processes creating and using objects that are instances of user-defined
  C++ classes?
- Can Tempo processes call Tempo's objects directly, instead of calling the functions
  provided by the kernel interface layer?

10.4.1 Using User-Defined C++ Classes in Tempo Programs

Tempo is compatible with C++ objects; in fact, we have used them in our programs since
the first example was presented in Chapter 2. The cout object used in our Tempo programs is an instance of the ostream class provided by the C++ stream I/O library, and
the output operator "<<" manipulates this object.

Any of the objects in this book's example programs could be implemented with
user-defined classes. At the processor level, calls to an object's interface functions (that is,
member functions and friend functions) are no different from ordinary function calls, and
as such they can be called by processes and ISRs.

Processes may create objects dynamically by using the new operator, and like any
calls to the C++ run-time library, mutual exclusion must be enforced by placing any use of
new in a critical section:

```
// create an instance of class Buffer
Buffer *buf;
CS(buf = new Buffer);
```

When developing classes for use in Tempo programs, we recommend that virtual
functions not be used unless you are confident that the code that performs the run-time
binding between objects and functions is reentrant. This can be difficult to determine
unless you have the source code for the C++ compiler's run-time library.

An object's interface functions do not enforce mutual exclusion by default, so
objects that are shared between processes or between processes and ISRs must be implemented as monitors using the techniques shown in Chapters 2 and 3. A monitor object that
is shared between processes will contain an internal mutual exclusion semaphore that is
waited on and signaled by the object's interface functions. For a monitor object that is
shared between processes and ISRs, the interface functions must provide mutual exclusion
through interrupt lockout.

10.4.2 Using Tempo's Objects

In Tempo programs, values of type `Process` are just pointers to PD objects (instances of Tempo's PD class) and values of type `Semaphore` are just pointers to Sem objects (instances of Tempo's Sem class). In all the Tempo programs presented so far, processes request kernel services by calling the kernel interface functions, which in turn call Tempo's objects by using the pointers to the objects. The kernel interface functions are coded as C++ inline functions, so requesting kernel services via these functions results in little or no additional overhead. For the sake of completeness, this section examines when Tempo processes can bypass the kernel interface functions and instead call PD objects and Sem objects directly.

Tempo's `create_process()` function should always be used to create new processes. It is possible to create a new process this way:

```
PD process1(root_function, priority);
```

but this is not a recommended approach. If `process1` is defined outside of any function, it will be created before the scheduler object during kernel initialization. Recall that when a new process is created, its PD object is placed in an appropriate ready-to-run queue in the scheduler. If the scheduler object does not yet exist, there will be no ready-to-run queue to hold the new PD object, and the program will fail. For this reason, processes should always be created this way:

```
Process process1;
process1 = create_process(root_function, priority);
```

Although we could create semaphores by declaring objects of class Sem, we prefer calling the `create_semaphore()` kernel function, for symmetry reasons. Both `create_process()` and `create_semaphore()` return pointers to objects, so we can use the same syntax to call both kinds of objects.

Calls to kernel interface functions that have a `Semaphore` argument can be replaced by calls to the corresponding Sem objects. For example,

```
signal_semaphore(sem1);
```

can be replaced by

```
sem1->signal(); // sem1 is a pointer to a Sem object
```

and

```
wait_semaphore(sem1);
```

can be replaced by

```
sem1->wait();
```

Calls to three of the kernel functions that deal with event queues specify the process that is to receive the signal or message. These can be rewritten as calls to the PD object for the destination processes. This call

```
signal(destination_process, queue);
// destination_process is a pointer to a PD object
```

can be replaced by

```
destination_process->signal(queue);
```

This call

```
send(destination_process, queue, msg, ack_queue);
```

 can be replaced by

```
destination_process->send(queue, msg, ack_queue);
```

and this call

```
reply(correspondent_process, queue, reply);
```

can be replaced by

```
correspondent_process->send(queue, reply, NO_ACK);
```

The other event queue functions provided by the kernel interface—wait(), receive(), mask_queue(), and unmask_queue()—map to calls to the PD object for the active process. Syntactically, our programs appear less cluttered if we continue to use these kernel functions in our programs. Interested readers should look at file kernel.h to see how these functions are implemented.

10.4.3 Converting a Skinny C++ Program to C++

To illustrate the ideas presented in the previous two sections, we now present examples from the MTU that have been recoded in full C++.

Recall that the transmission side of the MTU's L team contains a buffer-manager object, btxL, that holds up to two buffer objects. The skinny C++ code for this buffer-manager was shown in Figures 8.37 and 8.38. Figures 10.23 through 10.25 show how the buffer manager is implemented as a C++ class, BtxL. The class's header file (Figure 10.23) lists the buffer manager's public interface functions and its private member data.

```
// BtxL - buffer manager for tx buffer objects

class BtxL {
public:
    BtxL();
    void put_buffer_object(Buffer_object* tx);
    int remove_buffer_object();
    int get_char_from_buffer_object(char& ch);

private:
// The buffer object manager holds up to two tx buffer
// objects
Buffer_object* buf[2];

// The next tx buffer object will be stored in
// buf[nextbuf]
int nextbuf;

// When curbuf == 0 or 1, buf[curbuf] is the tx buffer
// that is currently being transmitted.  When no tx buffer
// is being transmitted, curbuf == -1.
int curbuf;

// tx buffer objects are transmitted one character at a
// time,so we need to keep track of how many characters
// have been transmitted.
int pos;
};
```

Figure 10.23 Buffer manager for tx buffer objects (part 1 of 3).

The class constructor, BtxL::BtxL() (Figure 10.24), corresponds to the skinny C++ function init_btxL(). Unlike init_btxL(), which is called explicitly by the L team's initialization function, the constructor is automatically called whenever a buffer-manager object is created.

Member function BtxL::put_buffer_object() (Figure 10.24) corresponds to function put_buffer_object_in_btxL() in the skinny C++ implementation; member function BtxL::remove_buffer_object() (Figure 10.25) corresponds to skinny C++ function remove_buffer_object_from_btxL(); and member function BtxL::get_char_from_buffer_object() (Figure 10.25) corresponds to skinny C++ function get_char_from_buffer_object().

```
// BtxL - buffer manager for tx buffer objects

BtxL::BtxL()
{
    buf[0] = NULL;
    buf[1] = NULL;
    nextbuf = 0;
    curbuf = -1;
}

void BtxL::put_buffer_object(Buffer_object* tx)
{
    short savedFlags = disable_ints();
    if (buf[nextbuf] != NULL)
        panic("btxL::put_buffer_object: no room");
    buf[nextbuf] = tx;
    // Now check to see if the UART transmitter is idle.
    // If it is, force a tx interrupt, to start
    // transmission of the packet in the buffer.
    if (tx_is_idle()) {
        // need to remember which buffer is being
        // transmitted
        curbuf = nextbuf;
        pos = 0;
        tx_is_now_busy();
        enable_tx_interrupt();
    }
    nextbuf = 1 - nextbuf;
    restore_flags(savedFlags);
}
```

Figure 10.24 Buffer manager for tx buffer objects (part 2 of 3).

The bodies of the member functions are nearly identical to their skinny C++ counterparts. Notice the statements

```
done = (pos == buf[curbuf]->packet_size());
buf[curbuf]->read_byte_from_buffer(pos, ch);
```

in BtxL::get_char_from_buffer_object(). These statements assume that the skinny C++ implementation of buffer objects (Figures 8.21 through 8.25) has been converted to full C++, so buffer objects are now instances of a Buffer_object class.

```
// After the tx buffer object in buf[curbuf] has been
// transmitted, call this function to remove the buffer
// object from the buffer manager.
// Returns 1 if the buffer manager contains another tx
// buffer object that has not yet been transmitted;
// otherwise, returns 0.
int BtxL::remove_buffer_object()
{
    short savedFlags = disable_ints();
    buf[curbuf] = NULL;
    curbuf = 1 - curbuf;
    if (buf[curbuf] == NULL) {
        // there are no other tx buffer objects stored
        // in the buffer manager.
        curbuf = -1;
        restore_flags(savedFlags);
        return 0;
    } else {
        // buf[curbuf] contains an unsent tx buffer object.
        pos = 0;
        restore_flags(savedFlags);
        return 1;
    }
}


// If the tx buffer object in buf[curbuf] contains unsent
// characters, returns 0, with the next character to send
// in ch.
// If all characters in buf[curbuf] have been sent,
// returns 1, and ch is undefined.
int BtxL::get_char_from_buffer_object(char& ch)
{
    int done;

    short savedFlags = disable_ints();
    done = (pos == buf[curbuf]->packet_size());
    if (!done) {
        buf[curbuf]->read_byte_from_buffer(pos, ch);
        pos++;   // position of next char to fetch
    }
    restore_flags(savedFlags);
    return done;
}
```

Figure 10.25 Buffer manager for tx buffer objects (part 3 of 3).

Figures 10.26 through 10.28 show how to implement a team as a C++ class, using the MTU L team as an example. Figure 10.26 contains the class declaration.

```
// Link (L) team for the MTU

class L_team {
public:
    L_team();
    void give_tx_buffer(Buffer_object *txbuf);
    void finalize();

private:
    Process rxL;
    BtxL* btxL;
    BrxL* brxL;
    Semaphore produced;
    static void rxL_root();
};
```

Figure 10.26 Implementing the L team as a C++ class (part 1 of 3).

In Figure 10.26, the root function for the rxL process is declared as a private member function of the class to ensure that it cannot be accessed from outside the class. To pass this function to `create_process()`, it must be declared `static`.

The constructor for the class, shown in Figure 10.27, corresponds to the skinny C++ function `init_L()`. This constructor creates instances of the BrxL and BtxL buffer managers and stores pointers to these objects in private variables `brxL` and `btxL`, respectively. The constructor also creates a semaphore and the rxL process by calling Tempo kernel functions in the usual manner.

Member function `L_team::give_tx_buffer()` (Figure 10.27) corresponds to skinny C++ function `give_tx_buffer_to_L()`. It calls the `btxL` buffer-manager object to store a buffer object for transmission.

```
// Link (L) team for the MTU

L_team l_team; // an L team object

L_team::L_team()
{
    // create the buffer manager objects
    CS(btxL = new BtxL);
    CS(brxL = new BrxL);

    produced = create_semaphore(0);
    rxL = create_process(rxL_root);

    init_uart_services();
}
// Store buffer object txbuf in the
// tx buffer-manager object
void L_team::give_tx_buffer(Buffer_object *txbuf)
{
    btxL->put_buffer_object(txbuf);
}

void L_team::finalize()
{
    shutdown_uart_interrupts();
}
```

Figure 10.27 Implementing the L team as a C++ class (part 2 of 3).

The root function for the rxL process is shown in Figure 10.28. Although the class declaration (Figure 10.26) declares the function to be static, the `static` keyword is not used in the function definition.

The rxL process waits on the `produced` semaphore by calling the Sem object directly instead of the `wait_semaphore()` kernel interface function:

```
l_team.produced->wait();
```

Because the root function for the rxL process is a static member of class `L_team`, the statement must specify the name of the L team object that contains the `produced` semaphore.

```
// The UART ISR (which is defined in another file) and the
// rxL process have a producer/consumer relationship,
// with the brxL buffer manager serving as the bounded
// buffer between them.  The ISR produces packets from the
// frames received by the UART (see the rx FSM).  Each
// packet is placed in a dynamically allocated buffer
// object, and buffer objects are stored in  brxL.
// The rxL process consumes buffer objects by removing
// them from the buffer manager and passing them to
// the P team.

// root function for the rxL process
void L_team::rxL_root()
{
    Buffer_object *rx_buf = NULL;
    for (;;) {
        // wait for a new packet to arrive
        l_team.produced->wait();
        rx_buf = brxL->remove_buffer_object();
        p_team.give_rx_buffer(rx_buf);
        rx_buf = NULL;
    }
}
```

Figure 10.28 Implementing the L team as a C++ class (part 3 of 3).

10.5 SUMMARY

In this chapter we have

- Described how Tempo is organized in terms of this book's component notation.
- Used CGs to explain what happens inside when a process calls a kernel functions. The behavior of the following functions was described: `create_process()`, `create_semaphore()`, `wait_semaphore()`, and `process_sleep()` (and its associated timer ISR).
- Explained the mapping between the components that comprise Tempo and C++ objects.
- Described how a kernel interface provides the skinny C++ interface to Tempo, by hiding the C++ objects inside the kernel from processes.
- Provided the C++ code for the CGs of the kernel functions.
- Provided guidelines for writing Tempo programs that use C++ classes and the objects inside the Tempo kernel.

Perspectives on Issues

This book has attempted to present the essence of designing and implementing *real-time systems* (remember that the term covers distributed systems also) through a combination of programming with concurrent processes, designing with system-oriented notations (UCMs and CGs), and studying examples that, though necessarily small scale, illustrate realistic system issues. In doing so, it has aimed to give a systems view of software that is very broad, certainly broader than the programming technology used to illustrate the ideas. Such a systems view is very important in a world in which the substrate for software applications is increasingly formed of many widely distributed computers, rather than a single computer (for example, the World Wide Web, aerospace vehicles, telephony) and the programming technology can change almost overnight (for example, the sudden emergence of Java as a language for programming distributed applications). In such a world, programming technology alone cannot provide the necessary concepts. People need to go outside programming technology to see things in system terms. This book has aimed to help satisfy that need.

An important question is this: From a student's perspective, how does the approach of this book relate to the real world of industrial practice? There are two sides to this question: What can a student take from this book to the real world that will be useful there? What should a student expect to find in the real world when he or she gets there? Readers who are not students may also be interested in the answers.

Another important question is this: What is the difference between the *process* of design on which this book has focused, which involves incomplete decisions expressed in relatively informal ways with notations that people can read but computers might find incomplete or troublesome, and the *product* of the process, which should, ideally, be a formal description of the artifact to be implemented?

This chapter aims to give a sense of the issues that are raised by these questions.

11.1 What a Student Can Take to the Real World

Students who have used this book as intended, as a supplement to programming experience, should be able to take the following from the book to the real world:

• Experience with programming interrupt-driven, concurrent, distributed systems that are complex enough to be interesting, even if not large scale. It does no harm that this experience is with a real world family of programming languages (C/C++). Java is strongly related to this family, so the experience should port easily to Java. The notations are particularly helpful in expressing the kind of structurally dynamic situations that result from moving Java byte code from place to place in a network. Such situations are becoming increasingly common in the world of distributed computing, with or without Java.

• Deep understanding of how concurrent, real-time systems function, derived from working with a minimal software infrastructure (a subset of C++ and the Tempo kernel) that does not depend on large, mysterious software layers to support concurrency and the delivery of physical events via interrupts.

• Knowledge of how to design into concurrent programs the ability to keep running in the presence of events and failures that occur in the environment of a distributed application at unpredictable times.

• Understanding that developing systems in which behavior emerges collectively from the actions of collaborating components, none of which sees the big picture, is very different from writing a program in which the behavior is embodied in an explicit algorithm.

• Ability to reason from application requirements for concurrency, performance, and robustness to process architectures that can realize them,   using the UCM notation that stands well back from the details of code. Paths through maps are inherently related to performance and robustness by their very existence. Performance problems arise due to overhead and general sluggishness along paths, to interference between paths, and to failure to start things moving down paths quickly enough. Robustness problems arise due to failures along paths that may result in a path—and the whole system—being in an inconsistent state. The map notation that forms the basis for this kind of thinking is so simple, common sense, and free of commitment to a particular type or scale of system that it is hard to imagine that it could not be applied to real-world systems of any type or scale. Furthermore, the notation is lightweight enough, and close enough to the way practical people think, to be used by busy practical people in an industrial setting.

- Ability to reason about structurally dynamic systems at a level above code. Such systems are difficult to conceptualize but can have such a strong effect on correctness, performance, and robustness that real-world designers must be able to deal with them at the same conceptual level and in the same terms as other factors that can affect correctness, performance, and robustness, such as IPC overheads along paths. UCMs provide the only design model known to us that provides a coherent context for such reasoning.

- A sense of how to design for system-level testing, based on the fact that the paths in UCMs naturally identify system test cases.

- Ability to translate process architectures into IPC structures, such as coupled pipelines, using a CG notation that is closer to code than UCMs but still stands back from code details.   This notation is not bound to the programming technology of this book but is equally useful (with some simple interpretation) for any other concurrent programming language or environment, for example, Java or Ada. Furthermore, its general nature is consistent with many other similar notations in use in the real world.

- Appreciation of how diagramming techniques that stand back from code help you to save work downstream in the development process (where mistakes cost more), in exchange for doing more work upstream.

- Bedrock understanding of the relationship between system issues and programs that will help you to be comfortable working with systems with many layers of support software and with design models and tools that are quite distant from code.

- Readiness to work in a team environment where technical matters must be communicated to others in a clear way (both informally and in formal documentation), software components must be developed separately without losing sight of system issues, and test plans must be developed guided by system requirements.

11.2 WHAT A STUDENT WILL FIND IN THE REAL WORLD

Development techniques in the area of this book are still in a state of ferment in industrial practice, with widely varying programming technologies and design methods/tools (or absence of them) in common use. The history of this field is that methods and tools have always had to catch up with new applications and programming technologies that have continually stretched old methods and tools to the breaking point. Most recently we have developments like Java and the World Wide Web starting to stretch things again. Although applications on the web are innocent-appearing initially, they are full-blown real-time systems with all the complexity factors that such systems entail. You can bet that systems are going to emerge out of this ferment that will be as large, complex, incomprehensible, and difficult to maintain as many of today's so-called legacy systems.

A few things remain constant. Developers of real-time systems cannot think in code alone. Developers explore concepts on paper, on whiteboards, on blackboards, in discussions over coffee, and in design review meetings, using a variety of techniques.

Wiring diagrams roughly like the CGs of this book are used, along with many other kinds of diagrams, many supported by CASE tools.

Use cases and scenarios have become quite popular and, in some places, UCMs are already being used even though they are still very new. Even if UCMs are not specifically used, the *concept* of causal paths traced by a literal or figurative finger over diagrams of components must somehow be in the minds of all experienced developers; otherwise how could they think about how stimuli propagate through a system as a whole without becoming bogged down in details?

Although the conceptual worlds explored by developers may have orderly models organized into orderly levels of abstraction, the actual design process may jump back and forth between different models and levels in a disorderly, opportunistic way, as something in one model or level triggers a thought about something in another that should be checked out or noted immediately. Diagrams scribbled on paper, whiteboards, or blackboards may be kept in that form for a while until the ideas in them jell, but then the diagrams may disappear. The concepts and final solutions are then captured with whatever computer-based tools are available and considered useful (for example, programming language editors, CASE tools, word processors, drawing packages), refined by adding details or changes, transformed into other forms manually or with computer assistance, and finally realized in code and tested.

Thus, at different stages, the system is a different thing. It starts out as a set of concepts that are captured in diagrams and ends up as a set of code files. If the contents of these files are not fully traceable back to the concepts, then the only description that can be trusted to define the system is the code.

This view of the real world indicates that the important issue is not whether you will find the specific techniques of this book there, but that you will find issues there with which the book has prepared you to grapple.

Although there are many CASE tools in everyday use, you will not find (at the time this is being written) any commercially available support tools for UCMs. This is an impediment to using this notation to create work products (UCMs) that can, over the lifetime of a system, be maintained, navigated, reused, edited, and kept in synchronization with other work products, including prose descriptions, models in existing CASE tools, and code. We expect graphical editors that understand UCMs to be available soon (one is already under development), but it will be a while before tools support UCMs in an integrated way with other design models.

The lack of integrated tools is not as much of a problem as it may at first seem, because practical people are quite used to having their minds provide the conceptual glue between concepts supported by different computer-based tools (or not supported at all). However, they are understandably reluctant to maintain sets of diagrams by hand.

The difficulty of the tool problem in general can be seen from the following shopping list of desirable capabilities of design-support tools:

- Support the range of conceptual models of the working culture, which may be quite wide (UCMs and CGs are but two of many possibilities).
- Support diagramming notations for the models that are already actively used by both beginners and experts in the working culture.
- Provide support in a way that leverages the design knowledge of expert designers, not just handholds novices.
- Provide traceability between related conceptual models in both directions (for example, between UCMs and CGs).
- Have Enough flexibility to enable experts to work opportunistically and arbitrarily with fragments of different conceptual models, and to move back and forth between models at any time without constraint.
- Support forward engineering, reverse engineering, and reengineering in a coordinated way.
- Support redundant design models that can be cross-checked against each other (for example, UCMs and communicating state machines).
- Support some diagrams as both input and output (for example, UCMs).
- Automatically generate code and documentation.
- automatically maintain consistency between diagrams of all kind and between diagrams and code.
- Support identification of multiple product lines and staged releases.
- support reusable design artifacts of many different kinds (not just code fragments).
- Make artwork easy for technical people who are not artists.

There are no current commercial CASE tools known to the authors that have all of these capabilities, and there are not likely to be any available soon. Some older CASE tools have so few of them as to be actually harmful for more than just handholding beginners. However, there a few newer ones with enough of these capabilities to be useful also for helping experts.

Although it may be a long time before you find magic tools that support everything in an integrated way, whatever methods or CASE tools you find in use in the real world in the near future, you can be sure that systems thinking of the kind you have learned from this book will be needed and that the notations will be either complementary or supplementary.

For example, let us see how the concepts from the book either complement or supplement those supported by a specific modern CASE tool of the variety that is actually helpful to expert designers in industry, ObjecTime (the Real Time Object Oriented Modeling technique, known as ROOM, supported by this tool is described in a book by Selic, Ward, and Gulekson: "Real Time Object Oriented Modeling", Wiley, 1994).

This tool supports modeling of systems in terms of components called *actors* that communicate by messages and are driven by internal state machines. Models entered mainly in diagram form (next figure) may be executed in the context of the entered diagrams, and may be automatically translated into target code in a variety of languages. The graphical interface describes actor structures as simple wiring diagrams analogous to the ones we used in Chapter 1 to introduce the concept. Messages flowing over the connections are described textually, along with the protocols they must obey. Self-modification is supported through additional visual notations (not shown) that identify slot-like actors; however, the actions that perform self modification are described textually. Actor diagrams may be organized into inheritance hierarchies to support reuse.

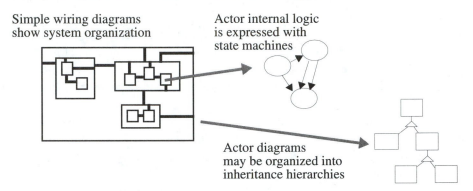

Simple wiring diagrams show system organization

Actor internal logic is expressed with state machines

Actor diagrams may be organized into inheritance hierarchies

Whether an actor is team-like, process-like, or object-like (in the terms of this book) is determined not by visual notation in actor diagrams, but by internal details of actors. Similarly, connection types, such as the asynchronous or synchronous IPC connections of this book, are determined by internal details. The internal details that determine these things are textual.

The approach of this book *complements* ROOM-style models at their own level of abstraction and also at the higher level of abstraction of UCMs. CGs give a richer visual picture than ROOM actor diagrams that can be translated into actor models and reverse engineered from actor models. The ObjecTime tool offers the ability to specify message sequence charts that give examples of required end-to-end behavior scenarios and then to observe message sequences from running the model and to compare them with required scenarios. This view of end-to-end behavior is much more detailed than UCMs, and the latter provide a useful *complement* to give a more compact system view at a higher level of abstraction.

Similar observations on complementarity and supplementarity apply to other methods and tools in use in industry or emerging (in particular, UML).

11.3 DESIGN: THE PROCESS VERSUS THE PRODUCT

This book has focused on the *process* of design, which involves making incomplete decisions expressed in relatively informal ways with design notations that humans can read but computers might find troublesome, because much is left to human interpretation.

In contrast, the *product* of the process should ideally be a formal description of the artifact to be implemented (formal in the sense that some automatable process can execute the description, analyze it, or compile it into code). Examples of formal descriptions are programs written in high-level languages that have standardized compilers and design models entered into CASE tools, such as ObjecTime, which can execute the models and translate them into executable code.

Experience tells us that, while formality is needed to capture the product, informality is essential to the process. It is a truism to say that one cannot proceed from the informal to the formal by formal means. Informality is essential to human understanding while making design decisions and to the translation by humans of these decisions into formal models.

This is so unless every aspect of the process of developing, maintaining, evolving and reengineering systems can be automated from the beginning, which it cannot because the process *begins informally*, by definition, and any human intervention along the line may invalidate formal descriptions (for example, modifying high-level-language code produced automatically by a CASE tool).

Even formal descriptions have informal aspects, such as names and comments, to make them understandable to humans. Change all the names in a formal description (say a program in some high level language) to nonsense names and remove all the comments and see how understandable is the result.

While many aspects of the design notations of this book can be formalized, this is not their purpose in this book. Their purpose is to help human designers with the thinking process.

A good set of design notations provides a context for adding and recalling details; an ability to express big-picture aspects in a way that helps designers explore the solution space in order to find good solutions; and a context for making use of design knowledge, making design tradeoffs, and understanding how to evolve designs to add new behavior or functionality. The notations presented in this book aim for all of these things.

Formal descriptions demand too much detail too soon for design exploration. They tend to be so narrowly focused on specific aspects of design that they leave out many issues that practical designers have to think about (recall the earlier list of desirable capabilities of design-support tools). Using a number of formal descriptions in combination to cover important issues tends to become mired in a tar pit of conflicting definitions at the detailed level. Stretching any one of them to try to make it cover all of the issues leads to conceptual difficulties.

In contrast, design notations like the ones of this book aim to express what designers really need to think about at the system level, without complicating it with all the formal details that are needed to get an executable or analyzable model, or an implementation.

They enable designers to draw diagrams that are meaningful in the large even when many details are missing, and thus to push detail down to a lower cognitive level. They can be used in combination without becoming mired in a tar pit of conflicting detail.

This is not to say they are completely informal; they must have sufficient formality to express relationships like causality and connectivity at a high level of abstraction with sufficient precision to help guide design thinking. However, additional human input is required to map them to executable or analyzable models, or to implementations. This should not be regarded as a weakness but as a strength, because it reflects the way practical people have to deal with the real world.

11.4 SUMMARY

We have attempted, in a short space, to give some sense of the issues raised by the following questions:

- What can a student expect to take from this book to the real world?
- What can a student expect to find in the real world that relates to this book?
- What is the difference between the *process* and the *product* of design?

Tempo Reference Manual

*T*he interface to the Tempo real-time kernel is through a small set of kernel functions. This appendix provides a programmer's quick reference to these functions. For each function, the function prototype is provided along with a brief description of the function.

For convenience, related kernel functions are grouped together in separate sections. A list of the functions, arranged in alphabetical order and cross-referenced to the appropriate sections, is provided on the following page.

Except for two of the functions in Section A.2, all Tempo functions can be called by user processes. Each section identifies those functions that can be called from interrupt service routines.

The second part of this appendix covers programming tips and hints. We describe several examples of the kinds of problems and bugs that novice real-time system developers are likely to encounter and provide guidance on how to avoid them.

A.1 ALPHABETICAL LISTING OF TEMPO KERNEL FUNCTIONS

A.2 KERNEL FUNCTIONS

```
void initialize_Tempo();
```

```
void become_idle();
```

```
void terminate_multitasking();
```

The first two functions are called from `main()` to transform a sequential C++ program into a concurrent Tempo program. (Tempo includes a `main()` function, which is shown in Chapter 2.) *These functions should never be called by processes or interrupt service routines.* The `initialize_Tempo()` call initializes the kernel's private data structures. When this function returns, Tempo's process creation and interprocess communication functions can be called. The `become_idle()` function causes its caller to become the idle process, which runs when no user processes are eligible to run. This function never returns.

   Function `terminate_multitasking()` can be called by any process to halt the currently executing Tempo program and exit to the operating system. Except for the system timer interrupt (which is handled by Tempo to provide timeouts), this function does not restore the system's interrupt vectors or the programmable interrupt controller's mask register to their original values. A Tempo program that installs its own ISRs *must* restore the original interrupt handlers before calling `terminate_multitasking()`; otherwise, spurious interrupts that occur after the program terminates will likely cause the computer to crash.

   The CG notation for `terminate_multitasking()` is shown in the following diagram.

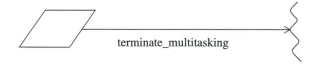

A.2.1 Interrupt Service Routines

None of these functions can be called by ISRs.

A.3 PROCESS FUNCTIONS

```
Process create_process(void (*root_fn_ptr)(),
                       int priority = 0);

void process_sleep(unsigned int ticks);
```

The create_process() call creates an instance of a process that starts execution in the root function pointed to by root_fn_ptr. If the process is successfully created, the new process's id is returned. The newly created process is left in the ready-to-run state. The new process has its own stack but shares external data with other processes according to the scope rules of C++.

Allowable process priorities run from 0 (the lowest possible) to 16 (the highest possible). It is not necessary that process priorities be unique. Any number of process may have the same priority.

If the new process's priority is higher than that of the creating process, an immediate context switch to the new process will occur.

A process may terminate by running off the end of its root function or returning (by means of a return statement) from its root function.

The process_sleep() function causes the calling process to relinquish the processor for the specified length of time. The function's argument is the integral number of ticks of the system timer, which is programmed to "tick" at 18.2 Hz.

The following diagram shows the relationship of these functions to the CG notation.

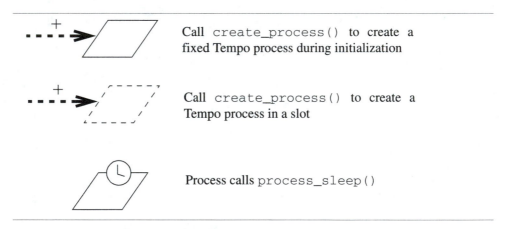

Call create_process() to create a fixed Tempo process during initialization

Call create_process() to create a Tempo process in a slot

Process calls process_sleep()

A.3.1 Interrupt Service Routines

None of these functions can be called by ISRs.

A.4 SEMAPHORE FUNCTIONS

```
Semaphore create_semaphore(int initial_count = 0);

void wait_semaphore(Semaphore semaphore);

void signal_semaphore(Semaphore semaphore);
```

Function `create_semaphore()` creates a counting semaphore with the specified initial signal count; if no initial count is specified, the value 0 is used by default. It is not permissible to specify a negative initial count. If the semaphore is successfully created, its id is returned.

Function `wait_semaphore()` checks the specified semaphore's signal count. If the count is 0, the calling process blocks and is placed on the semaphore's queue; otherwise, the signal count is decremented by 1 and calling process continues to run.

Function `signal_semaphore()` dequeues the process at the head of the specified semaphore's queue, makes that process ready-to-run, and reschedules. If the queue is empty when this function is called, the semaphore count is incremented by 1.

The following diagram shows the relationship of these functions to the CG notation.

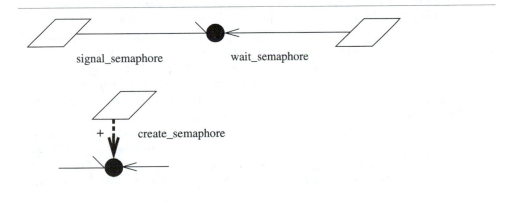

A.4.1 Interrupt Service Routines

ISRs can call `signal_semaphore()`.

A.5 EVENT QUEUE FUNCTIONS

```
void signal(Process process_id, int queue);

int wait();

void send(Process destination, int queue, message msg,
          int ack_queue);

int receive(message &msg, Process &correspondent,
          int &ack_queue);

void reply(Process correspondent, int queue, message reply);

void mask_queue(int queue);

void unmask_queue(int queue);
```

Each process has eight event queues that belong to it. Event queues can be signaled by processes, like semaphores. In addition, event queues support asynchronous message passing between processes.

Function `signal()` signals the specified event queue belonging to the specified process. This function has the same semantics as `signal_semaphore()`.

The `wait()` function is called by a process to wait for a signal to arrive at one of its unmasked event queues. This function is similar to `wait_semaphore()`, with one exception: `wait()` checks each of the process's unmasked event queues for a signal. This function returns an `int` that indicates which of the process's queues was signaled.

Function `mask_queue()` is called by a process to mask the specified event queue. Masked event queues are ignored by `wait()` and `receive()`; that is, `wait()` returns after removing a signal from one of the calling process's unmasked event queues, and `receive()` returns after removing a signal or a message from an unmasked event queue. When a masked event queue is signaled, the signal is not lost; instead, it simply increments that event queue's signal count. Similarly, messages sent to a masked event queue are stored in the queue.

The `unmask_queue()` function unmasks the specified event queue so that it will be checked by subsequent calls to `wait()` and `receive()`.

Function `send()` sends message `msg` to the specified `destination` process, placing the message in `queue`. Messages are pointers to blocks of memory that are cast to type `message`. Parameter `ack_queue` specifies a queue belonging to the sending process, where the sender will wait for a reply. (`NO_ACK` is specified if no reply is required.) This function may return before the receiving process has consumed the message.

Function `receive()` is called to wait for a message to arrive at one of its unmasked event queues. When this function returns, `msg` contains the message (a pointer to a block of memory), `correspondent` contains the process identifier of the process that sent the message, and `ack_queue` contains the queue where the correspondent process will wait for a reply. This function returns the queue where the message was found.

The receive() function waits for both signals and messages. Signals take precedence over messages: receive() will return a message only if there are no signals in any of the process's unmasked event queues. To indicate that it has received a signal instead of a message, receive() assigns NULL to the msg, correspondent, and ack_queue parameters.

The reply() function is typically used to reply a message to a correspondent process. It has the same semantics as send(), except that an acknowledgment queue is not specified.

The following diagram shows the relationship of these functions to the CG notation.

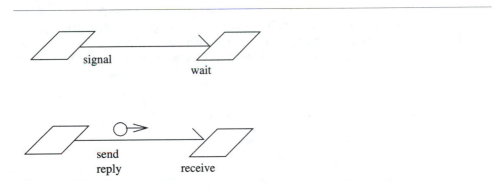

There is no notation corresponding to mask_queue() and unmask_queue()

A.5.1 Interrupt Service Routines

ISRs can call signal() and reply(). ISRs can also call send() but should specify NO_ACK for the acknowledgment queue, because they cannot wait for a reply.

A.6 TIMEOUT FUNCTIONS

```
int wait_semaphore(Semaphore semaphore, int timeout);

int wait(int timeout);

int receive(message &msg, Process &correspondent,
            int &ack_queue, int timeout);
```

Tempo maintains a count of the number of ticks of the system timer that have occurred since the kernel was initialized. The kernel provides versions of `wait_semaphore()`, `wait()`, and `receive()` that time out and return if the waiting process does not receive the desired event within the number of clock ticks specified by parameter `timeout`. If a timeout occurs, these functions return the value `TIMED_OUT`.

The following diagram shows the relationship of these functions to the CG notation.

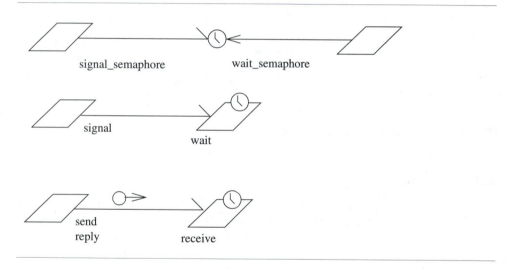

signal_semaphore   wait_semaphore

signal

wait

send
reply   receive

A.6.1 Interrupt Service Routines

None of these functions can be called by ISRs.

A.7 INTERRUPT FUNCTIONS

```
short disable_ints();

void enable_ints();

void restore_flags(short saved_flags);
```

Function `disable_ints()` disables interrupts by clearing the interrupt bit in the processor's flags register. This function records the value of the flags register before interrupts are disabled and returns that value.

Function `enable_ints()` reenables interrupts by setting the interrupt bit in the processor's flags register.

Function `restore_flags()` sets the processor's flags register to the value `saved_flags`. Usually, `saved_flags` is the value returned by a previous call to `disable_ints()`.

None of these functions alter the interrupt mask register in the computer's programmable interrupt controller (PIC).

When an interrupt service routine and a process communicate through a monitor, the monitor's interface functions must ensure mutual exclusion by bracketing all operations on the shared data with calls to `disable_ints()` and `restore_flags()`:

```
type monitor_interface(param_list)
{
    short saved_flags;

    saved_flags = disable_ints();  // begin mutual exclusion
    // code to access shared data placed here
    restore_flags(saved_flags);    // end mutual exclusion
    return value;
}
```

A function written this way can be called by interrupt service routines (which typically run with interrupts disabled) as well as processes (which typically run with interrupts enabled). The function will return with interrupts disabled when called by code that is running with interrupts disabled. The same function will return with interrupts enabled when called by code that is running with interrupts enabled. This eliminates the need for the monitor to provide two kinds of interface functions: namely, functions that always disable interrupts on entry and enable interrupts on exit (and consequently can only be called by processes) and functions that always return with interrupts disabled (and consequently can only be called by ISRs).

There is no notation that directly corresponds to these functions; however, their use is implied by a diagram showing a monitor shared by a process and an ISR.

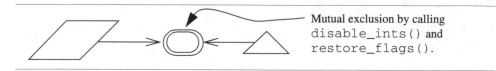

Mutual exclusion by calling
`disable_ints()` and
`restore_flags()`.

A.7.1 Interrupt Service Routines

These functions can be called by ISRs.

An ISR begins execution with interrupts disabled, so it does not need to lock out further interrupts by calling `disable_ints()`. Calling `disable_ints()` while interrupts are disabled is permitted (for example, see the example monitor interface function).

Because an ISR is normally short, interrupts are usually disabled while the ISR runs. If necessary (for example, to allow another interrupt to be recognized while a long ISR is running), interrupts can be enabled by calling `enable_ints()`.

A.8 PROGRAMMING TIPS AND HINTS

Over several years of helping teams of students with their programming projects, we've gathered numerous examples of the kinds of problems and bugs that novice real-time system developers are likely to encounter. Well-known C/C++ sequential programming bugs are the most common source of problems, but some problems are related to the use of concurrent processes. This section describes these difficulties and provides guidance on how to avoid them.

A.8.1 Pointer Variables and Dynamically Allocated Memory

Bugs related to the incorrect use of pointer variables and dynamically allocated memory are perhaps the most frequent source of grief for novice programmers in both sequential and multitasking programs. The nature of pointer bugs means that their effects often do not become apparent until well after the incorrect C/C++ statements are executed, so locating these bugs can be tedious and time-consuming. Multitasking programs increase the challenge—a pointer bug in one process can cause a bug-free process to exhibit incorrect behavior. Programmers may then waste considerable time looking for bugs in processes that are actually correct.

The most common pointer bugs are as follows:

- Dereferencing a pointer variable before it has been pointed to a dynamically allocated block of memory.
- Deferencing a pointer variable after the memory that it points to has been deallocated (returned to the system memory pool).
- Having two or more processes with pointer variables that point to the same block of memory, and reading/writing that memory without synchronizing their accesses.
- Forgetting to deallocate the block of memory that is pointed to by a pointer variable before assigning a new value to the pointer variable (memory leaks).

By following the programming conventions listed next, our students find that their multitasking programs have few pointer bugs. The intent of these conventions is to ensure that each pointer variable is dereferenced only when it points to a block of memory that can be read and written through that pointer. In other words, we must ensure that

1. Each pointer variable is NULL whenever it does not point to a block of memory.
2. Each pointer variable is non-NULL only when it points to a block of memory that can be read and written through the pointer.

The programming conventions that accomplish this are as follows:

- Assign NULL to pointer variables when they are not pointing to blocks of memory.
- Check that the value returned by the C++ new operator is not NULL, to verify that

memory was allocated correctly. (If new cannot allocate memory, it returns NULL).

- Before dereferencing a pointer variable, verify that it points to a valid memory address by checking that it is not NULL.
- Before using the C++ delete operator to deallocate a block of memory, verify that its argument (the pointer to the memory) is not NULL.
- After using the C++ delete operator to deallocate a block of memory, assign NULL to the pointer that pointed to the memory.
- When ownership of a dynamically allocated buffer is passed from one process to another by passing the pointer to buffer, the process that relinquishes ownership of the buffer should NULL the pointer variable after it has passed the pointer.

The following code fragments were extracted from functions in the MTU for managing buffer objects. These fragments illustrate typical pointer bugs and show how the programming conventions detect them.

In the following version of create_buffer_object(), memory for the buffer object is deliberately not allocated to illustrate an error. The statement

```
CS(p = new Buffer_object);
```

is missing.

```
Buffer_object *create_buffer_object(char msg[])
{
   Buffer_object *p;

   // Missing statement would go here in a
   // correct function.

   // Check if memory was allocated.
   if (p == NULL)
     panic("create_buffer_object: new failed");
   ...
   return p;
}
```

Because pointer variable p is assigned NULL when it is declared, this error of leaving out the allocation at run-time is detected at run time by the statement

```
if (p == NULL) {
  panic("create_buffer_object: new failed");
```

When the missing statement is added to the function, the if statement verifies that the buffer object has been allocated correctly, because new returns a NULL pointer if it cannot obtain the required amount of memory.

The next example shows the importance of checking pointer variables before accessing the memory to which they point. The version of set_packet_type()

shown next, is called with two arguments: a pointer to an MTU buffer object (containing a data packet, an ack packet, or a nak packet), and a character that represents the type of packet. The function assumes that pointer variable p points to a buffer object, and simply assigns the packet type character to the `type` field in the packet header.

```
void set_packet_type(Buffer_object *p, char type)
{
    p->ph.type = type;
}
```

A more robust version of the function, shown next, verifies that the pointer is not NULL before performing the assignment operation. (It also verifies that the packet type argument is a legal value.)

```
void set_packet_type(Buffer_object *p, char type)
{
    if (p == NULL)
        panic("set_packet_type: NULL pointer");
    if ((type == DATA) || (type == ACK) || (type == NAK)) {
        p->ph.type = type;
    } else {
        CS(cout << "set_packet_type: bad packet type"
                << type << endl);
        panic("");
    }
}
```

Similarly, `destroy_buffer_object()` verifies that its argument, a pointer to a buffer object, is not NULL before it uses `delete` to deallocate the object:

```
void destroy_buffer_object(Buffer_object *p)
{
    if (p == NULL)
        panic("destroy_buffer_object: NULL pointer");
    CS(delete p);
}
```

The following fragments from the MTU's M team illustrates how processes and interface functions that use dynamically allocated buffers should be coded according to our programming conventions.

```
void txM_root()
{
    ...
    handle_send_command(cmd);
    ...
}
```

```
void handle_send_command(char cmd)
{
    // Ensure that the initial state of the pointer to
    // the buffer object is NULL.
    Buffer_object *tx_buf = NULL;

    for (;;) {
        ...
        // Allocate a new buffer object.
        tx_buf = create_buffer_object(s);

        // tx_buf now contains a non-NULL pointer, and
        // points to a valid buffer object (this is
        // guaranteed by the pointer checks in
        // create_buffer_object)

        // Pass the buffer to P
        give_tx_buffer_to_P(tx_buf);

        // We've relinquished ownership of the buffer
        // object, so NULL our pointer to it.
        tx_buf = NULL;
        ...
    }
}
```

Interface function `give_rx_buffer_to_M()` verifies that its argument (a pointer to a buffer object containing a data packet) is not NULL before it sends the pointer to the rxM process.

```
void give_rx_buffer_to_M(Buffer_object *rx_buf)
{
    if (rx_buf == NULL)
        panic("give_rx_buffer_to_M: NULL rx_buf");
    send(rxM, GIVE_RX_BUF, (message)rx_buf, NO_ACK);
}
```

Given that `give_rx_buffer_to_M()` ensures that the pointer sent to rxM is not NULL, the rxM process assumes that it has received a non-NULL pointer when it returns from `receive()`. The process ensures that the variable that holds the pointer is nulled when it is not pointing to a buffer object.

```
void rxM_root()
{
    ...
    // initially, the buffer object pointer is nulled
    Buffer_object *rx_buf = NULL;

    for(;;) {
        // wait for a new rx buffer object to arrive
        queue = receive(msg, correspondent, ack_queue);
```

```
    rx_buf = (Buffer_object *)msg;
    ...
    // code to proces the packet data removed
    ...
    // deallocate the buffer object
    destroy_buffer_object(rx_buf);

    // rx_buf no longer points to a buffer object,
    // so NULL it.
    rx_buf = NULL;
    }
}
```

A.8.2 Initialization Bugs

Many of the bugs in our students' programs are caused by incorrect system initialization. Here are a few common examples.

Sometimes a programmer forgets to call a team's initialization function. The following version of the root function for MTU's Main process is supposed to initialize all the MTU teams; however, the call to the P team's initialization function is missing.

```
void Main(){
    init_C();   // init the control team
    init_S();   // init the status team
    init_M();   // init the Message team
    // call to init_P() missing
    init_L();    // init the Link team
    // init the UART/PIC hardware and ISR support
    init_uart_services();
}
```

The easiest way to locate this kind of bug is to review the CGs showing system initialization and verify that every connection to an initialization function has a corresponding function call in the code.

Other common initialization bugs include forgetting to create a process. If a call to create_process() is missing, the Process variable for the process is uninitialized. These bugs are easily detected by reviewing the CGs and code. Every arrow in a CG that asserts the creation of a process must have a corresponding call to create_process(). A similar kind of bug is forgetting to create a semaphore.

A.8.3 Synchronization Bugs

A surprising number of novice programmers make the following errors:

- Forgetting a call to signal_semaphore().
- Forgetting a call to wait_semaphore().

- Calling `wait_semaphore()` **instead of** `signal_semaphore()`.
- Calling `signal_semaphore()` **instead of** `wait_semaphore()`.

The following code is from an incorrect version of root function for the L team's rxL process:

```
// The UART ISR (which is defined in another file) and the
// rxL process have a producer/consumer relationship, with
// the brxL buffer manager serving as a bounded buffer
// between them. The ISR produces packets from the frames
// received by the UART (see the rx FSM). Each packet is
// placed in a dynamically allocated buffer object, and
// buffer objects are stored in brxL. The rxL process
// consumes buffer objects by removing them from the
// buffer manager and passing them to the P team.
//
// Because the buffer manager has a fixed capacity, the
// normal synchronization protocol between a producer and
// a consumer must be followed; namely, the consumer must
// be signaled when a new buffer is available and the
// producer (the ISR) must be signaled when a buffer is
// removed from the buffer manager.

Semaphore produced, consumed;

void rxL_root()
{
    Buffer_object *rx_buf = NULL;

    for(;;) {
        // wait for a new packet to arrive
        // (semaphore produced is signaled by the ISR)
        wait_semaphore(produced);
        rx_buf = get_buffer_from_brxL();
        // the ISR waits on the consumed semaphore
        signal_semaphore(consumed);
         give_rx_buffer_to_P(rx_buf);
         rx_buf = NULL;
    }
}
```

The comment describing the protocol between the rxL process and the UART ISR sounds plausible but contains a serious error, indicated by the highlighted phrase. The assumption is that the UART ISR will wait on semaphore `consumed`, which is signaled by the process. For reasons explained in Chapter 3, an ISR must never synchronize with a process by calling a Tempo kernel function that can cause the ISR to wait. As such, the `consumed` semaphore and the highlighted call to `signal_semaphore()` must be removed from the process.

A.8.4 Interrupt Service Routine Bugs

The two most common ISR bugs are as follows:

- Calling a Tempo kernel function that may wait. Chapter 3 contains a detailed explanation of why this should not be done.
- Forgetting to send an EOI command to the PIC. As discussed in Chapter 3, this should be the first statement in any ISR. Because EOI stands for *end*-of-interrupt, students sometimes send EOI at the end of the ISR, not at the beginning.

Collaboration Graph Reference Manual

B.1 STRUCTURALLY STATIC SYSTEMS

The following diagram shows the notations for fixed components and summarizes their relationships to Tempo and to ordinary code.

Teams are design abstractions of compound operational units, the internal organization of which will be shown in a nested fashion. They have nothing in particular to do with multitasking. They are committed as implementation units (modules) only if they are given interfaces in CGs. Modules may be coded in many ways (commented groupings, instances of classes, files).

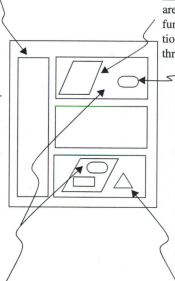

Processes implement multitasking. They are coded as ordinary functions (*root* functions) with some special conventions and then made known to Tempo through create calls.

Objects are abstractions that have nothing to do with multitasking and not necessarily anything to do with OO programming. They are the minimal *diagrammatic* representation of raw data and raw procedure. For C/skinny C++, they represent related sets of (optionally) raw data and functions; for C++, they represent literal objects (or abstractions of sets of them). Diagrammed objects are primitive visual entities (never decomposed visually).

Nesting of components inside other components is an operational abstraction that helps system understanding even though it may not describe the organization of the code accurately (for example, nothing is literally nested in process code except raw data).

ISRs link hardware to processes outside the kernel. They are coded as ordinary functions with some special conventions. Except for one ISR of its own to handle timer interrupts, the kernel is unaware of the existence of ISRs.

The following diagram summarizes the elements of the wiring notation for structurally static systems. Remember that although connections are *conceptualized* as fixed, they are mostly established dynamically in code. A system is characterized as structurally static if we can conceptualize all connections between actual components as fixed, otherwise it is structurally dynamic.

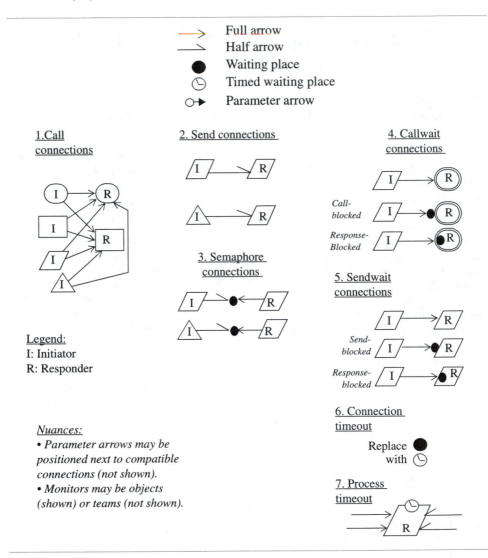

Legend:
I: Initiator
R: Responder

Nuances:
• *Parameter arrows may be positioned next to compatible connections (not shown).*
• *Monitors may be objects (shown) or teams (not shown).*

B.1.1 Some Important Connection Conventions

The following diagram summarizes some important connection conventions. Rectangular boxes stand for *any component*. Arrows stand for *any connection*, unless otherwise indicated.

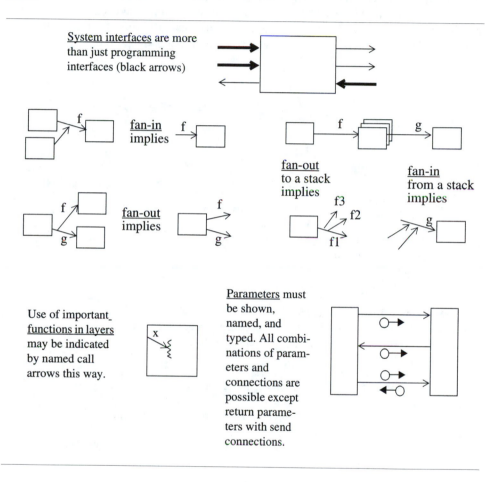

B.1.2 IPC Connections

The following diagram summarizes the relationship of the connection notation to the current version of Tempo. Numbers refer to the numbered list of Tempo functions at the bottom and identify where calls to these functions are made to perform interactions over the connection. Callwait and sendwait connections are not shown here because they are not specifically supported by the current version of Tempo (later diagrams for them refer back to the list of Tempo functions in this diagram). Tempo functions not shown in the examples of this diagram (1,2,10,11,15,16,17) have no interpretation as IPC connections.

List of Tempo Functions

1. create_process(void (*root_fn_ptr)(), int priority = 0)
2. create_semaphore(int initial_count = 0)
3. wait_semaphore(Semaphore semaphore)
4. signal_semaphore(Semaphore semaphore)
5. void signal(Process process_id, int queue)
6. wait()
7. send(Process destination, int queue, message msg, int ack_queue)
8. receive(message &msg, Process &correspondent, int &ack_queue)
9. reply(Process correspondent, int queue, message reply)
10. mask_queue(int queue)
11. unmask_queue(int queue)
12. wait_semaphore(Semaphore semaphore, int timeout)
13. wait(int timeout)
14. receive(message &msg, Process &correspondent, int &ack_queue, int timeout)
15. disable_ints()
16. enable_ints() (an additional restore_flags functions used with this is not listed here)
17. terminate_multitasking

The following diagram summarizes the relationship between callwait connections for monitors and the current version of Tempo (numbers refer back to the list of Tempo functions).

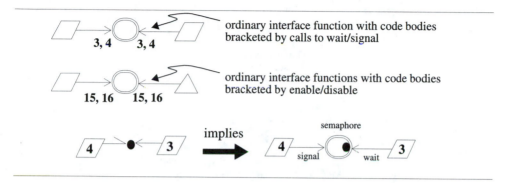

ordinary interface function with code bodies bracketed by calls to wait/signal

ordinary interface functions with code bodies bracketed by enable/disable

The following diagram summarizes the relationship between sendwait connections and ordinary Tempo send connections. It includes a useful shorthand notation that is not in the CG overview diagram. (Tempo may eventually support sendwait, but in the meantime, this is how to think about sendwait.)

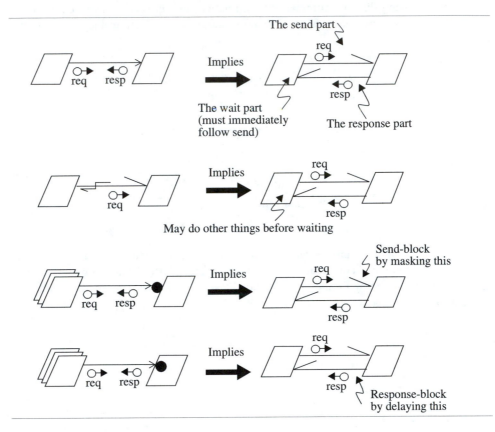

Because the notation for IPC connections implies the use of an underlying kernel layer to implement the connections, it also implies the existence of queues for signals and messages and of queues for processes where they may wait for signals, messages, or responses. *There is no need for extra notation to indicate the existence of such queues and it is a mistake to try to represent them in CGs by tricks such as showing PID (process identifier) parameters going into and out of objects identified as queue objects—feeling compelled to do so is an indicator that you do not understand the notation.*

The queueing implications are summarized next for all connections (omitting only the call-blocked, send-blocked and response-blocked variants, which add nothing new to this summary). The kernel's ready-to-run queues are not included in this summary because, in principle, all processes in them are running concurrently. Parameter arrows are omitted, for simplicity. Fan-in of connections from different processes is shown, for generality.

- There is no queueing at the interfaces of objects or teams. Processes may execute interface functions concurrently. Tempo is not involved in the interactions.

- Each separate connection or set of fanned-in connections indicates a Tempo event

queue at the responder. There are no queues for initiators, only for the signals or messages they send. There is a single-process queue for the responder where the responder may wait for the first signal or message arriving on any of its connections. This waiting is FIFO, except Tempo prioritizes connections by message queue number to handle situations in which many signals or messages have arrived on different connections.

- There is nothing new at the initiator end for a semaphore but there is a many-pro-

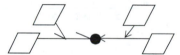

cess queue for responders. Because all queues are FIFO, there is no way of arranging for a specific signal to go to a specific responder.

- Initiators are queued in FIFO order at the responder (the monitor) in a many-process

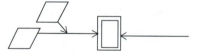

queue from which they are served one at a time. Different connections are not distinguished in this queue.

- Initiators are queued in FIFO order at the responder in a separate queue for each

connection (recall that fan-in indicates a single connection from the responder's perspective). Different initiators for the same connection are responded to in the order in which they are queued.

B.2 STRUCTURALLY DYNAMIC SYSTEMS

The following diagram identifies the components of the notation that are used for structurally dynamic systems and summarizes their relationships to Tempo and to ordinary code.

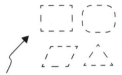

Slots indicate places where dynamic components may appear (become visible) or disappear at any time. They are metaphors for changing visibility, not necessarily representations of actual code elements. If they are represented explicitly in code, it will be as pointer variables located where the slots are shown.

Pools store dynamic components while they are not occupying slots (components may be aliased between pools and slots). For code, *storing components* means storing pointers. Pools are, in effect, data objects but are shown in a special way to indicate their special role. Pools may be used to indicate queueing of processes for slots, but *not* to indicate process queues supported by Tempo.

Note: The term *pointer* covers plain pointers in languages like
C as well as quantities such as process identifiers returned by
create calls to Tempo.

The following diagram summarizes the elements of the CG notation for representing structural dynamics. Remember that the dashed arrows are not regarded as connections because they are not paths for interaction; they are really assertions about things that must happen.

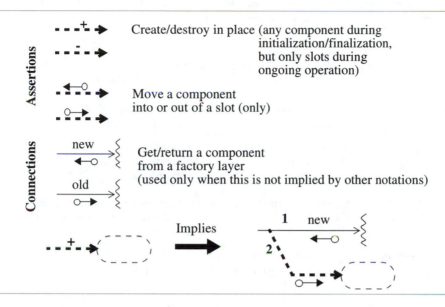

For moving components into and out of pools, use ordinary connections, because pools are, in effect, ordinary data objects.

Ordinary connection arrows touching a slots indicates connections with the component in the slot. Exercising the connections requires that a component be in the slot.

Assertions are *not connections*. They eliminate the need for a separate notation for the creation of connections because they imply connections will be dynamically established (how this is to be done is left as an implementation detail).

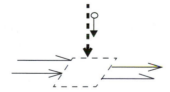

The following diagram summarizes the relationship of these notations to Tempo (only create is shown, but destroy is symmetrical).

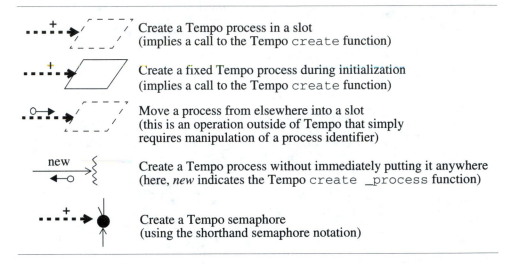

Create a Tempo process in a slot
(implies a call to the Tempo `create` function)

Create a fixed Tempo process during initialization
(implies a call to the Tempo `create` function)

Move a process from elsewhere into a slot
(this is an operation outside of Tempo that simply requires manipulation of a process identifier)

Create a Tempo process without immediately putting it anywhere
(here, *new* indicates the Tempo `create _process` function)

Create a Tempo semaphore
(using the shorthand semaphore notation)

Everything else supported by Tempo is represented as a connection; there is no notation provided (or needed) to indicate creation of connections. Semaphores are schizophrenic. They are actually monitors supported by Tempo but a shorthand notation represents them as connections; the creation notation for semaphores in the previous diagram is therefore a somewhat odd hybrid.

B.3 SOME HELPFUL HINTS FOR USING THE NOTATION

This section presents a grab bag of do's and don'ts for using the notation, drawn from experience designing it, teaching it, and observing students trying to use it.

B.3.1 Ways of Looking at Teams

The next diagram shows three ways (among others) of indicating implementation commitment for teams with CGs. In (a), the team has no direct representation in the implementation. In (b), the team is a container unit with internal components. Our convention is to call such a unit a *module* in cases where we want to explicitly indicate an implementation commitment (although we often continue to use the term *team* when the meaning is clear from the context). In (c), the team is implemented as a switchboard object. Recall that the term *object* is a slippery one. Nothing prevents the container module in (b) from being implemented as an object in an object-oriented programming language or the switchboard object in (c) from being implemented as a module in a language that supports modules— the diagrammatic distinction is more a matter more of what we want to show and hide in system level diagrams than of programming commitment. The only programming commitment here is to concept in (a), container in (b), and switchboard in (c). This begs the question: Why, if we wanted (c) in the implementation, would we not show it that way in the concept diagram at the top? The answer is that we would just have a cluster of apparently unrelated objects.

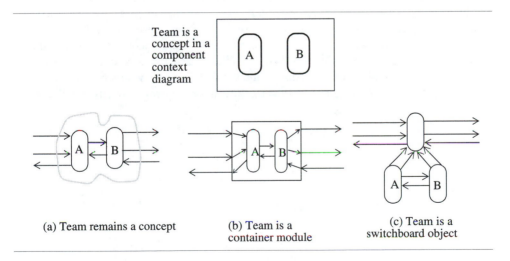

(a) Team remains a concept   (b) Team is a   (c) Team is a
                                         container module   switchboard object

B.3.2 Interaction Sequences

Annotating connections with sequence numbers to indicate standard sequences of interactions may often be helpful for getting a system view. There is no notation to distinguish connection *names* (which may also be numbers) from sequence numbers, so this must be resolved by context. An indented numbering notation may be used to indicate causally related sequences of interactions in cases where they can be conveyed clearly this way. Putting the same sequence number on different connections means the order in which they are exercised is not important. Here are two obvious examples, for the simplified bounded buffer problem. The left-hand example indicates that Buffer must be initialized before the processes that use it are created. The right-hand example identifies causally connected call chains *get-get-print* and *put-put-print*.

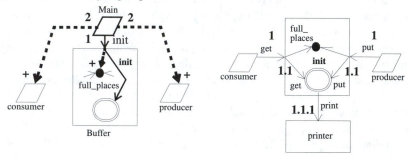

When developing designs at this level of detail from use case maps, remember that the direction of a path in a use case map indicates a causal sequence, not necessarily an interaction sequence. In general, interaction sequences may be out of order relative to causal sequences. For example, a causal sequence along a path may be implemented as a sequence of returns from a chain of calls made in the reverse direction of the path (instead of as a sequence of calls in the direction of the path), or a process anywhere along a path may wait for work to arrive along a path via a callwait or sendwait interaction in the opposite direction of the path.

B.3.3 IPC Connections

Remember that there is no way of identifying which process sent the signal or which process will receive it in semaphore connections that have multiple processes at either or both ends.

The following configurations are meaningless.

Although event queues are like internal semaphores of processes, we do not show semaphores internally (next diagram). It seems as if this diagram could be read to mean a signal is sent to an internal semaphore waited on by the internal mainline of the process. However, if this is meant to be a real semaphore that is operationally local to the process, then the intent is silly because event queues do the job. If this is meant to be a metaphor for how event queues work, we do not need it because the notation implies this is how they work.

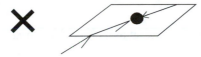

Don't use IPC connections in meaningless ways.

In general, understandability is improved by hiding by IPC connections between processes in different teams behind call connections between teams. This enables the big picture to be presented free of IPC clutter. The following diagram gives some examples.

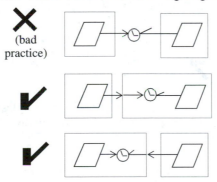

The exception to this rule is structurally dynamic systems in which dynamic visibility of processes may be useful between teams (but then use the slot notation to indicate local visibility of processes in other teams, as described in Section B.3.9 of this appendix).

B.3.4 Timeouts

A common mistake is to draw a connection like this, imagining that the full arrow indi-

cates the path for setting the timer (true) and the half arrow the path for propagating the timeout event (false).

The correct notation and its meaning are as follows. The timeout event is propagated in the reverse direction of the full arrow.

There are no separate start or cancel arrows for the timer. Start automatically occurs when waiting starts and cancel automatically occurs when a signal or message arrives.

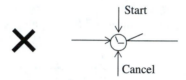

The following notation is sufficient to indicate that a process may put itself to sleep for a period.

Here are correct and incorrect ways of indicating timeout on a synchronous interaction. Remember that, although the notational convention places the timer at the responder end, the meaning is that the initiator waits.

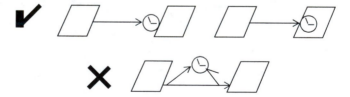

Timeout out on an asynchronous interaction is meaningless because the initiator never waits, yet this notation implies that it does (this notation does *not* mean that the responder waits with timeout).

Here is the correct notation to indicate the responder waits with timeout. The key is that the timer is associated with the responder, not the connection.

Here is how to show the initiator waiting with timeout for a response.

The following configurations do *not* mean sending a timeout notification to another process (they do not mean anything).

B.3.5 Think Out IPC Connections Carefully

Designs submitted by students are often good sources of insight into how not to do things. Here are some examples.

Example B.3.5 (a)

In a Tempo program, a service team has an interface function `ask-service` that is used by external client processes to ask for service. This function sends a request to an internal server process of the team. The server then starts a chain of events to service the request that may involve messages to other processes and, ultimately, messages back to the server. Each client waits for the service to be completed in such a way that it returns from the ask-service call with the results. The question is, how should a client wait? Here are some examples of answers to this question (some incorrect). For simplicity, only one client is shown; not shown are the other processes and the message parameters.

The following solution works but fails to satisfy the requirements, because the client returns from the ask-service call without the results.

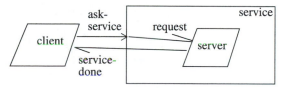

The following solution may work but is unsafe in general. The idea is that the client waits in the ready-to-run queue for the service to be completed. This is arranged by giving the server process higher priority than the client, so that when the client makes a request, the server starts running immediately. The assumption is that the client will not run again until after the server blocks to wait for the next request, after calling `put`. This will not work if priorities are changed. Even if the priorities remain as assumed, what if the server, while interacting with other processes, is forced to block before calling put? Then there must be other high-priority processes ready to run to fill the gap, or else the client will run again and call `get` before the server can call `put`. In general, priorities should be used only to affect performance not to implement program logic.

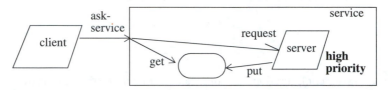

The following solution can be made to work but is unsatisfactory because of its non-uniform implementation of IPC and its lack of modularity (it requires access to internal event queues of a process from a global interface function of a module). The look of this diagram is different from most other IPC diagrams in this book because it shows IPC in terms of calls to the kernel instead of connections between processes. This is because the client's call to receive a message is in a different part of the system from the process itself, namely in the `ask-service` function of the service team. This IPC arrangement can be made to work if `receive` and `send` refer to the same event queue of the client. Because the `ask-service` function is executed in the context of the client process, calling `receive` from there for a client event queue is legitimate. However, the nonuniform treatment of IPC makes the logic of the system obscure when reading the code, which is reflected in the awkward way we are forced to diagram the solution.

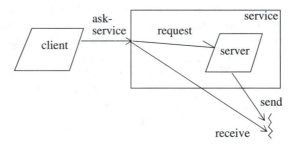

The following solution works and satisfies the requirements. Before returning from the ask-service call, the client waits on a service-done semaphore signalled by the server and then gets the result. Note that the availability of synchronous send would greatly simplify this solution.

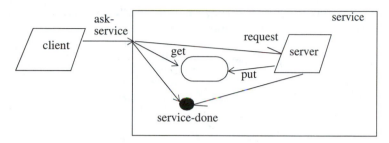

Example B.3.5 (b)

A server process A receives requests from other processes and passes them on for action to a set of identical but distinct worker processes B (for example, A might be a communications server and B a set of communication line drivers). When work is completed, process A sends a yes message to the done event queue of the requestor of that work. If work is not completed within a certain timeout period, A sends a no message via the same route. A must always be ready to receive requests. The IPC arrangements between A and B are undefined. Here is a poor IPC solution, actually submitted by a student (message parameters are omitted for simplicity).

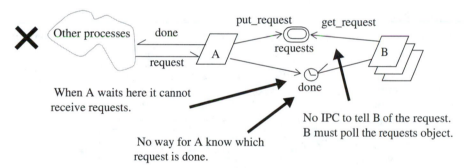

A better solution is shown below.

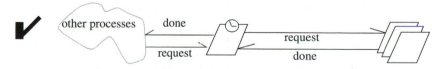

Example B.3.5 (c)

Process A sends a request to process B and then waits with timeout for a result from pro-cess B.   Here is a poor solution to this problem.

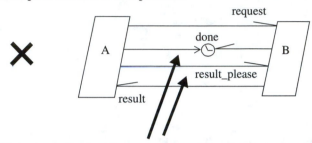

These are redundant because the result can be sent when it arrives.

Here is a better solution.

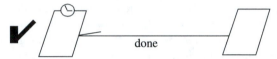

Example B.3.5 (d)

In the following diagram, the incorrect solution provides no way of waiting for a result.

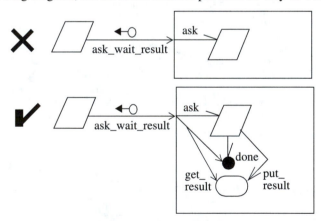

Using sendwait connections greatly simplifies such designs because the result can be passed back as a returned parameter. The response-blocked connection indicates that the initiator must routinely expect to wait after the request has been decoded by the responder (the implication would be that the responder interacts with other processes not shown to get the result).

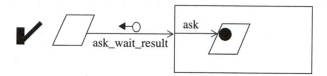

Example B.3.5 (e)

Don't use processes unnecessarily. For example, don't use processes where monitors would do, as in the following adaptation of the bounded buffer example (the buffer process replaces an earlier monitor object). Nothing is gained and performance is lost due to extra process switching overhead.

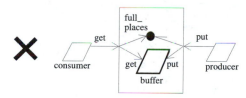

Don't use processes as unnecessary intermediaries. The middle process in the next diagram is redundant if its only role is to relay ask messages to a server process. Redundant processes create unnecessary IPC overhead and thereby reduce performance.

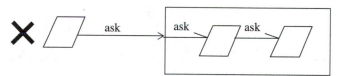

B.3.6 ISRs

The following combinations are illegal because the implied synchronization could require

the ISR (really the interrupted process, dragging the ISR along with it) to wait for the process, which could delay interrupt processing drastically or even cause deadlock (if the process on the right happened to be itself waiting for a sendwait interaction with the interrupted process).

This combination is illegal because, by our diagramming conventions, interrupt ser-

vice routines cannot be called by software. Triggering an ISR from software can always be indicated with a connection from a software component to the hardware component that generates the interrupt.

The following does *not* mean signaling all processes at once (they are signaled one

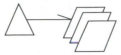

at a time, with a separate call required for each).

Avoid clumsy event notification chains, such as the following one from a student submission that aims to get an event from an ISR to a process via a flag and a stack of notifier processes that poll for events. This is both clumsy and inefficient.

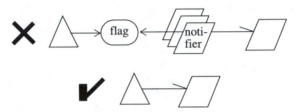

Special tricks are needed with ISRs; for example, as shown in the next diagram, to kickstart output (meaning sending something initially from a process to get an interrupt chain going that will take over).

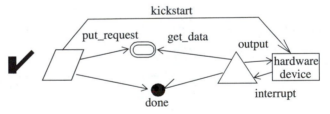

B.3.7 Chaining Connections Across Interfaces

Connections may be chained across component boundaries to show external-internal connections, where appropriate. There are legal and illegal combinations.

Call arrows (and callwait or sendwait arrows) imply a response is returned by the same path, so do not use separate arrows like the ones highlighted here (from student submissions) to indicate a response action.

Send arrows do not imply a response is returned by the same path. However, a separate send connection is required to return a response, not just some arbitrary arrow symbol like the one highlighted next (from a student submission).

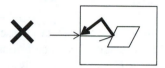

Any outgoing arrow from an *object* implies that a call from an outside initiator is

chained through the object. The outside initiator must ultimately be a process (or ISR). This process (or ISR) is required to act as the ultimate initiator because the object itself is not an autonomous component. Concurrent programs may have many ultimate initiators, sequential programs may have only one (for a sequential program, the single initiator process would correspond to the mainline).

Discontinuities in incoming connection chains across process boundaries indicate

the process acts as an autonomous initiator for the internal connections at times of its own choosing. Discontinuities in outgoing connection chains are illegal because they violate interface conventions, given next.

Discontinuities in incoming connection chains across team or object boundaries are

meaningless because neither type of component can be an autonomous initiator in its own right. There is always a call chain. When drawing a diagram of a component in isolation, its interface must be shown to indicate the continuity of connection.

To avoid confusion about what is meant by connections across boundaries from inside a compound component to outside it, the general convention is to show arrowheads only on the outside part (arrowheads on the inside part might be interpreted to mean the component interacts with itself).

Components interacting with themselves (such as some internal part of a team calling an interface function of the team) should be shown as follows.

Be careful with processes. Self-communication can cause deadlock and, even when it does not, is questionable (sending yourself a message to remind yourself to do something later saves programming, relative to doing it explicitly with local data, but adds IPC overhead).

B.3.8 More on Connections

Here are correct and incorrect ways of representing the existence of isolated functions in CGs. Use this notation sparingly only to identify the need to invoke important layer services that are not implied by any other notations. (Nothing significant is meant by positioning the arrow inside the process instead of outside. It could equally well be outside.)

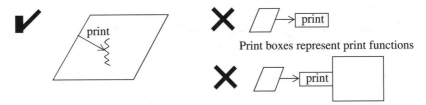

Print boxes represent print functions

Pay careful attention to the meaning of the arrowhead shapes; don't interchange them, reinterpret them, or invent your own.

Name connections to identify their application meaning. Do not name IPC connections with the names of the kernel functions that must be called to implement them. Normally a name should indicate how the connection is seen by the initiator. Stick to a consistent naming convention in this regard, otherwise designs can be very confusing (in the last example in the next diagram, `put` is how the initiator sees one connection and `get` is how the responder sees the other).

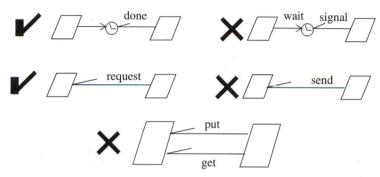

Be careful not to leave passive components dangling without any ultimate initiators (initiators can be in separate diagrams but make sure they exist somewhere).

Be sure that connections are complete relative to the intended purpose of a diagram. For example, in the next diagram, there is no `put` to correspond to the `get`.

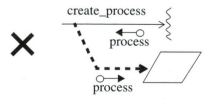

B.3.9 Structural Dynamics

Do not use the style of the next diagram to indicate normal initialization of fixed components (illustrated by Tempo processes here) that are structurally static afterward. The *move* assertion is specifically restricted to having slots as the target; its use with a fixed component is wrong, and replacing the fixed component with a slot would be inappropriate if a fixed component is intended.

Programming Interrupt Controllers and UARTs

*T*his appendix provides basic information about interrupt handling and UART programming for Intel-standard computers. Chapters 3 and 8 assume that the reader has some knowledge of these topics, and this appendix provides additional background for those who are on unfamiliar ground. Students who have completed a first- or second-year course in computer organization and assembly language programming should have sufficient background to understand the machine-level details of I/O programming. Our coverage is not exhaustive; entire books have been written about these topics, so we can present only the essential ideas here. Suggestions for further reading can be found in the bibliography.

C.1 INTERRUPT STRUCTURES

Interrupts are a way for a computer's external devices to provide real-time notification of events to the processor. The processor has an interrupt request signal, and if the processor is running with interrupts enabled, it checks this signal as during its normal instruction cycle (fetching instructions from memory and executing them). If the interrupt signal has been asserted, it immediately begins to process the interrupt. The processor pushes the contents of its flags register on the run-time stack, followed by the address of the instruction that would have been executed next if the interrupt had not happened. The processor then determines the appropriate *interrupt service routine* for the interrupt (how it does this is described later) and starts to execute it. In effect, an interrupt is a function call that is triggered by hardware instead of by the processor's call-function instruction.

Interrupt handling finishes when the processor executes an interrupt-return instruction. This pops the flags register and the saved address from the stack, causing the processor to resume execution where it was interrupted.

The processor disables interrupts when interrupt processing begins, so ISRs run with interrupts disabled until they explicitly enable interrupts. When the processor returns from the ISR, interrupts are reenabled.

Intel-standard processors support interrupts that are *vectored* and *prioritized.* By vectored, we mean that each hardware device capable of generating interrupts has its own interrupt service routine. When one of these devices interrupts the processor, support hardware causes the processor to begin executing code from the ISR associated with that device.

Different interrupt sources have different *priorities* (which are not the same thing as Tempo process priorities). If two devices attempt to interrupt simultaneously, support circuitry determines which device will interrupt the processor first, according to their interrupt priority levels. In addition, interrupt priorities provide a mechanism for higher-priority devices to interrupt the processor while it is executing a lower-priority device's ISR.

The interrupt structure of the basic 8086-family architecture is split between the processor and a separate 8259A programmable interrupt controller (PIC) chip (see Figure C.1). The processor has two interrupt input signals, NMI and INTR. NMI is the nonmaskable interrupt input, but as this type of interrupt is not used by Tempo programs, we can ignore it. INTR is the vectored interrupt input. The lowest 1K of memory is reserved for use as an interrupt vector table. It contains 256 four-byte interrupt vectors, numbered 0 through 255, and each vector holds the starting address of an interrupt service routine. When the INTR line is asserted, the processor is provided with the interrupt number of the device that is requesting the interrupt. The processor then reads the ISR address from the corresponding interrupt vector and transfers control to the ISR.

The circuitry that prioritizes interrupt requests and provides the interrupt number to the processor is contained in the 8259A PIC. Hardware devices that generate interrupts are not directly connected to the processor. Instead, the PIC's INT output signal drives the processor's INTR input, and interrupting devices are connected to the PIC's eight interrupt request inputs, IR0 through IR7. Figure C.1 shows how the programmable timer, the keyboard interface, and two UARTs are connected to the PIC in an Intel-standard computer. When the computer boots, the PIC is programmed so that interrupt requests IR0 through IR7 generate interrupt numbers 8 through 15, respectively (the programmable timer, connected to IR0, causes type 8 interrupts; the primary UART, connected to IR4, causes type 12 interrupts). Each IR input can be individually masked or unmasked by writing the PIC's Interrupt Mask Register. When an IR input is masked, that signal is ignored by the PIC (see Section C.1.1).

The PIC is programmed so that its interrupt request inputs are prioritized, with IR0 (the timer interrupt) having the highest priority and IR7 having the lowest priority. If multiple interrupt requests are asserted at the same time, the highest-priority unmasked request is processed first, and lower-priority requests are handled after the higher-priority interrupt has finished.

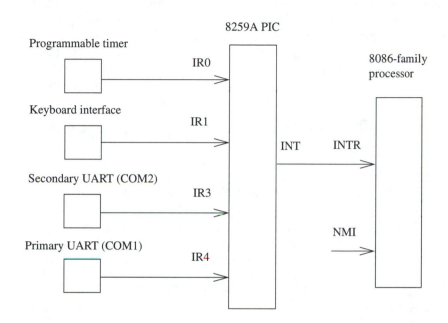

8259A PIC

Programmable timer

IR0

8086-family
processor

Keyboard interface

IR1

INT   INTR

Secondary UART (COM2)

IR3

NMI

Primary UART (COM1)

IR4

Figure C.1 Block diagram of the interrupt hardware.

The PIC prioritization logic permits nested interrupts: Higher-priority interrupt requests can interrupt lower-priority ISRs. Suppose the ISR associated with IRm is currently running and interrupts have been enabled at the processor. If an unmasked, higher-priority request IRn ($n < m$) occurs, the processor will transfer control to the ISR for IRn. The interrupted ISR will resume when the higher-priority ISR returns. On the other hand, if an unmasked, lower-priority request IRl ($l > m$) happens while the processor is executing the ISR for IRm, the request is ignored until the ISR finishes.

How does the PIC determine that an ISR has finished, so that it can process further interrupt requests at the same or lower priorities? The PIC is not part of the processor, so it cannot "see" the execution of an ISR's interrupt-return instruction, which transfers control back to the interrupted code. Instead, every ISR must output an end-of-interrupt command to the PIC's command register before it exits. In Borland C++, this is accomplished by the following statements:

```
#define PIC_CMD 0x20   // port address of PIC
                       // command register
#define EOI     0x20   // end-of-interrupt command
```

```
outportb(PIC_CMD, EOI);
```

Additional devices not shown in Figure C.1 (for example, disk controllers) are usually connected to the other IR inputs. Many computers have multiple PICs in order to support more than eight interrupt sources; the INT outputs of the slave PICs are connected to the IR inputs of the master PIC, which is connected to the processor. Details of the interrupt structure vary between different computers, so readers should consult the technical documentation for their particular model; however, backward compatibility is usually maintained, so the structure described is supported by most Intel-standard machines.

C.1.1 Enabling and Disabling Interrupts

For a device to interrupt the processor,

- interrupts must be enabled at the processor, and
- the IR input that connects the device to the PIC must be unmasked.

Let's start by looking at how interrupts are enabled and disabled at the processor.

The processor's flags register contains several 1-bit flags. One of these bits, called the interrupt flag (IF), determines whether interrupts are enabled. When the IF is set to 1, interrupts are enabled and the processor recognizes interrupt requests from the PIC. When the IF is cleared to 0, interrupt requests are ignored. The processor provides the STI instruction to set the IF and the CLI instruction to clear this bit. In addition, this bit is automatically cleared (interrupts are disabled) when the processor jumps to an ISR, and restored when the ISR finishes and the processor returns to executing the interrupted code.

Interrupt requests are masked and unmasked at the PIC by writing to its interrupt mask register (IMR). When bit n in the IMR is 0, input IRn is unmasked (enabled). When bit n in the IMR is 1, input IRn is masked (disabled) and interrupt requests at this input are ignored.

A common source of confusion should be noted: In the processor, the IF bit is *set* to enable interrupts, but in the PIC, bits in the IMR are *cleared* to enable interrupts.

Figure C.2 shows one way to visualize this. Think of the PIC's interrupt mask register as a set of switches connecting the IR inputs to its internal interrupt processing logic. Clearing (unmasking) a bit in the IMR closes the corresponding switch, allowing that interrupt request to pass through. Setting (masking) a bit in the IMR opens the corresponding switch, so interrupt requests on that input will be ignored.

The processor's IF bit is like a switch connecting its INTR input to its internal interrupt processing logic. When this bit is cleared, as in the diagram, the switch is open and interrupts are disabled at the processor. Setting the bit enables interrupts by closing the switch.

This diagram shows that in order for a device connected to the PIC at IRn to interrupt the processor, the corresponding bit in the interrupt mask register must be unmasked (cleared) and interrupts must be enabled at the processor (IF set).

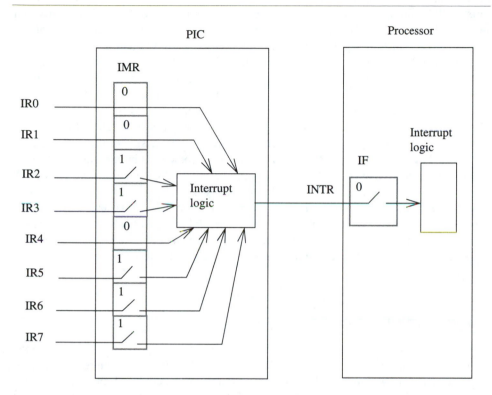

Figure C.2 Enabling and disabling interrupts at the processor and PIC.

The three functions provided by Tempo to enable and disable interrupts modify the IF. Function `disable_ints()` disables interrupts at the processor by clearing the IF. This function records the value of the flags register *before* interrupts are disabled and returns that value. Function `restore_flags()` loads the processor's flags register with the value of its argument, which is usually the value returned by the previous call to `disable_ints()`. Depending on this value, the IF is set or cleared; that is, interrupts are enabled or disabled. Function `enable_ints()` enables interrupts by setting the IF.

These three functions do not modify the PIC's IMR. Every Tempo program that uses interrupts is responsible for masking and unmasking the appropriate bits in the IMR, depending on which interrupts the program has been designed to handle.

C.2   THE 8250 FAMILY OF UARTS

Most Intel-standard PCs have at least one serial communications port (also known as

COM1), many are equipped with a second serial port (COM2), and some have four serial ports (COM1 through COM4). In most computers, the bulk of the electronic circuitry that provides the interface between the computer's processor and the serial communications link is packaged in an integrated circuit chip called a *universal asynchronous receiver and transmitter* (UART). The UART used in the original IBM Personal Computer was National Semiconductor's 8250 ACE (Asynchronous Communications Element). Each serial port (COM1, COM2) required its own 8250. A slower version of this chip, the 8250-B, was used in many of the early IBM-compatible computers. A revised version of the 8250 that corrected a number of its flaws was released as the 8250A. The IBM Personal Computer AT (and many compatible machines) used a faster version of the 8250A called the 16450. Each of these UARTs has been found in the computers in our real-time laboratories, so we refer to them collectively as the 8250 family, and we have evolved our UART device drivers over the years to handle all of these chips.

The 8250 UART is programmed through 10 registers that are accessed by Borland C++ programs through the compiler's `inportb()` and `outportb()` functions. There are two data registers (for reading characters received from the serial link and transmitting characters), three status registers, and five control registers that allow the UART to be configured under software control.

C.3 A UART DEVICE DRIVER

The software that handles an input/output device is called a *device driver*. A well-designed device driver hides the complex details of hardware and provides a clean interface for processes to read and write data and control the device. The remainder of this appendix presents the code for a device driver for the 8250 family of UARTs. It consists of several functions that support an interrupt-driven serial link through COM1 or COM2. This software underlies the MTU's L layer and is also used by the interrupt examples in Chapter 3.

Over the course of writing several UART drivers, we have observed that the functions that initialize the UART and handle the basic operations (receiving and transmitting individual characters), once tested and debugged, evolve slowly and tend to be used as is over several projects. In contrast, UART ISRs are often modified for each program. Their design is dependent on several factors, including the character reception and transmission protocol, the scheme used to buffer data, and the synchronization with processes. For these reasons, we organize the driver as shown in Figure C.3.

The team labeled UART provides the software interface to the UART. Processes do not access any of the 8250's registers directly; instead, they call the UART team's interface functions to control the UART and transfer characters. The UART ISR is not part of the team. By keeping it separate, the ISR can be tailored for a specific application without necessarily causing changes to the UART team. The ISR calls the team's interface functions to read and write the 8250's registers.

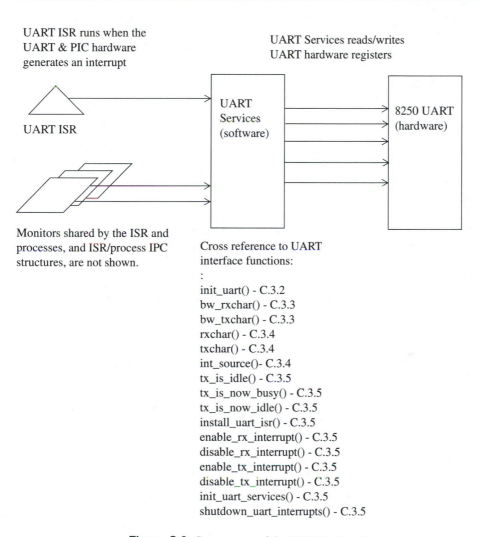

UART ISR runs when the
UART & PIC hardware
generates an interrupt

UART Services reads/writes
UART hardware registers

UART ISR

UART
Services
(software)

8250 UART
(hardware)

Monitors shared by the ISR and
processes, and ISR/process IPC
structures, are not shown.

Cross reference to UART
interface functions:
:
init_uart() - C.3.2
bw_rxchar() - C.3.3
bw_txchar() - C.3.3
rxchar() - C.3.4
txchar() - C.3.4
int_source()- C.3.4
tx_is_idle() - C.3.5
tx_is_now_busy() - C.3.5
tx_is_now_idle() - C.3.5
install_uart_isr() - C.3.5
enable_rx_interrupt() - C.3.5
disable_rx_interrupt() - C.3.5
enable_tx_interrupt() - C.3.5
disable_tx_interrupt() - C.3.5
init_uart_services() - C.3.5
shutdown_uart_interrupts() - C.3.5

Figure C.3 Components of the UART device driver.

C.3.1 The UART Team: Register Definitions

The device driver begins with a terse description of the 8250's registers. Symbolic identifiers are defined for the register port addresses. Comments describe the individual bits within the registers, and symbolic constants are defined for useful bit patterns.

```
// 8250 port addresses and bit definitions
// ------------------------------------

// The primary 8250 ("COM1") is located at I/O ports 0x3f8
// through 0x3fe.

#define COM1     0x3f8

// The secondary 8250 ("COM2") is located at I/O ports 0x2f8
// through 0x2fe.

#define COM2     0x2f8

// This module supports COM1.

#define UART_BASE    COM1

// The following three registers are accessible when the
// DLAB bit in the Line Control Register is 0.

#define    RBR  UART_BASE+0  // Receive Buffer Register
#define    THR  UART_BASE+0  // Transmitter Holding Register
#define    IER  UART_BASE+1  // Interrupt Enable Register

// When DLAB = 1, the two divisor latches are located at
// these ports.
#define    DLL  UART_BASE+0  // Divisor Latch -
                            // least significant byte
#define    DLM  UART_BASE+1  // Divisor Latch -
                            // most significant byte

// The remaining registers are accessible at all times

#define    IIR  UART_BASE+2  // Interrupt Id Register
#define    LCR  UART_BASE+3  // Line Control Register
#define    MCR  UART_BASE+4  // Modem Control Register
#define    LSR  UART_BASE+5  // Line Status Register
#define    MSR  UART_BASE+6  // Modem Status Register

// Bit masks in the LSR

#define    DR    0x01   // Data Ready: 1 == character
                       // available in RBR
#define    THRE  0x20   // Transmitter Holding Reg Empty:
                       // 1 == can output char to THR

// Bits in the LCR
//
// Bit 7 is the Divisor Latch Access Bit (DLAB).
// When this bit is 1, ports UART_BASE+0 and UART_BASE+1
```

```
// are the two divisor latches.
// When this bit is 0, port UART_BASE+0 is the RBR
// (read-only) and the THR (write-only), and port
// UART_BASE+1 is the IER.

#define     DLAB_HIGH   0x80   // access DLL, DLM
#define     DLAB_LOW    0x00   // access RBR, THR, IER

// Bits 0 and 1 select the word length: bit 1 = 1, bit 0 = 0
// for a 7-bit character length; bit 1 = 1, bit 0 = 1 for an
// 8-bit character length.
// Bit 2 is cleared to select 1 stop bit, set to select 2
// stop bits.
// Bit 3 is cleared to disable parity, set to enable parity.
// If bit 3 is set, bit 4 is set to select even parity, cleared
// to select odd parity.
// Normally, bit 5 is cleared. If bit 5 and bit 3 (parity
// enable) are both set, then setting bit 4 forces space
// parity (parity bit always 0) and clearing bit 4 forces
// mark parity (parity bit always 1).
// Bit 6 is normally cleared (we don't want to transmit BREAK)
// Bit 7 is DLAB; see above.

#define     LEN_7          0x02
#define     LEN_8          0x03

#define     STOP_1         0x00
#define     STOP_2         0x04

#define     NO_PARITY      0x00
#define     ODD_PARITY     0x08
#define     EVEN_PARITY    0x18
#define     MARK_PARITY    0x28
#define     SPACE_PARITY   0x38

#define     NO_BREAK       0x00

// Bits in the MCR

// Bits 0 and 1 are set/cleared to assert/negate the UART's
// DTR and RTS outputs.
// Bit 2 controls the OUT1 output; negate this signal, as
// it's not used.
// Bit 3 controls the OUT2 output. For some reason, IBM used
// the OUT 2 line to enable the logic which passes the 8250
// interrupt through to the PC bus, and hence to the PIC.
// When enabling interrupts, remember to set the OUT2 bit
// to 1.  It's not enough to enable interrupts at the IER
// and PIC!
// Bit 4 enables loop mode, which is used for test purposes.
// This bit is cleared to disable loop mode.
```

```
#define     MCR_INIT  0x3    // DTR, RTS asserted, OUT1 and
                             // OUT2 negated, loop mode off
#define     OUT2      0x8    // OUT2 asserted

// Bits in the IER

#define NO_INTS  0x00 // all 8250 interrupt sources disabled

#define ERBFI    0x01  // Bit 0: Enable Received Data
                       //        Available Interrupt
#define ETBEI    0x02  // Bit 1: Enable Transmitter Holding
                       //        Register Empty Interrupt
#define ERLSI    0x04  // Bit 2: Enable Receiver Line
                       //        Status Interrupt
#define EMSI     0x08  // Bit 3: Enable Modem Status Interrupt

// Bits in the IIR

#define INT_PENDING    0
#define NO_INT_PENDING 1

#define RLSI           0x06  // receiver line status
                             // interrupt pending
#define RDAI           0x04  // received data available
                             // interrupt pending
#define THREI          0x02  // transmitter holding register
                             // empty interrupt pending
#define MSI            0x01  // modem status interrupt
                             // pending

// A 1.8432 MHz crystal provides the input clock for the
// 8250's Baud Generator. The Baud Generator divides this
// input clock by a 16-bit divisor. This divisor is chosen
// so that the output of the Baud Generator is 16 X the
// desired Baud Rate (divisor = 1.8432 Mhz/(baud rate x 16).
// The divisor latches are loaded with the divisor when the
// UART is initialized.

// For 1200 baud, the divisor = 1.8432E6/(1200 * 16)
//                            = 96 decimal
//                            = 0060 hex

#define DLM_INIT  0x00    // most sig byte of divisor
#define DLL_INIT  0x60    // least sig byte of divisor

// PIC registers

#define PIC_CMD   0x20    // command register
#define PIC_MASK  0x21    // interrupt mask register
```

```
#define EOI    0x20      /// end-of-interupt command

// The primary 8250 (COM1) is connected to the PIC's IR4
// input, causing type 0x0c interrupts

#define UART_INT_TYPE   0x0c
#define UART_IRQ_BIT    0x10   // bit in PIC_MASK for IR4
```

C.3.2 UART Initialization

Function `init_uart()` configures the 8250 for the number of data bits per character,
the number of stop bits, parity generation and checking, and the baud rate (the rate at
which data bits are transmitted and received across the serial link). It also asserts the
chip's request-to-send and data-terminal-ready output signals (depending on the wiring of
the cable connected to the computer and the hardware attached to the other end, this may
not be needed). When this function returns, the UART can receive and transmit characters
through polled I/O; however, interrupt-driven communications are disabled until additional interface functions, described in Section C.3.5, are called.

```
// void init_uart()
// Initialize the 8250 UART for a 7 bit character length,
// 1 stop bit, even parity, 1200 baud. Modem output signals
// (RTS, DTR) are asserted. General output lines OUT1 and
// OUT2 are negated. Loopback mode is disabled.
// All 8250 interrupt sources are disabled.

void init_uart()
{
    unsigned char temp;

    // init the line ctrl register
    outportb(LCR, DLAB_HIGH + NO_BREAK + EVEN_PARITY
             + STOP_1 + LEN_7);

    // Wait 1 ms before accessing another UART register.
    // Slow 8250s seem to need this when used in fast machines.
    delay(1);

    // DLAB is 1, so we can now access divisor the latches
    outportb(DLL, DLL_INIT);  // load baud rate divisor
    delay(1);
    outportb(DLM, DLM_INIT);
    delay(1);

    // clear DLAB bit in LCR, leave other bits unchanged
    temp = inportb(LCR) & (~DLAB_HIGH);
    delay(1);
    outportb(LCR, temp);
    delay(1);
```

```
    // DLAB is 0, so we can now access the RBR, THR, and IER.

    outportb(IER, NO_INTS);    // init intr. enable reg
    delay(1);
    outportb(MCR, MCR_INIT);   // init modem ctrl. reg
    delay(1);

    // clear out any pending characters or interrupt requests
    temp = inportb(IIR); // Interrupt Id Register
    temp = inportb(LSR); // Line Status Register

    temp = inportb(IIR); // Interrupt Id Register
    temp = inportb(RBR); // throw away any garbage character

    temp = inportb(IIR); // Interrupt Id Register
    temp = inportb(MSR); // Modem Status Register

    temp = inportb(IIR); // Interrupt Id Register
}
```

C.3.3 Polled I/O

Two functions support polled (busywait) I/O. Function bw_rxchar() repeatedly checks the Data Ready bit in the 8250's Line Status Register until it indicates that a new character has been received. It then reads the character from the UART's Receiver Buffer Register. Function bw_txchar() performs busywait transmission of the character passed by its caller. It loops, reading a byte from the Line Status Register and checking its Transmitter Holding Register Empty bit. When this bit indicates that the holding register is empty, the character is sent to the Transmitter Holding Register and sent across the serial link. Calling these functions in a multitasking program is strongly discouraged. The calling process does no useful work while it polls, waiting for the UART to receive a character or become ready to transmit a character (hence the phrase that it is *busy,waiting*). Instead, it should relinquish the processor, allowing Tempo to schedule other processes until a character arrives or can be transmitted. We've already seen how a UART ISR and Tempo's IPC primitives permit this. Nonetheless, these functions are included in the driver because they are useful for testing the serial link.

```
// char bw_rxchar()
// Read a character from the 8250, busywaiting until a
// character is available. Returns the character read from
// the Receiver Buffer Register.

char bw_rxchar()
{
    while ((inportb(LSR) & DR) == 0)  // poll...
        ;
    // ensure bit 7 is 0 (ASCII chars have 7 bits)
```

```
        return (inportb(RBR) & 0x7f);
}

// void bw_txchar(char ch)
// Output ch via the 8250, busywaiting until the
// Transmitter Holding Register is empty.

void bw_txchar(char ch)
{
    while ((inportb(LSR) & THRE) == 0)   // poll...
        ;
    outportb(THR, ch);
}
```

C.3.4 Register Access Functions

The next two functions provide an interface to the UART's input and output buffers. Function `rxchar()` reads a character from the Receiver Buffer Register and returns it. It expects that there is an unread character in the buffer. Function `txchar()` writes its argument to the Transmitter Holding Register. It expects that this register is empty.

```
// char rxchar()
// Return the character read from the Receiver Buffer
// Register. Expects that the RBR contains an unread char.

char rxchar()
{
    // ensure bit 7 is 0 (ASCII chars have 7 bits)
    return (inportb(RBR) & 0x7f);
}

//void txchar(char ch)
// Output ch via the 8250. Expects that the Transmitter
// Holding Register is empty.

void txchar(char ch)
{
    outportb(THR, ch);
}
```

Function `int_source()` returns the current value of the UART's Interrupt Identification Register. This function can be called by the UART ISR to determine which condition caused the 8250 to interrupt the processor.

```
// char int_source()
// Returns the value of the 8250's Interrupt Identification
// Register.

char int_source()
{
```

```
        return(inportb(IIR));
}
```

C.3.5 Interrupt Support

The remaining code provides support for interrupt-driven communications. Function install_uart_isr() is passed the address of the interrupt function that handles UART interrupts while the Tempo program runs. Before pointing the appropriate UART interrupt vector to the new ISR, it saves a copy of the original interrupt vector so that it can be restored before the program exits. This function also asserts the UART's OUT2 output signal. This enables interrupt requests from the 8250 to be passed to the PIC. Finally, the bit in the PIC's interrupt mask register that corresponds to the interrupt request connection to the UART is *cleared* (not set). Interrupt requests from the UART are now unmasked and will be processed by the PIC.

```
// olduartisr will be used to save a copy of the default uart
// interrupt vector
static void interrupt (*olduartisr)(...);

// void install_uart_isr(void interrupt (*uartisr)(...))
// Installs uartisr() as the interrupt service routine for
// the 8250 interrupt, saving the original interrupt vector
// in olduartisr. Enables 8250 interrupts at the PIC.
// General output line OUT2 is asserted (to pass the 8250's
// interrupt output to the PIC), but all 8250 interrupt
// sources are left disabled.

void install_uart_isr(void interrupt (*uartisr)(...))
{
    unsigned char temp;

    tx_is_now_idle();

    olduartisr = getvect(UART_INT_TYPE);
    setvect(UART_INT_TYPE, uartisr);

    temp = inportb(MCR);
    delay(1);
    outportb(MCR, temp | OUT2);   // assert OUT2 line
    delay(1);

    // unmask UART IRQ bit in the PIC
    temp = inportb(PIC_MASK);
    delay(1);
    outportb(PIC_MASK, temp & (~UART_IRQ_BIT));
    delay(1);
}
```

Even after install_uart_isr() is called, the 8250 will not interrupt the processor. The 8250 can generate an interrupt request when a new character is received, when the transmitter holding register becomes empty (that is, when another character can be written to the UART for transmission), when a UART error occurs, and when the UART inputs corresponding to modem control signals change state. Each of these four interrupt conditions can be individually enabled and disabled by writing to the 8250's Interrupt Enable Register. The following four functions enable and disable interrupt generation for character reception and transmission. (Functions to enable and disable the other two interrupt conditions are not provided but would be very similar.)

```
// void enable_rx_interrupt()
// Enables the 8250 received data available interrupt.
// Expects that install_uart_isr() has been called.

void enable_rx_interrupt()
{
    outportb(IER, inportb(IER) | ERBFI);
}

// void disable_rx_interrupt()
// Disables the 8250 received data available interrupt.

void disable_rx_interrupt()
{
    outportb(IER, inportb(IER) & (~ERBFI));
}

// void enable_tx_interrupt()
// Enables the 8250 transmitter holding register empty
// interrupt. Expects that install_uart_isr() has been called.

void enable_tx_interrupt()
{
    outportb(IER, inportb(IER) | ETBEI);
}

// void disable_tx_interrupt()
// Disables the 8250 transmitter holding register empty
// interrupt.

void disable_tx_interrupt()
{
    outportb(IER, inportb(IER) & (~ETBEI));
}
```

Function `init_uart_services()` initializes the 8250 for interrupt-driven character reception through an ISR called `uartisr()` which is supplied by the user, and is tailored for a particular application.

```
// void init_uart_services()
```

```
// After this function returns, interrupt-driven character
// reception through ISR uartisr() is enabled.

void init_uart_services()
{
    init_uart();
    install_uart_isr(uartisr); // see uartisr.h
    enable_rx_interrupt();
}
```

The device driver provides the following three functions to help processes and ISRs to keep track of whether or not the UART is currently performing interrupt-driven transmission. The MTU code in Chapter 8 provides an example of how these functions are used.

```
static int txState;
#define TXIDLE 1  // 1 == UART transmitter is idle
#define TXBUSY 0  // 0 == UART currently transmitting

// int tx_is_idle()
// Returns 1 if the UART transmitter is idle, 0 otherwise.

int tx_is_idle()
{
    return txState;
}

// void tx_is_now_busy()
// Records that the UART transmitter is busy.

void tx_is_now_busy()
{
    txState = TXBUSY;
}

// void tx_is_now_idle()
// Records the UART transmitter is idle.

void tx_is_now_idle()
{
    txState = TXIDLE;
}
```

To finish cleanly, any Tempo program that uses this driver must call shutdown_uart_interrupts() before it terminates. This function restores the UART interrupt vector to point to the original ISR, masks UART interrupts at the PIC, and disables interrupt request generation at the 8250.

```
// void shutdown_uart_interrupts()
// Restores the original UART isr, masks out the UART
```

```
// interrupt at the PIC, negates the 8250's OUT2 line, and
// disables all 8250 interrupt sources.

void shutdown_uart_interrupts()
{
    setvect(UART_INT_TYPE, olduartisr);
    outportb(PIC_MASK, inportb(PIC_MASK) | UART_IRQ_BIT);
    outportb(MCR, inportb(MCR) & (~OUT2));
    delay(1);
    outportb(IER, NO_INTS);
}
```

Reading List and Bibliography

D.1 Suggestions for Further Reading

Real-Time Systems

Analysis and design of real-time systems is a large subject and we have not attempted to cover it in all its ramifications. There are many other books devoted to complementary approaches that may be used to supplement the approach of this book, and we recommend turning to them to get a broader perspective after absorbing and applying the material of this one.

Burns, A. and Wellings, A.: *Real-Time Systems and Programming Languages*, 2nd Ed. This book contains a comprehensive survey of fundamental real-time systems principles. It's approach is more theoretical than our book, with less emphasis on design and implementation, so we recommend it for a different perspective on the same subject. Of particular interest is their treatment of programming language support for implementing real-time systems.

Gomaa, H.: *Software Design Methods for Concurrent and Real-Time Systems*. Describes and compares several design methods that are extensions of popular methods for developing sequential software. Two methods developed by the author, called

ADARTS and CODARTS, are also presented and applied to four case studies. The chapter on performance analysis and real-time scheduling theory should be within the grasp of undergraduate engineering and computer science students.

Levi, S. and Agrawala, A.: *Real-Time System Design.*
Presents a design method for hard real-time systems in which timing constraints and timing issues are central. Suitable for advanced undergraduates and graduate students.

Son, S. H. (ed).: *Advances in Real-Time Systems.*
The contributing authors summarize recent results in various areas of real-time systems research. Aimed at professionals, researchers, and graduate students.

Real-Time and Object-Oriented Systems

Many experts in the field believe that object-oriented technologies are well-suited to developing real-time systems. The three books listed here describe new approaches to designing real-time systems that use the object-oriented paradigm as a cornerstone, and we encourage students to read any (or all) of them after mastering the material in our book to deepen their understanding of real-time system design.

Buhr, R. J. A. and Casselman, R. S.: *Use Case Maps for Object-Oriented Systems.*
The UCM notation was introduced in this book; however, it is not needed to understand the one you are holding. The UCM book gives a stand-alone description of everything about UCMs that is needed to understand its examples and case studies and to apply the notation to object-oriented and real-time design problems.

Selic, B., Gulekson, G., and Ward, P.: *Real-Time Object-Oriented Modeling.*
This is the book that is discussed in Chapter 11. Highly recommended for its emphasis on thinking about programs as systems.

Douglass, B.: *Real-Time UML: Developing Efficient Objects for Embedded Systems.*
This is the UML book that was mentioned in the preface.

Object-Oriented Methods and Notations

Fowler, M.: *UML Distilled: Applying the Standard Object Modeling Language.*
This slim volume summarizes the notation that has been proposed as a standard for modeling object-oriented systems, and as such, it is a useful companion to Douglass's book. The book's bibliography lists most of the classic texts on object-oriented analysis and design.

Jacobson, I, Christeron, M., and Overgaard, G.: *Object-Oriented Software Engineering: a Use Case Driven Approach*.
This is the book that introduced use cases to object-oriented software development. We recommend this book for its approach to specifying and designing systems from a systems perspective, not a programming language perspective.

Operating Systems Design

Tanenbaum, A. and Woodhull, A.: *Operating Systems: Design and Implementation*, 2nd Ed.
This book explains fundamental operating systems principles and describes the design and implementation of a small, Unix-like operating system called MINIX. Highly recommended for readers who are interested in operating system internals. Exercise for the student: reverse engineer MINIX into collaboration graphs and use case maps.

Comer, D.: *Operating System Design, the Xinu Approach*.
This book describes the Xinu operating system, including a detailed presentation of the C source code.

I/O Devices

Slater, M.: *Microprocessor-Based Design: a Comprehensive Guide to Hardware Design*.
Chapter 3 describes interrupt structures and the PIC. Chapter 8 describes fundamental principles of data communications and provides an overview of the 8250 family of UARTs.

D.2 Bibliography

Advances in Real-Time Systems. Sang H. Son (Ed.). (Englewood Cliffs, NJ: Prentice-Hall Inc., 1995).

Microprocessor-Based Design: a Comprehensive Guide to Hardware Design. Michael Slater. (Mountain View, Calif.: Mayfield Publishing Company, 1987).

Object-Oriented Software Engineering: a Use Case Driven Approach. I. Jacobson, M. Christeron, and G. Overgaard. (Reading, Mass.: Addison-Wesley Publishing Company, Inc., 1992).

Operating System Design, the Xinu Approach. Douglas Comer. (Englewood Cliffs, NJ: Prentice-Hall, Inc., 1984).

Operating Systems: Design and Implementation, 2nd Ed. Andrew S. Tanenbaum and Albert S. Woodhull. (Upper Saddle River, NJ: Prentice-Hall, Inc. 1997).

Real-Time Object-Oriented Modeling. Bran Selic, Garth Gullekson, and Paul T. Ward. (New York: John Wiley & Sons, Inc., 1994).

Real-Time System Design. Shem-Tov Levi and Ashok K. Agrawala. (New York: McGraw-Hill, Inc., 1990).

Real-Time Systems and Programming Languages, 2nd Edition. Alan Burns and Andy Wellings. (Harlow, England: Addison Wesley Longman Limited, 1997).

Real-Time UML: Developing Efficient Objects for Embedded Systems. Bruce Powel Douglass. (Reading, Mass.: Addison Wesley Longman, Inc., 1998).

Software Design Methods for Concurrent and Real-Time Systems. Hassan Gomaa. (Reading, Mass.: Addison-Wesley Publishing Company, Inc., 1993).

UML Distilled: Applying the Standard Object Modeling Language. Martin Fowler.(Reading, Mass.: Addison-Wesley Longman, Inc., 1997).

Use Case Maps for Object-Oriented Systems. Raymond J. A. Buhr and Ronald S. Casselman. (Upper Saddle River, NJ: PTR Prentice Hall, 1996).

Index